Palgrave Studies in Literature, Culture and Human Rights

Series Editor
Alexandra S. Moore
Binghamton University
New York, NY, USA

This series demonstrates how cultural critique can inform understandings of human rights as normative instruments that may at once express forms of human flourishing and be complicit with violence and inequality. The series investigates the role of genre and the aesthetic in shaping cultures of both rights and harm. Essential to this work is an understanding of human rights as at once normative and dynamic, encompassing egregious violations as well as forms of immiseration that have not always registered in human rights terms.

More information about this series at
http://www.palgrave.com/gp/series/16248

Alexandra S. Moore · Samantha Pinto
Editors

Writing Beyond the State

Post-Sovereign Approaches to Human Rights in Literary Studies

palgrave
macmillan

Editors
Alexandra S. Moore
Binghamton University
New York, NY, USA

Samantha Pinto
University of Texas at Austin
Austin, TX, USA

ISSN 2524-8820 ISSN 2524-8839 (electronic)
Palgrave Studies in Literature, Culture and Human Rights
ISBN 978-3-030-34455-9 ISBN 978-3-030-34456-6 (eBook)
https://doi.org/10.1007/978-3-030-34456-6

Cover image: Jason deCaires Taylor, Young Charles sculpture at entrance to the Coralarium in Maldives

This Palgrave Macmillan imprint is published by the registered company Springer Nature Switzerland AG
The registered company address is: Gewerbestrasse 11, 6330 Cham, Switzerland

Dedicated to Chloë, Samantha, Finn, and Tegan

Acknowledgments

We are grateful for permission to reprint the images in this collection as follows.

Our cover photograph from Jason deCaires Taylor's The Sculpture Coralarium, Sirru Fen Fushi, Maldives, appears with the generous permission of the artist. We thank Georgetown University for supporting the use of this image.

In Chapter 1, Theophilus Marboah's image from "Echoes and Agreements" is comprised of Plan of the Slave Ship Brookes, from Thomas Clarkson's "The history of the rise, progress, and accomplishment of the abolition of the African slave trade by the British Parliament" (1808), used courtesy of the British Library Board, and Massimo Sestini's photograph of the migrant boat crossing, reprinted by permission (©Massimo Sestini). We thank Mr. Marboah for recreating the diptych from his "Echoes and Agreements" series for this volume.

Amnesty International USA (AIUSA) has generously granted permission for the use of and quotations from its archives, material which appears in Chapter 4.

Chapter 5 includes a still from the VR film, *Clouds Over Sidra*, reprinted with permission of the director, Chris Milk. We're grateful to Richard Mosse and the Jack Shainman Gallery for permission to reprint Mosse's image: *Moria in Snow*, Lesbos, Greece, 2017, Digital C on metallic paper, 35.5" × 120", from *The Castle* by Richard Mosse, published by Mack Books in 2018.

Chapter 6 features three photographs from the Humans of New York blog by Brandon Stanton and are reprinted with his permission.

The map of "voluntary departure" survivors' routes from Israel, discussed in Chapter 10, appears curtesy of authors Lior Birger, Shahar Shoham, and Liat Bolzman of the 2018 Report, "Better a Prison in Israel Than Dying Along the Way: Testimonies of Refugees Who 'Voluntarily' Departed Israel to Rwanda and Uganda and Gained Protection in Europe," translated by Elizabeth Tsurkov and published by the Hotline for Refugees and Migrants.

We thank the author and artist Tings Chak for permission to reprint two of her images in Chapter 11. We are grateful to Aage A. Mikalsen and Kunstall Trondheim for permission to reprint the "Encyclopedia" installation image in Chapter 13.

Finally, we thank Ben Doyle and Camille Davies for their support for this project from its inception.

Contents

Notes on Contributors

Stephanie Athey is Associate Professor of English at Lasell University (USA) and author of *Torture's Echo and the National Security Imagination* and editor of *Sharpened Edge: Women of Color, Resistance and Writing*, collecting transnational feminist scholarship on women's armed resistance, resistance in the arts, and development strategies in Africa, India, and the Americas. She guest coedited the 2016 *Prose Studies*, "Revaluing the Human: The Moral Economy of Human Rights" (with K. M. Ferebee and Wendy S. Hesford), and has published refereed articles on race, gender, colonial discourse, slavery and lynching, eugenics, and reproductive technology. She has held research appointments at the Trotter Institute for the Study of Black Culture and Columbia University's Center for the Study of Human Rights.

Kerry Bystrom is Associate Professor of English and Human Rights and Associate Dean of the College at Bard College Berlin, A Liberal Arts University in Germany. She is author of *Democracy at Home in South Africa: Family Fictions and Transitional Culture* (2016) as well as co-editor of collections including *The Global South Atlantic* (with Joseph R. Slaughter, 2017) and "Humanitarianism and Responsibility," a special issue of *Journal of Human Rights* (with Glenn Mitoma, 2013).

Emily S. Davis is Associate Professor of English and Women and Gender Studies at the University of Delaware, USA. She is the author of *Rethinking the Romance Genre: Global Intimacies in Contemporary Literary* *and Visual Cultures* (2013) as well as articles on the intersections of gender, globalization, genre, and race.

Peter Hitchcock is Professor of English at the CUNY Graduate Center and Baruch College of the City University of New York, USA. He is also on the faculty of Women's Studies and Film Studies at the Graduate Center. He is the Associate Director of the Center for Place, Culture, and Politics at the Graduate Center. His books include *Dialogics of the Oppressed*; *Oscillate Wildly: Space, Body, and Spirit of Millennial Materialism*; *Imaginary States: Studies in Cultural Transnationalism*; *The Long Space: Transnationalism and Postcolonial Form*; and, most recently, *Labor in Culture, or, Worker of the World(s)*. He has also coedited two essay collections, *The New Public Intellectual: Politics, Theory, and the Public Sphere* and *The Debt Age*. Recent essay publications include, "History and Class Struggle," "Resistance is Futile: The Cultural Politics of Transformation in the Digital Age," "Kant at the Federal Reserve," and "The Speed of Place and the Space of Time: Toward a Theory of Postcolonial Velo/city." Books in progress include "The World, The State, and Postcoloniality," "Trading Objects: Finance, Commodities, and Culture," and "Serial, Seriality, and Serialization." He is currently editing a special issue of the *Minnesota Review* on the Commons.

Marike Janzen is Associate Professor of Humanities at the University of Kansas, USA. She is the author of *Writing to Change the World: Anna Seghers, Authorship, and International Solidarity in the Twentieth Century* (Camden House, 2018). She has published articles and chapters on German literature and the literature of human rights. Her current book project, "Readers and Refugees as World Citizens in the Contemporary German Literary Sphere," explores how Germany's public culture initiatives engage the voices of noncitizens in the country.

Mukti Lakhi Mangharam is Associate Professor of English at Rutgers University, USA. Her book, *Literatures of Liberation: Non-European Universalisms and Democratic Progress* (Ohio State University Press, 2017), explores local traditions of democratic liberation in Indian and South African literatures. She has published widely on postcolonial and world literatures in journals including *ELH*, *Economic and Political Weekly*, *Journal of Commonwealth and Postcolonial Studies*, *Diacritics*, *ARIEL*, and *Safundi*.

Alexandra S. Moore is Professor of English and Co-director of the Human Rights Institute at Binghamton University, USA. Her most recent publications include the monograph, *Vulnerability and Security in Human Rights Literature and Visual Culture* (2016), and several coedited collections: *Witnessing Torture: Perspectives of Survivors and Human Rights Workers* (with Swanson, 2018); *The Routledge Companion to Literature and Human Rights* (with McClennen, 2015); *Teaching Human Rights in Literary and Cultural Studies* (with Goldberg, 2015); and *Theoretical Perspectives on Human Rights and Literature* (with Goldberg, 2012). Her current research is on cultural representations of rendition, torture, and indefinite detention in the war on terror.

Ramona Mosse is Lecturer in Theatre, Film, and Media Studies at the Goethe University, Frankfurt, Germany. Her current research focuses on the intermedial relationships between theatre, sound studies, and virtual reality in contemporary performance practices. She is the co-editor of Erika Fischer-Lichte's *Routledge Introduction to Theatre and Performance Studies* (with Arjomand, 2014). Her work on metatheatricality, intermedial performance, tragedy, and philosophy has been published in a range of edited book collections and journals, among them *Theatre Journal*, *Anglia*, *Shakespeare Survey*, and *The Baffler*. She is also a Core Convenor of the Performance Philosophy Network.

Greg A. Mullins is Academic Dean at The Evergreen State College in Olympia, Washington, USA. His research centers on the cultural practices of human rights and on literary engagements with the cultural politics of rights. He is the author of *Colonial Affairs*, a study of colonialism and queer sexuality in American expatriate literature. Recipient of a Fulbright grant in Brazil, he has published essays on literature, sexual rights, and human rights in Brazil and in the United States, and has served as guest editor for human rights issues of *Cadernos de letras* and *College Literature*.

Hanna Musiol is Associate Professor of English and Deputy Director of NTNU ARTEC at the Norwegian University of Science and Technology, Norway. Her research interests include American literature, transmedia storytelling, theory, and critical pedagogy, with emphasis on decolonization, migration, rights, and political ecology. She traffics in metaphors and transmedia theory in her scholarship, pedagogy, and editorial, curatorial, and transnational civic engagement work, and she publishes frequently on literary and visual aesthetics and justice.

Angela Naimou is Associate Professor of English at Clemson University, USA, co-editor of *Humanity* journal, and an associate editor for the journal *Contemporary Literature*. She is the author of *Salvage Work: U.S. and Caribbean Literatures amid the Debris of Legal Personhood* (Fordham University Press 2015), which won the Association for the Study of the Arts of the Present (ASAP) Book Prize and honorable mention for the William Sanders Scarborough Award from the Modern Language Association. Her current research examines forms and practices of contemporary literature in relation to the politics of migration, refuge, and asylum.

Samantha Pinto is Associate Professor of English and affiliated faculty of Women's and Gender Studies, African and African Diaspora Studies, The Warfield Center for African American Studies, and LGBTQ Studies at the University of Texas at Austin, USA. Her book, *Difficult Diasporas: The Transnational Feminist Aesthetic of the Black Atlantic* (NYU Press, 2013), was the winner of the 2013 William Sanders Scarborough Prize for African American Literature and Culture from the MLA. Her work has been published in journals including *Meridians*, *Signs*, *Palimpsest*, *Safundi*, *Small Axe*, and *Atlantic Studies*, and she has received fellowships from the National Endowment for the Humanities and the Harry Ransom Center. Her second book, *Infamous Bodies* (Duke University Press, 2020), explores the relationship between eighteenth- and nineteenth-century black women celebrities and discourses of race, gender, and human rights. Currently, she is at work on a third book, "Under the Skin," on race, embodiment, and scientific discourse in African American and African Diaspora culture.

Terri Tomsky is Associate Professor in the Department of English and Film Studies at the University of Alberta, Canada. Her research examines memory politics and memory economies in postcolonial and post-socialist literatures. She is the co-editor (with Eddy Kent) of *Negative Cosmopolitanism: Culture and Politics of World Citizenship after Globalization* (McGill-Queen's University Press, 2017). She has published articles in *parallax*, *Journal of Commonwealth Literature*, *Life Writing*, *Biography*, and *The Australian Journal of Human Rights*, as well as contributed chapters to several book collections, including *Cosmopolitan Animals* (2015) and *Security and Hospitality: New Literary Perspectives* (2016).

Diren Valayden is Assistant Professor of Human Development at Binghamton University, USA. His research focuses on critical theories of race and the human, the intersection of race and human rights, and military urbanism. He is currently writing a book on "Racial Feralization" in which he argues that racial governance is increasingly legitimated in terms of the management and violent regulation of those characterized as feral beings.

List of Figures

CHAPTER 1

Beyond Sovereignty: New Cultural Imaginaries of Human Rights

Alexandra S. Moore and Samantha Pinto

Sovereignty serves as the crux of the human rights project: the source of its juridico-political structure and its deepest conceptual and political paradoxes, if not abuses. Much critical work has demonstrated, first, how human rights might secure the state's monopoly on legitimate violence and, second, sovereignty's twinned role as guarantor of human rights and perpetrator of their abuses. Another strand of critique has focused on the sovereign subject of human rights, and the efficacies and limitations of the figure of the liberal subject in responding to egregious human rights abuses and to the pernicious effects of incremental degradation. At the same time, human rights remain a discursive and juridico-political framework for the definition and pursuit of certain forms of human flourishing. That framework has proven to be, yes, imperfect or even detrimental in

A. S. Moore
Binghamton University, New York, NY, USA
e-mail: amoore@binghamton.edu

S. Pinto (✉)
University of Texas at Austin, Austin, TX, USA
e-mail: samantha.pinto@utexas.edu

A. S. Moore and S. Pinto (eds.), *Writing Beyond the State*,
Palgrave Studies in Literature, Culture and Human Rights,
https://doi.org/10.1007/978-3-030-34456-6_1

some circumstances, but also at times resilient, dynamic, and efficacious in responding to atrocity and harm.

Informed by trenchant analyses of the role of sovereignty in normative human rights, *Writing Beyond the State* moves into the space beyond those critiques, taking them as a point of departure and exploring how literature, the arts, and culture give us new aesthetics, methods, and modes of articulation for human rights imaginaries. In doing so, we collectively argue that literature and literary study can shift perspectives on the category of human rights, rather than continuing to beat the drum of sovereignty and its limits. These shifts are not intended to be salvific of normative human rights, but rather to open up new forums for imagination, representation, and critique. Our hope is that as readers and critics, we have written to push collectively the borders of human rights; we hope that from starting at the recognition of the impossible binds of our reading practices, so hemmed in by statist discourse and limits, we might acknowledge but also find new ground beyond the either/or of celebrating or abandoning the human rights project. This collection thus seeks to reorient critical and aesthetic attention to alternative cultural imaginaries of rights, to forms of representing human rights that do not depend upon sovereignty of the subject or nation as their sole currency.

As a point of departure, we might consider Theophilus Marboah's representation (Fig. 1.1) of desperate human movement. Marboah's pairing of the diagram of the "Brookes" slave ship (circa 1790) with Massimo Sestini's 2014 photograph of asylum seekers traveling across the Mediterranean from North Africa toward Italy links not just the history of enslavement and the contemporary status of refugees in Fortress Europe, but visually renders the deep relationship between statelessness and rightlessness in modernity. While theorists such as Paul Gilroy have imagined the ship as a modern vehicle of ineffable pain but also of masculine freedom and mobility (Gilroy 1993), this piece from Marboah's "Echoes and Agreements" series stages the ship as a floating, startling rebuke to ideals of mobility between states. It showcases displacement beyond sovereignty, giving a structural view of the asymmetrical relations between subject and subjected, between historical articulations of modernity's limited notion of the subject of human rights, and of the human itself, and its present-day refusals and trite witnessing of a seemingly anachronistic echo. Although each image may signal human traffick between nation-states, the images more forcefully focus attention

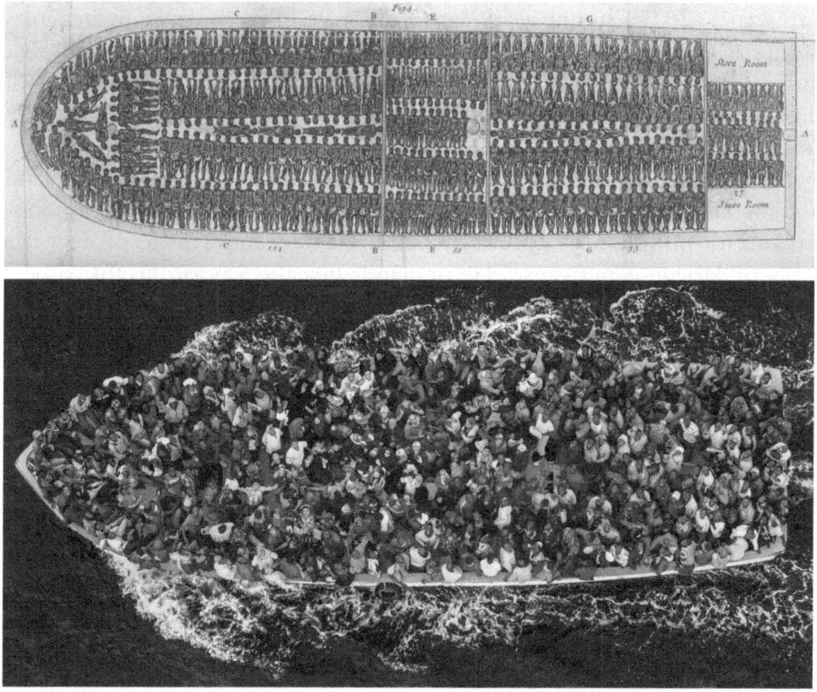

Fig. 1.1 Theophilus Marboah, selection from "Echoes and Agreements," 2018. "Plan of the Slave Ship Brookes," from Thomas Clarkson's "The history of the rise, progress, and accomplishment of the abolition of the African slave trade by the British Parliament" (1808), appears courtesy of the British Library Board. Massimo Sestini, photograph of the migrant boat crossing, is reprinted by permission (©Massimo Sestini)

on the life- and death-worlds of the ship and of the journey that often refuses to resolve into the teleology of national belonging.

Upon first glance, this conclusion that the artwork foremost represents potential refusal would seem to confirm Hannah Arendt's thesis that human rights require citizenship to become fully realized. Such a reading does little to shift our understanding of normative human rights, and instead underscores a familiar critique of their reliance on citizenship as an expression of sovereignty. Shifting the focus to the inbetweenness of the journey, however, opens up another line of inquiry, following Ayça

Çubukçu's (2017) recent work, about the role of ***potentiality*** in structuring normative human rights and, thus, regarding human rights as implicitly hierarchical. As Çubukçu demonstrates in a comparative reading of Malcolm X and Arendt, Arendt's attention to citizenship, argued in the context of her deeply troubling and under-examined chapters in *Origins of Totalitarianism* on "Race-thinking before racism" and "Racism and bureaucracy," is undercut by Malcolm X's forceful and contemporaneous demand for human rights precisely because citizenship fails to protect the rights of African Americans.[1] He demands first the a priori "right to be a human being" in order "to be given the rights of a human being in this society" (Malcolm X 1970, 56, qted Çubukçu 2017, 253). In the work of both thinkers, human rights are at once aspirational and marked by the category of humanity as at once inclusive and discriminatory in categorizing some members according to their full or potential realization of its ideal attributes. In Çubukçu's words,

> the very inscription of particular qualities to human beings (be it agency, autonomy, rationality, or whichever other quality is thought to differentiate humans from non-humans) helps construct the human as *potentially* autonomous, developed, sane, rational, civilized and *therefore potentially* entitled to, and capable of enjoying, human rights. Human rights, in other words, are the potential rights of proper human beings ... (256; see also 262)

Çubukçu's reading of Malcolm X and Arendt concludes in deep skepticism of the category of humanity as foundational to liberal human rights for the ways in which "such conceptions of human rights attach particular qualities to the concept and the person of the human" (255). Rather than pursue "justice without borders" through the concept of a collective humanity, she argues for solidarity between and meaningful justice for "human and non-human alike" (266).

Marboah's work takes up the problem of racial hierarchies within humanity and human rights and offers a different trajectory through the critiques of humanity's exclusions, representing and responding to the historical violence in the deployment of humanity by troubling its terms. As a diptych, Marboah's work raises the question of the relationship between the two parts. Although it runs the risk of intimating an equivalency between halves, the form need not imply a decontextualized narrative of centuries-long Afropessimism. Rather, Marboah's work, with its close attention to the aesthetic dimensions of composition, framing, perspective, and what he calls the "rhyme" in form and content between images, unsettles interpretations of each half on its own (this effect is magnified by reading the work above in the context of Marboah's larger body of images in this series in which he consistently pairs canonical images with lesser known photographs and film stills). Unsettling generates inquiry into the images of the Black diaspora he presents as well as alternative relationships he constructs between subjects. For Marboah, the "dialogue" within a pair of images can offer "reminders of the category of universality in which we all dwell, despite the time and space that separate us" (Marboah), both aspects of which are represented through the lens of the African diaspora. This artwork, then, does not seek the slave ship as metaphor or analogy but tries to align itself to failures of thought, our inability, despite decades of critique, to transcend appeals to the nation-state to repair and restore the category of the human.[2]

Our reading of Marboah's work hews to Ida Danewid's recent trenchant critique of the affectual modes of contemporary theory that focus on empathy or the work of mourning: "By privileging a focus on the ontological—as opposed to historical—links that bind humankind, these ethical perspectives contribute to an ideological formation that disconnects histories that are intimately connected, and that removes from view the many afterlives of historical and ongoing colonialism" (Danewid 2017). When affective identification replaces or elides historical understanding, the "result is a veil of ignorance which [...] allows the white subject to re-constitute itself as 'ethical' and 'good,' innocent of imperialist histories and present complicities" (Danewid). Marboah's work, with its insistence on critical distance and hence difference, confronts the viewer as potentially complicit in the historical confluence of human rights violations (including differential access to full humanity), denying the vicarious affectual bond of sentimental feeling for the refugee. The diptych sticks to the colonizer's formal point of view as it deploys the medium of aerial photography—a capture technology of the security state—to make its aesthetic and political imaginary, as well as the ongoing crisis of human rights, visible. The structure of white feeling and the categories it produces (sovereignty, nationalism, property, and human cargo) become the subject of the piece, displacing the question of whether and how to incorporate the "non-citizen" into the nation-state (although Marike Jansen's essay in this volume provides a compelling blueprint for that topic in the realm of theater). This powerful re-aestheticization of the material forms of transnational, cross-historical violations of human rights provides an example and a reflection of this volume's focus on the capacity of literature and expressive arts in the political realm.

Marboah's invocation of at once universality and historical differentialization often takes place through the juxtaposition of known and unknown or familiar and unfamiliar, however his is not a reassertion of classical humanism with all of its embedded, embodied exclusions. His formal rhyming occurs through the indexicality of gestures and perspectives, insisting on specificity, context, and material grounding for comprehension. Rather than erase the differences between the slave ship and refugee boat, the pairing magnifies the conditions that informed each crossing, raising questions about directionality and outcome, movement versus the finality of death (at either end of the journey or in its midst), the claims of either group pictured to recognizable subject positions, and the position of the viewer vis à vis the image. Note, for instance, the startling recognition that passengers in Sestini's image are looking back up at the viewer, at once calling attention to and interrogating the structural inequities that inform humanitarian spectatorship (including the choice to look away). The interpellation of the viewer by the photograph's subjects also underscores the depersonalization of figures on the slave ship in legal, material, and representational terms. The pairings, in other words, return the viewer to the particular forces catalyzing these journeys and the contemporary conditions of their visuality. This doesn't insist on equivalencies but rather showcases the ways that art and culture might wrestle with and represent a sense of contingency and irresolution in the wake of (to echo Christina Sharpe 2016) individual and state sovereignty's historic, recurring failures to secure human rights.

Thinking Through Post-Sovereignty

In his analysis of the conceptual underpinnings of the *Universal Declaration of Human Rights* (1948), Johannes Morsink draws attention to what he calls "special international (human) rights" which require international cooperation between nation-states (Morsink 1999, 72). Articles such as Article 15 (1), "Everyone has the right to a nationality," he writes, provide "real test cases for any list of human rights, for in their case *the question of the problem of sovereignty* can longer be hidden behind the veil of positive constitutional law" (73, emphasis added). Morsink traces the impetus for Article 15 to Nazi Germany where revoking Jewish citizenship provided a crucial stepping stone in the process of dehumanization and genocide. When the Third Committee drafting the UDHR eventually passed "Everyone has the right to a nationality," although not without dissent, it was with the recognition that this right would necessitate "UN involvement" (82). The debates that informed the drafting and inclusion of Article 15 emphasize the extent to which the framers of the UDHR took the political necessity of the nation-state for granted even as they acknowledged the tension between the United Nations and individual state sovereignty. These assumptions and concerns lay bare several of the oft-rehearsed, foundational paradoxes of international human rights: that they are idealistic and unenforceable precisely to the degree that they at once shore up the sovereign power of the nation-state and depend upon its voluntary participation; that they have relied on Western notions of individual rights over collective duties or responsibilities; that they concern themselves with political and civil rights over thornier, transnationally interlocking social, economic, environmental, and cultural rights; that they have set up a larger Western, undemocratic, capitalist body to determine which states "deserve" humanitarian aid and intervention, and on what terms and in what forms these interventions will manifest.

In this volume, we put pressure on what Morsink describes circuitously as *the question of the problem of sovereignty* from a different direction. Rather than read human rights as fatally tainted by paradox, we begin with the assumption that the current state of human rights is already post-sovereign—at once untethered from its original political building blocks of the nation-state and the liberal subject and nonetheless responsive to the state's capacity for violence and to its potential as a bulwark against neoliberalism. Instead of rehearsing critiques of a legal and moral field still invested in the promise of the sovereign state and individual or undone by paradox, this collection works on reimagining the normative terrain of human rights beyond the conceptual and political boundaries that have been the necessary focus of critique for at least the founding quarter century of the field of human rights and the humanities. Contributors to this volume engage directly with the forces that shape the imagination of human suffering and rights—neoliberalism, the security state, post-humanism. Each essay also analyzes how creative forms and representational practices might generate alternative human rights social imaginaries for our collective present and future.

We take Marboah's image as our starting point for this collection to signal the volatile inbetweenness of theorizing human rights at our current moment. We know that human rights discourse is in crisis. Or rather, human rights discourse has been in crisis for quite some time, with a long history of academic and activist critique from Left, feminist, critical race, and postcolonial politics (e.g., Bunch 1990; Grewal 2005; Kennedy 2005; Slaughter 2007; Douzinas 2000, 2007; Perugini and Gordon 2015). Some of that critique responds to the very normativity of human rights—to the ways in which human rights discourse has entered the public sphere, even if its institutions remain limited in power and effectiveness. But the contemporary shape of the crisis, its scale and its urgency, have ballooned in the face of the mounting and open challenges to even the basic tenets of human rights and personhood on a global scale: mass incarceration; police, military, and other state violence and surveillance; refugee death, displacement, and disavowal; unchecked corporate capitalism and oligarchy, accompanied by the distribution of debt as a form of social control; and a radical denial of environmental devastation even as its consequences become deeply present and material. How, in the face of these debilitating and existential threats to human and nonhuman life, are we to imagine the work of human rights? Are they the dismal failure of a capitalist modernity in decline, or do we redouble our claims to their tenets, or try to rework them, in the face of their radical erosion in the contemporary moment?

For scholars of human rights, this disingenuous choice between embrace and disavowal is, in so many ways, an old question, a false constitution of the crisis of late capitalism in a global frame. Rights, as many have shown, are constructed through not just political systems but through narrative, through culture, and through representation. What scholars in the field have been diagnosing for years are the possibilities and the pitfalls that consciously and unconsciously lay in not just our appeals to and for human rights, but also in our critiques of their efficacy that keep wrapping back into the frame of the nation-state and questions of state enforcement. On the one hand, human rights are paradoxical in their appeal to the very state from which the claimant seeks protection. On the other hand, especially given the scale of violations produced in the wake of neoliberalism, is it possible that states might be one of the only entities powerful enough to respond to egregious human wrongs as well as to the slow violence (Nixon 2011) that immiserates specific populations? Or can we imagine other forms of solidarity that might incorporate some of human rights' core values around conditions of human flourishing?

In a moment when we might say that the limits of appeals to sovereignty (as well as the endless critique of sovereignty the field has produced in the wake of the failures of individual civil and political entitlement rights and nation-state enforcement) have collapsed under the weight of global atrocity and inequity, where else can human rights conceptually travel? What are the possibilities that the study of literature, art, and culture can bring to the field in this post-sovereign moment, including but also exceeding representations of transnational belonging and unbelonging? How might the displacement of sovereignty, both at the limits of the formal state and the boundaries of personhood-as-individual-property, offer us new modes of representation that are not necessarily mimetic reflections of human rights as they are but as they could be refigured in this moment of crisis? How might crisis itself be a temporality we exploit, explore, and explode in our attempt to think about literature, art, and culture's enduring entanglements with human rights?

As nationalist parties re-entrench racist and xenophobic borders in fictions of purist pasts in many parts of the world, these dangerous and material performances of sovereignty have also given heightened attention to the un-sovereign roots of the Western nation-state (and many of the postcolonial states that emerged in empire's wake), built through the violence of slavery capitalism and natural resources extraction in the colonial era, and from the historical conditions of the post-world war era of decolonization, Cold War imperialism, neoliberal policy, and the soaring international debt for the "developing" world left in this historical wake (Beckart and Rockman 2016; Moyo 2009; Baptist 2014; Browne 2015). The optics and technologies of the security state—which bring sovereignty and biopower together, in our view, rather than mark a transition from the former to the latter—have always been meant to surveil intranational difference and do the work of transnational reach beyond the formal borders of the state, asserting sovereignty as a mobile and devouring entitlement from infrastructure to sexual identity (Hoad 2006; Weber 2016; Amar 2016; Alexander 2006). Post-sovereignty, then, is a *historical*, *conceptual*, and *political* relation: *historical* in its description of an ongoing state of affairs for the most vulnerable populations of the globe that have had their individual and national sovereignty treated as secondary to the West's own rights to the globe as white property; *conceptual* in its insistence on not retreating to the totalizing remedy of the nation-state for repair and redress even as it finds immanent critique at the site of the nation-state as well as in the rehearsal of some human rights discourses; *political* in its will to locate something beyond critique in this recognition of being beyond the state. We argue that the expressive arts, then, can offer us not just reflections of but new methods of thinking through post-sovereign relations, ways to imagine political forms that face us in the modern-day security archipelago (Amar 2013; Grewal 2017) as well as those yet to come.

We maintain, then, a dual insistence on both emphasizing the possibilities of a "beyond" in human rights studies of the state and sovereignty and a transparency about the deep conceptual, methodological, and linguistic difficulty—even inevitable failure—to transcend or escape the modes of critique of the state that haunt the field. The collection stands not as a disavowal of previous modes of reading and reading for human rights and its failures, but a deep engagement with the seductive and pervasive promise of rights discourse and its enduring power in a modernity founded on and upon the nation-state.

And what of the subject facing that future? After laying out a critique of the particular binds of human rights discourse in regards to another border—that of the body—critic Elizabeth S. Anker (2012), drawing on phenomenology, suggests reading against an imperative for bodily integrity while still taking corporeality, in all its messiness, into account in human rights discourse. One can read in her work a feminist imperative against the object/subject binary, a way to read past the impasse of paradigms of sovereignty of both self and state. Moore (2016) examines the limitations of the sovereign subject of human rights through recent developments in vulnerability theory, including the risk it runs of transforming the potential human rights claimant into the recipient of humanitarian benevolence. Crystal Parikh, in her recent *Writing Human Rights* (2017), would in fact levy most critiques of human rights as critiques of the limits of humanitarianism, a mode of looking at the "other" as "object" in need of saving. Parikh examines human rights in the work of US writers of color to locate a creative ethical imperative away from the limits of the racist domestic state and toward the complex transnational terrain of social, cultural, and economic rights, or what Parikh deems the "political imaginaries" that link literary and human rights production beyond the state. In many ways, Marboah's image suggests the ways we have always been post-sovereign—the ways that fictions of the security state are undergirded and undone by the long legal and labor history of human trafficking and the transnational economies of enslavement that built the nation-state.

As the opening image suggests, the question of the human, the question of rights, and their yoking to state's rights and sovereignty, has always been asked in the transnational networks of the Middle Passage, indigenous and ethnic genocide, refugee "crises," and other events of mass violence that undergird efforts to secure national borders and individual citizenship for some (Cacho 2012; Brandzel 2016). Without attempting to rescue human rights or literature, this introduction and collection, like Parikh's recent work, takes seriously the ethics of aesthetics in asserting something beyond the state, beyond domestic law, to something like an ethical imaginary—something that is at once imagined through the representation of hyper-localized bodies and spaces but also goes beyond the pragmatic politics of the state or the impossibility of statist discourse in human rights studies. It is precisely by drawing attention to the formal dimensions—material and aesthetic—of representation that the expressive arts can help us reconsider the formal dimensions of political and legal representation. Something like the visual pairing of the slave ship diagram and the migrant ship aerial photo offers repetition with a difference, connection across historical, national, and trans-political "crisis" that forces an ethical confrontation beyond the borders of the state, and the ways that human rights have spoken to and intimately recognized the limits of the state in the global (mis)recognition of who counts as a human with rights. Crucially, Marboah's piece poses this as a structural question—rather than giving a close up of individualized suffering that appeals to the humanitarian object in need of rescue, his work offers the ship as the object of scrutiny, as the spectacular technology that lays bare human rights failures in the name of and in between sovereign states (a method repeated in a different way in several essays in this collection, most notably by Angela Naimou and Diren Valayden). *Writing Beyond the State* traces how expressive cultural work like Marboah's diptych inhabits, creates, arbitrates, and imagines new forms and relations of human rights in the wake of sovereignty and its critiques (Sharpe 2016).

This collection, at its core, focuses on these questions, and on how different literary, visual, and political technologies are reimagining both human rights and their claimants. Contributors examine the possibilities of the forms, genres, and affects of human rights, covering a multimedia terrain of documentary photography, poetry, science fiction, and theater, as well as the narratives of human rights discourse itself produced in legal instruments, manifestos, and appeals for change. Rather than simply critique normative discourses of human rights that are built upon the foundations of sovereignty, the authors of the chapters that follow explore creative possibilities for the future of rights—futures that may include the failure of rights. They analyze the structures of how it is we do and might do human rights work through literary and cultural analysis, thinking through both the material and conceptual edifices that remain in the wake of sovereignty. We define the failures of discourses and politics of sovereignty through the deconstruction of the welfare state, the collation of international human rights politics into the forms of neoliberal governance bodies and the NGO industrial complex, and the large-scale material and human losses of the decolonial, postcolonial, and, in the US, post-Civil Rights era that we are now living out. The ramifications have been stark: the criminalization of poverty and the privatization of basic human rights as moral entitlements; the rampant distribution of wealth, access, opportunity, and life chances to a miniscule percentage of the world's population; the continued transformation of the nation-state and the individual citizen as "property"—with all of the attendant weight of that term as a white patriarchal supremacist vision of violent protectionism.

In the shadow of this breakdown of democratic, liberal humanist, as well as radical "freedom dreams," this collection asks how we might build anew human rights imaginaries, discourses, and representations that incorporate multiplicity and flexibility rather than originalism and purity (Kelley 2002). Thus, our contributors engage critiques of human rights proffered by other contemporary theorists working on social justice issues, without necessarily abandoning human rights themselves. *Writing Beyond the State* looks to arts and literature to generatively disorient our critical sensibilities rather than bring our already honed, rational tools of recognition and critique to the cut and dried labor of both interpretation and world-building that human rights studies promises. In acknowledging this labor, this unlearning, as the work of the volume writ large and in individual contributions, we then organize the intellectual project of the collection and field around innovative, risky, and speculative modes of understanding the project of human rights studies—as well as its history and its futures. The essays herein explore how strands of materialist, affective, posthumanist, eco-critical, and leftist theory might work together to help us to recognize and to reimagine human rights for our present and future.

Post-Sovereign Sites: The Chapters

Marboah's work implores us not to take in "the other" to our own sovereign state but to imagine the massive scale of structural violence that constructs, connects, and confronts the viewer across time and space. This sense of the scale of the theoretical, historical, and cultural networks in which our contributors participate haunts each essay's individual intervention into the dynamic field of human rights and literary/cultural expression.

The six essays in Part I, Refiguring Human Rights and Humanitarianism from Decolonization to Capitalist Globalization, ask us to rethink the terms of contemporary human rights, beginning with its comparativist and transnational humanist underpinnings in the era of decolonization. This historiographic approach challenges Samuel Moyn's thesis that contemporary human rights were launched in the late 1970s and engages with recent scholarship on the productive use of human rights in the Global South (e.g., Jensen 2016) during this period. Such research reveals that the post-Enlightenment liberal subject of rights was only ever a partial and compromised conception of rights' scope and flexibility. Essays in this section present a wide range of aesthetic and political orientations to rights beyond state apparati and individual entitlement. In their chapters, Samantha Pinto and Emily Davis reconceptualize the subject of human rights as embodied, racialized, gendered, and politically constituted across different literary genres, time periods, and representations of African, African diaspora, and indigenous subjects. Pinto recasts the rise of the United Nations as a site of definitional human rights alongside decolonial movements in continental Africa in the 1960s as a key tension point in the articulation of women and girls' rights. She looks to literature by African feminists of the period, shut out of official cultural and political channels for rights intra- and internationally, as an underexplored avenue where ambivalence about the state's protection of women's rights as human rights becomes most vividly articulated. For Davis, utopic and yet critically informed investments in international human and posthuman rights frameworks that take feminism, anti-colonialism, and indigeneity as their core principles saturate the imagined worlds of African science fiction.

The next three essays in this section examine the role of style, empathy, and affect in normative human rights genres through examination of the archives of Amnesty International, multimedia platforms (the Humans of New York series in the *New York Times*), and the deployment of virtual reality technologies by humanitarian organizations and the technologies' potential to disrupt the "empathy machine" of human rights appeals. Greg Mullins focuses on the historic shift to what we now consider the paradigmatic "style" of humanitarian industry, insisting that we take seriously the politics of affect and its ability to structure human rights work. Also addressing the role of affect, here in the relationship between immersive technologies and the production of empathy, in their essay, Kerry Bystrom and Roberta Mosse engage with the complex pitfalls and potentials of virtual reality technologies in humanitarian campaigns as an effort to destabilize Western conceptions of "the other" in relationship to rights.

This section concludes with two essays on neoliberalism and political economy. Mukti Lakhi Mangharam presents the innovative use and difficult translations of contemporary multi- and social media forms of mobilizing human rights affects and discourses through her essay's astute analysis of the wildly popular and now much-copied form of Humans of New York. The final contribution is a far-reaching essay by Peter Hitchcock on the political economy of rights in our current moment of neo-populist, nationalist, anti-rights retrenchment. He provocatively posits securitization against risk as a model of rights that can look beyond neoliberalism by decoupling personhood and property. All of the essays in this section then recast the history and current moment of human rights beyond the state and law by focusing on the forms and styles of humanitarian and human rights-focused literature and culture.

Part II, Securitization, Toxicity, and the Future of Rights, extends the collection's focus on form and aesthetics to three of the overriding human rights crises of our time: the rise of the security archipelago (Amar), displacement and the search for refuge, and the endangerment of human and nonhuman life by environmental catastrophes both dramatic and incremental. Drawing on a wide range of interdisciplinary methodologies and analyzing institutional norms, data surveillance collections and technologies, graphic narratives, poetry, drama, and eco-fiction, the six essays in this section examine the structural, formal, and technological sources of human rights abuse as well as the structures, forms, and technologies of reimagining human rights claims and claimants through creative expression.

We begin with Valayden's essay on the detailed history and form of maritime sovereignty in the littoral, the high-traffic, high-risk areas that connect mainlands to islands to ocean, and its implications for reading the conditions facing refugees unfolding today. The collection then moves from the concept of liquid sovereignty to a focus on the networks in which human rights abuses and responses take place. In her essay, Stephanie Athey analyzes the ways in which violence in the name of securitization (specifically in the US war on terror) is made possible by institutional norms of professionalism—here legal professionalism as well as the norms articulated by the American Psychological Association. Athey's approach demonstrates a vital new area of scholarship in human rights, and applies network theory developed largely in sociology to the analysis of discourse, culture, and politics. She focuses on the infrastructures of structural violence and, crucially, potential futures of rights organizing apart from individual and state entity culpability for singular violations or events.

The essay's focus on material and institutional structure flows into the next three essays, which look at the contested status of citizenship vis à vis the contemporary refugee crisis. Naimou thinks through contemporary poetics' reconfiguration of the data of death, loss, and grief as a powerful movement away from state accounting of refugee death and loss, but also away from the aesthetics and politics of individualization and/as humanization that plague the field. Taking up the material conditions of securitization, Terri Tomsky analyzes the architecture of detention in her essay on the holding of refugees and immigrants along with the secrecy and refusal of sociality that accompany the built space of xenophobic deprivations of rights. Marike Janzen offers a powerful ethnographic examination of state-funded theater engagement with refugee performers in Germany, arguing for a reconceptualization of human rights aesthetics and politics away from the citizen and toward the figure of the refugee that extends into practice.

We end this section with Hanna Musiol's dive into the productive intersection of posthumanist, eco-critical, and human rights discourses in her reading of innovative contemporary art and literature focused on climate change. She brings attention to new forms and genres of cultural expression in conjunction with a vital reformulation of rights away from personhood. This volume concludes with a brief epilogue that takes sculptor Jason deCaires Taylor's underwater Museo Atlántico installation (deCaires Taylor also provides the cover image for this volume) as a point of departure for considering how the aesthetic might figure violations of human rights that are inseparable from other life forms, ecologies, and histories unbounded by legal personality or sovereign states.

Notes

1. See also Kathryn T. Gines, *Hannah Arendt and the Negro Question* (Indiana University Press, 2014) for an important analysis of the role of race in Arendt's thought.
2. Marboah's seemingly comparative frame for the dual images also engages the work of art historians, poets, and artists who have reconceptualized the slave ship icon in and for the twentieth and twenty-first centuries. Cheryl Finley's powerful work on the slave ship form's repurposing by Black artists, *Committed to Memory: The Art of the Slave Ship Icon* (Princeton University Press, 2018), posits the image of the slave ship as a site of radical and radicalized memorialization—beginning with abolitionist appropriation of the icon of the ship in eighteenth- and nineteenth-century work toward emancipation. The shock of its human brutality and cost is reimagined in the stark organizational image in Marboah's work, another moment where "data" as incorporated by artists can give voice to a human rights beyond sentimentalism (as argued by several essays in this collection). But if Marboah joins a number of artists and writers (including Amiri Baraka, Betye Saar, and Claudia Rankine) in a modern-day reworking of the slave ship icon, he departs from the use of it as a sight of communal memory and memorialization. Nor does he embody critiques of art such as J. M. W. Turner's *Slave Ship* (or *Slavers Throwing Overboard the Dead and Dying—Typhoon Coming On*, 1840) that note its aesthetic and affective white humanitarian translation of the Middle Passage.

Works Cited

Alexander, M. Jacqui. 2006. *Pedagogies of Crossing: Meditations on Feminism, Sexual Politics, Memory, and the Sacred*. Durham: Duke University Press.

Amar, Paul. 2013. *The Security Archipelago: Human-Security States, Sexuality Politics, and the End of Neoliberalism*. Durham: Duke University Press.

———. 2016. "Plural Global Perversions and Curious International Relations." Online forum on Queer IR. *International Studies Quarterly*, August 30.

Anker, Elizabeth S. 2012. *Fictions of Dignity: Embodying Human Rights in World Literature*. Ithaca: Cornell University Press.

Baptist, Edward E. 2014. *The Half Has Never Been Told: Slavery and American Capitalism*. New York: Basic Books.

Beckart, Sven, and Seth Rockman, ed. 2016. *Slavery's Capitalism: A New History of American Economic Development*. Philadelphia: University of Pennsylvania Press.
Brandzel, Amy. 2016. *Against Citizenship: The Violence of the Normative*. Urbana: University of Illinois Press.
Browne, Simone. 2015. *Dark Matters: On the Surveillance of Blackness*. Durham: Duke University Press.
Bunch, Charlotte. 1990. "Women's Rights as Human Rights: Toward a Re-vision of Human Rights." *Human Rights Quarterly* 12 (4, November): 486–498.
Cacho, Lisa. 2012. *Social Death: Racialized Rightlessness and the Criminalization of the Unprotected*. New York: New York University Press.
Çubukçu, Ayça. 2017. "Thinking Against Humanity." *London Review of International Law* 5 (2): 251–267.
Danewid, Ida. 2017. "White Innocence in the Black Mediterranean." *The Disorder of Things*, June 7. https://thedisorderofthings.com/2017/06/07/white-innocence-in-the-black-mediterranean/.
Douzinas, Costas. 2000. *The End of Human Rights*. Oxford: Hart Publishing.
———. 2007. *Human Rights and Empire: The Political Philosophy of Cosmopolitanism*. London: Routledge-Cavendish.
Gilroy, Paul. 1993. *The Black Atlantic: Modernity and Double Consciousness*. Verso.
Gines, Kathryn T. 2014. *Hannah Arendt and the Negro Question*. Indianapolis: University of Indiana Press.
Grewal, Inderpal. 2005. *Transnational America: Feminisms, Diasporas, Neoliberalisms*. Durham: Duke University Press.
———. 2017. *Saving the Security State: Exceptional Citizens in Twenty-First Century America*. Durham: Duke University Press.
Hoad, Neville. 2006. *African Intimacies: Race, Homosexuality, Globalization*. Minneapolis: Minnesota University Press.
Jensen, Steven L. B. 2016. *The Making of International Human Rights: The 1960s, Decolonization, and the Reconstruction of Global Values*. New York: Cambridge University Press.
Kelley, R. D. 2002. *Freedom Dreams: The Black Radical Imagination*. New York: Beacon Press.
Kennedy, David. 2005. *The Dark Sides of Virtue: Reassessing International Humanitarianism*. Princeton: Princeton University Press.
Malcolm X. 1970. *By Any Means Necessary: Speeches, Interviews, and a Letter by Malcolm X*, edited by G. Breitman. New York: Pathfinder Press.
Marboah, Theophilus. 2018. "Echoes and Agreements." *Afrosartorialism*, September 4. https://www.afrosartorialism.net/2018/09/04/talents-theophilus-marboah-echoes-and-agreements/.

Moore, Alexandra Schultheis. 2016. *Vulnerability and Security in Human Rights Literature and Visual Culture*. New York and London: Routledge.
Morsink, Johannes. 1999. *The Universal Declaration of Human Rights: Origins, Drafting and Intent*. Philadelphia: University of Pennsylvania Press.
Moyo, Dambisa. 2009. *Dead Aid: Why Aid Is Not Working and How There Is a Better Way For Africa*. New York: Farrar, Straus & Giroux.
Nixon, Rob. 2011. *Slow Violence and the Environmentalism of the Poor*. Cambridge: Harvard University Press.
Parikh, Crystal. 2017. *Writing Human Rights: The Political Imaginaries of Writers of Color*. Minneapolis: University of Minnesota Press.
Perugini, Nicola, and Neve Gordon. 2015. *The Human Rights to Dominate*. Oxford: Oxford University Press.
Sharpe, Christina. 2016. *In The Wake*. Durham: Duke University Press.
Slaughter, Joseph R. 2007. *Human Rights, Inc.: The World Novel, Narrative Form, and International Law*. New York: Fordham University Press.
Weber, Cynthia. 2016. *Queer International Relations: Sovereignty, Sexuality and the Will to Knowledge*. London: Oxford University Press.

PART I

Re-figuring Human Rights and Humanitarianism from 1960 to the Present

CHAPTER 2

Feminist Drift: Africa, Gender, and Ambivalent Histories of Human Rights Beyond the State

Samantha Pinto

Rebecca Njau's 1960 one act play, *The Scar*, startles in its articulation of feminist transformation:

> This is a new land; it is not the land of
> your birth.
> The old has gone with its teaching;
> The young girls must learn new things;
> They must receive something deeper –
> something to uplift
> Them – something to raise their dropping
> heads.
> A 'physical operation' is as empty as a cave;
> It is meaningless.
> They must go through a different initiation
> that will
> Make no man or even women like you shake them. (14)

S. Pinto (✉)
University of Texas at Austin, Austin, TX, USA
e-mail: samantha.pinto@utexas.edu

A. S. Moore and S. Pinto (eds.), *Writing Beyond the State*,
Palgrave Studies in Literature, Culture and Human Rights,
https://doi.org/10.1007/978-3-030-34456-6_2

This essay takes up a brief, important moment in modern African history—1960, the crossroads of independence movements across Africa and the nascent moment of United Nations/nongovernmental organization development discourse around Human Rights and Africa—to think through the national, historical, ideological, academic, and institutional limits of the state and its role in feminist human rights critique. I will read *The Scar*, an award-winning, one act play from Kenyan author Rebecca Njau,[1] as an early scene of ambivalence about feminist human rights, cultural nationalism, and their anticipated critiques. In doing so, this essay engages a set of questions that refuse the polarizing binds of representation that mark African women as cultural signifiers of pre-modernity, or romanticize them as resistant local and global agents in the history of transnational feminist discourse.

Playwright and eventual novelist Njau, a Kikuyu-identified woman from Kenya, won first prize in the 1960 Ugandan Drama Festival for her brief play.[2] Circulating among the literary and cultural energy of the continent at this time, including publication in the East African arts and letters magazine *Transition* in 1963, the play is also part of larger decolonization dynamics that paralleled and buoyed this public focus on developing and showcasing the arts and cultural talents of the continent in the early nineteen-sixties.[3] As a prize winning play, *The Scar* was also clearly accepted as part of an existing if exciting dialogue on the Pan-African literary scene—no political aberration, even as its "theme" would be belatedly interpreted as controversial by standard debates around Kikuyu loyalty and anti-colonial sentiment.[4] The play anticipates Ngugi wa Thiong'o's own ambivalent novel dealing with female genital cutting and rebellion, *The River Between*, in 1965, which also dramatizes (although more as a complex metaphor for the anti-colonial struggle) the difficult questions surrounding the practice that entangle colonialism, tradition, and Christianity.

Though the above lines suggests a definitive "stance" on African feminist practice—one that is defiant and even oppositional in its claiming of the "new land" of decolonized Kenya—the play in fact stages an ambivalence not about the practice of female genital cutting which it speaks forcefully against, but about the long, messy process of claiming feminist victory within the bounds of the state and its disciplining cultural narratives. Instead of culminating in this triumphant declaration of new-ness, the play points us toward a more tragic theory of "drift"—a disengagement with binaries of national sovereignty and critiques of the Western universalism of human rights in favor of a feminist ethic of ambivalent institutional engagement. Focusing on the extralegal and cultural spheres represented in the play maps a critical "drift" away from an all-encompassing and inevitable focus on the law and the state without losing their formative presences. This focus on local institutional and social relations—the kinds of intimate yet simultaneously public regulation of women's bodies and education—allows for failure, disruption, and deferral as part of a feminist process of human rights study beyond statist definitions of political success.

The play centers around a schoolteacher guarding a group of young girls from village women who seek to perform infibulation, and guarding her own secret as an unmarried woman confronted with a nonconsensual sexual act from her past in the form of an unrepentant pastor threatening exposure of his previous relationship with the teacher, the revelation that one of the village girls is their child, and an irate community of women bent on enforcing uneven gendered correctives for this vulnerable past and the future of the school girls. With its ambivalent narrative resolution—the teacher leaves town and her mission but seems to pass on her protective mandate—and incessant critique of political possibilities for African women, the text stages what I'm characterizing as a feminist "drift" away from prescriptive human rights remedies and toward attention to structural and cultural inequities. This drift haunts the structural and cultural work of contemporary African Studies as well as transnational feminist debates on the historical and methodological role of Western feminism in feminist human rights in the Global South. My reading of the play, which has not been critically analyzed before, engages a version and a vision of feminist human rights that embraces ambivalence, failure, and uncertainty. It also establishes a genealogy of feminist ambivalence through African and African diaspora black feminist thought, a line traced as an alternate history to one that recovers black diaspora feminist subjects as recognizably resistant, community-oriented, or endlessly mourning/tragic subjects of social death. How do we recognize and critique the pervasive structural violence of modernity for black subjects without collapsing into appeals to the state and the individual, even if they take on seemingly revolutionary forms? This essay pushes on this question in the explicit context of the complicated history of "women's rights as human rights" as they intersect with the history of decolonization in Africa, and the ensuing rise of the Cold War and human rights discourse. It both imagines these as co-constitutive events and thinks of them as historical narratives and habits of thought that drift alongside, against, and away from each other in configurations of African feminist thought in the 1960s, and reading protocols for feminist human rights today.

This moment of 1960, in Kenya specifically and in Africa's self- and global image more broadly, is a time when the transnational economy and ideology that enacted slavery and colonialism were in flux, bordering on hopeful rupture. Independence, though largely bequeathed by former colonial powers abdicating their responsibility and cost to build infrastructure and in order to set up a series of future debts, led to a different scramble for Africa than the previous iteration. Here, Africa was a light to self-rule and political change that third world peoples around the globe looked to as a contemporary example, not just historical sample. At the same time, institutions like the UN and UNESCO were beginning to shape narratives of human rights that would come to be seen as "universal" from the perspective of the West, belying their often multi-authored, multivalent frame during this era (Jensen 2016; Burke 2010). These international human rights institutions reframed the African continent in terms of moral responsibility and financial aid in transformative ways as the twentieth-century progressed and visions of rights as responsibilities and duties were often crowded out by issues of state sovereignty, individual rights, and national citizenship. The play stages not the question of for -or- against these formations, but of an already deeply felt ambivalence—even cynicism or pessimism—about the space of the state for feminist thought in decolonized culture, and about the difficulty of building progressive structures and institutions—commonly thought of as part of "development"—while also having to attend to ideals of individual rights, cultural-historical identity, and anti-colonial politics. *The Scar* stages structural critique rather than individual characterization, refusing to have the one stand-in for the many, and hence refusing feminist rhetorics of "choice" that continue to be critiqued today as the Western basis for rights and freedom. Instead of seeking exclusive models of agency, resistance, and autonomy, *The Scar* presents both action and inaction as feminist responses to human rights binds.

The Scar dramatizes a critical distance or "drift," back to 1960, presciently locating African women as the casualties of comparative thought in human rights, African nationalist, and feminist studies, as they objectified the sign of "African women" into action as the similes for the continent, "good" and "bad." This binary mode is taken as the object of inquiry by the play and by this essay, staging an ambivalent tragedy that questions the fetishization of individual choice, especially in the quest for women's human rights. This move away from prescriptive rights and statist implementation is also a response to an understandable move toward localization in transnational feminist studies that seeks community and group identity for women as political solutions against national and global frames of rights. This essay then negotiates the tensions of seeking "feminist human rights" by investing not in representations of individual triumph or failure but in Njau's play as a mode of cultural production through which the "sign" of African women—and the ideological capital that sign brings with it—anticipates, explores, and exceeds the structural limits of such bounded, binary questions in the moment of their formation, rather than as "late" critiques of the state and of human rights itself.

Dilemma and Drift

Critical conversations on female genital cutting abounded in the late 90s and early aughts—largely from African feminist thought itself, which responded to how the practice was taken up as the defining "case" of women's human rights in Western thought, thus limiting African women to the state of perpetual ahistorical victims in need of intervention, and leveling the state of African feminism to pro or con positions on the practice. Scholars and practitioners of African feminism pushed not just against such a reductive reading of African women's bodies and politics, they also sought and have continued to expand the field of reference, much as US reproductive rights debates have been reframed as reproductive justice platforms by scholars and activists of color. From recovering matriarchal relations to property and social development through reinterpreted pasts of particular African cultural norms (Mikell 1997) to staging a speculative meta-critique of all of Western thought as fixated on gender difference due to its obsessive relation to the visual as the site of rational analysis and truth claims (Oyewùmí 1997), scholars of African feminisms consistently grounded conversations around women's human rights beyond the state in historical and political senses that went beyond cause and remedy.[5]

In taking up *The Scar*, an early, transition-era critique of the way knowledge production and knowledge claims around "African Women" are made, this essay continues those African feminist and human rights studies' critical shifts, relocating the narrative of African women as responders to Western intervention in the 1990s and 2000s. This essay expands on the histories of human rights that critics such as Steven Jensen have laid out that renarrate the ways that human rights have been authored by decolonized peoples, as well as the work of transnational feminist studies, particularly anthropologists such as Rogaia Mustafa Abusharaf who have recontextualized debates around women and development as central to understanding the economic and political stakes of globalization. Analyzing Njau's work against nearly a century's worth of rhetoric around the stakes of female genital cutting, I argue for the transition to decolonization as an era of deep African feminist critique rather than one of only masculinist investment and feminist hope in the project of nationalism. *The Scar*'s staging of ambivalence toward female genital cutting and the national decolonial politics that undergird it also points to the early, complex role of African feminist thought and cultural production in the formation of human rights not just as a system of positive entitlements but as a mode of thought and international activism that has, since its own founding, promoted critical distance from the state as a valuable if not the most valuable asset to the decolonized subject—where critique and failure are both inevitable and both deployed as methods of human rights beyond or in the wake of the state.

The Scar characterizes this critical distance and ambivalence around rights as a way of negotiating the seemingly impossible space of thinking and acting through the competing binds of ideological, political, and representational protocols that attempt to hail one into totalizing narratives of subjectivity and resolution. In *The Scar*, African feminist thought arrives not as a belated traveler, a reactor or responder to existing human rights debate, but as a generative author of a school of feminist thought which values ambivalence and deconstruction as tools for rather than against institution building, a mode of thinking human rights that always already recognizes the limits of the state as a site of protest or repair.

In making these failures and ambivalences clear while also continuing to do institutional work for political change, *The Scar* also merges transnational and black feminist concepts of "wandering" (Abusharaf 2002; Cervenak 2014) and "waywardness" (Hartman 2019) as anthropological, philosophical, performative, and historical modes of human rights politics beyond the boundaries of individual subjectivity and rational knowledge. What Abusharaf, who focuses on women's migrant labor in a transnational economy, Cervanak, who studies African American women's literary and performative engagements with and against Enlightenment thought, and Hartman, who theorizes the political import of studying young black women in the early twentieth century who seek out quotidian pleasures, dangers, and desires, construct in their archives and arguments is a way of understanding minoritized women's lives in between the seemingly hard lines of coercion and consent, agency and submission. Instead, they locate a politics of feminist drift, one that runs alongside of theorist Jean-François Lyotard's in the 1970s, in the wake of the decolonial upheaval in the 1960s, a moment of global shifts in the racial, sexual, and governmental world order that form the backdrop of his own move away from Marxism and reason and toward the messy economies of desire and the corporeal. He writes of:

> Driftworks in the plural, for the question is not of leaving one shore, but several, simultaneously: what is at work is not one current, pushing and tugging, but different drives and tractions. Nor is just one individual embarking here, or even a collective of individuals, but rather, as in Bosch's ship, a collection of fools, each fool being an exaggerated part of the normal subject, libido cathected in such and such a sector of the body; blocked up in this or that configuration of desire, all these fragments placed next to each other... for an aimless voyage, a collection of fragments impossible to unify for it drifts with the Ship, its very drift giving the advantage of the strongest resonance now to one Trieb-fool, now to another, in accordance with the diversity of the times and sceneries wafted through. Not at all a dislocated body, since there has never been anything but pieces of the body and there will never be a body, this wandering collection being the very affirmation of the non-body. (10)

I give you a sense of Lyotard's "driftworks" not to claim him as the post-dated author of African feminist drift as exhibited through *The Scar* but as its student, belatedly recognizing the ways that political agency, and bodily agency, are fictions unsuited to the experience of embodied modernity, and uncontained/unable to be remedied by the state. Though he imagines a material metaphor but an increasingly immaterial body for the political subject, Njau (and today's contemporary interlocutors Abusharaf, Cervenak, and Hartman) stages how African female subjects must contend with the literal pull on the body. Njau, with her inclusion of female genital cutting, rape, and women's education, dramatizes the major conflict of contemporary feminist political thought—the way feminism must engage with the body, but also must be careful to note its vulnerability without constructing that as a limit case, a problem to be absolutely solved by local, national, or international custom and law. In this, it mirrors and rejects various colonialist visions of colonized women's subjectivity, from the practice of sati to the veil, that come to synecdochally stand in for all women of certain ethnic, cultural, or religious groups (Spivak 1988; Moallem 2005). In Njau's play, African women's bodies "drift" with no clear solution to the fact that they are subject to multiple pathologizing gazes. With no clear shore to call an autonomous home, Njau's women experience a sense of the impossibility of fulfilling the competing critical desires that try to hail them into political being much as the term "African Women," like Chandra Mohanty's much-exercised category of "Third World Women" in her classic essay "Under Western Eyes," has come to stand in for a set of ideological battles, all the binaries of which should be read in scare quotes: between the West and Africa, writ large; between tradition and modernity; between men and women on the continent; between diaspora black identities and continental African ones; between feminism and nationalism; between human rights and cultural relativism; between the pre-colonial and the colonial periods; between the individual and the collective; between working class and rural poor women and middle class educated women of the continent; and between theory and practice, object and subject, author and object in the academic pursuits of African studies and transnational feminist studies, among other fields (Mohanty 1991, c.1984).[6]

The Scar is a play that dramatizes, in part, the dilemma of female genital cutting—otherwise known through a list of clinical and moral-ethical monikers, such as infibulation, clitorectomies, female genital circumcision, and female genital mutilation.[7] Infibulation stands as an illustrative and continuing case study of the constructed bind of local, national, and international intervention into African feminism, and African women's representation. A flashpoint practice that varies in execution, origin, and explanation as well as in religious, geographic, and cultural presence, female genital cutting is most often marked as an "initiation" rite for girls of varying ages. It is varyingly a measure of property, sexuality, marriage rites, paternity, childbirth, and group leadership. In Kenya, the practice became the source of much debate among colonial missionaries and governance, who marked it as a "savage" and "backwards" custom (a typical formulation of colonial power to any differing local custom), and hence it became a major source of resistance from the leaders of the Kikuyu ethnic group. Both sides entrenched: Britain sought to define itself and its presence as "civilizing" Africa's "traditions," with African woman being "saved" by white men from brown men, in Spivak's formulation (Spivak 1988). African women's bodies were marked as the ultimate site and sign of culture in the Kikuyu leadership, the sacred and unchanging terrain of so-called tradition, as if it was a static notion, and as if female genital cutting was its defining formation.

Such was the background in Kenya by 1960, post the eight-year Mau-Mau rebellion (1952–1960), a brutal war with the British that included torture, imprisonment, and labor camps. But it was also a time when more and more women were moving to the newly industrializing urban center of Nairobi, and when more women were gaining access to education in the immanent transition to independence in 1963. This urban migration and institutionalization of education was fostered by decolonial industry but also NGO money from international human rights organizations created in the wake and place of colonial rule. UNESCO's non-binding convention document in 1960 outlined the imperative of non-discriminatory and non-segregated access (based on religion, sex, race, etc.) to education in the "developing" world—the new target of human rights-based campaigns (even as the "developed" world was still dealing in segregation and a lack of civil and political rights) during the moment of decolonization, with a new neocolonial "sensitivity" to local concerns present in that document's call to allow education in native languages. This positivist human rights focus led to large-scale shifts in women's potential roles in the state and abroad, and created the beginning of the false pull between cultural nationalism and feminism, with feminist critiques of patriarchy coded as Western and feminist claims on African women to break to with non-conforming aspects of cultural identity locked to Western feminist ideals of personal choice and bodily sovereignty. The UN Council on Social, Economic, and Cultural Rights characterizes this neocolonial emphasis on "rights" with cultural "understanding" or "sensitivity" (instead of the earlier model of blatant cultural superiority), commissioning the World Health Organization in 1960 for a report on female genital cutting—the beginning of UN and NGO focus on the issue.

These moves begin to crystallize a "rights" discourse that paints choice and culture as antithetical. As this language inhered in human rights discourse, it retrospectively cast those categories—choice and culture—as existing in binary tension. Thus choice was perceived as the province of the modern nation state, and culture rendered the static forms to be tolerated or included into the more enlightened state and international human rights frameworks. Such totalizing narratives—not just of rightness or wrongness, but of the very frame of the debate as the only possible conception of the question of gendered rights—continue to inform the way we read the history of African feminist critique as necessarily weighing in on some side of the female genital cutting "debate," rather than navigating the impossibility of these demands in a long-term process of institutional change that involves but is not limited to the state or state apparatuses. The supposed split between choice and culture either demanded allegiance from or named the victimization of African Women, and was reproduced in the institutionalization of women's studies in the US, and the rise of women's rights as human rights doctrine that assumed the cultural ideals of so-called western feminism as universal. Feminist proponents such as Charlotte Bunch and feminist critics such as Inderpal Grewal and Karen Engle have attempted to navigate the nuance and thorniness of these iterations of transnational feminist politics, while scholars such as Lisa Levenstein have documented the US domestic development of solidarity politics as women of color feminists authored the original slogan, "Women's Rights are Human Rights," not as call to universality but as a recognition of the ways that the gendering of civil rights and nationalist movement goals excluded the embodied political realities of women, especially poor and nonwhite women, from meaningful access to and central conversations around political rights (Bunch 2001; Grewal 2005; Engle 1992; Levenstein 2018). Female genital cutting was at the heart of this "debate" that emerged between Western academic feminism and African feminism (broadly defined, and certainly not as monolithic as it sounds), one that dehistoricized a cross-cultural practice that was still prevalent in early twentieth-century European populations, in fact. The name itself was polarizing, with each iteration hoping to mark the most specific political vantage point for description, such as marking the difference between male circumcision and infibulation, for instance, as a way to speak about the cultural value of the rite versus the medical risks, another iteration of trying to get culture's supposed static forms "right" in opposition to "choice."

Female genital cutting then became the dominant way that African women entered into the feminist and human rights public political sphere in the west, over-stating its prevalence and significance and painting it as the only way into feminist subjectivity for African women. Scholarship, memoirs, and NGOs—all had to traffic in the debate and made hay of the currency of the topic—capitalizing off of its sensational focus on African women's sexuality and their bodies either in rigorous anthropological context or in the neocolonial discourse of rights. The individual was pitted against the collective, and African feminists and their allies, including diaspora feminists, were asked to take sides—nuanced as that "side" might be, it still had to be for or against. Those who were "pro" sided with the patriarchy, or with diluted and deluded senses of cultural relativism that ensured that no change could ever take place; those who were against were elitist, brainwashed by the West, and culturally dislocated from an imagined homogenous cultural past, even as they occupied anti-racist, feminist subjectivities as, for example, in Parmar and Walker's documentary and edited collection *Warrior Marks* (1996). This, in a long-ish and brutally drawn nutshell, is the dilemma of the state and state critique for and under the sign "African Women," for feminist practice in the 1990s, and it informs the ways that African feminists scholars resisted and fought for access and visibility in Western feminist publications with more contextualized, historicized politics of rights.

These debates and this particular question of African women's bodies are still salient in the twenty-first century as definitive of representations of African Women, if not in the academy, then in the Western popular imagination (a "case" that still resounds in media and the production of memoirs around Islam).[8] Infibulation has been constructed as a flashpoint of the binary bind of African feminist thought, even as African feminist thought in the form of cultural productions like *The Scar* has long foreseen and drifted from the for or against model, refusing to see local, state, or international intervention as "remedies" for the problem of disciplining gender, sexuality, and embodiment. Instead, *The Scar* argues that the fundamental conception of rights needs to shift to accommodate the inevitable failures and conflicts of prescriptive rights around intimate contact between the self and the community that defines cultural norms.

To understand this ambivalent method of extra-state rights critique, we must first acknowledge that critiques of female genital cutting exist not just in the 1990s transnational feminist debates of the practice but far earlier in Africa itself, by African women and feminists who locate it within patriarchal cultural modes that, under the banner of "tradition," were allowed to extend power to elite men, even and especially during processes of decolonization. Soon to be canonical male writers at this mid-century turning point levied heavy critiques of the role of gender politics in colonization and decolonization as well—from Achebe's blistering and unsympathetic portrait of patriarchal masculinity in 1959's *Things Fall Apart*, set in the 1890s just as colonization hits interior Nigeria, to the opening sequence of Ousmane Sembene's 1975 film *Xala* (based on his 1973 novel), which lampoons the mimicry of Western power and corruption by Black African politicians amidst their continued calls to cling to "Africanicity" by continuing polygamous arrangements that privilege these men not just socially, but as moments to consolidate capital, prestige, and political power through the traffic in women. "The woman question" of African cultural studies and decolonization has been, then, mischaracterized within discourses of tradition versus modernity, as if these two categories are geographically and temporally distinguishable, much like culture and choice. Since the late 1990s and early aughts, of course, transnational feminism has taken on this false bind as exactly that, largely in the context of false debates around fundamentalism and the veil. Gender politics were a primary way of upholding and maintaining power for decolonized elites, and for how narratives of Africa as a revolutionary new frontier of political promise in a changing world shifted—and were compressed into—stories of aid, intervention, and the foreign policies and cultural moves of the West that have materially redefined the continent in the past 40 years. Looking back to the 1960s, at a moment of promise, upheaval, and heightened publicity for the continent gives us a window into this shift. African feminist critique and cultural expression from the period stands as a refusal to engage women's and children's status as justification for a range of difficult responses to and from colonial/neocolonial and nationalist forces. In this way, looking at gender, sexuality, and embodiment always brings us to the impossible bind of the state and beyond it—with writers like Njau expressing ambivalence about decolonial national projects and politics in the quotidian lives of women and girls, and in the symbolic order that marks women's bodies as static objects of disciplinary rights and as the false subjects of a cultural-evacuated notion (and fetishization) of "choice."

Drifting Beyond the State

The Scar subtly dramatizes not just the emergent comparative debates that attempt to fix and to hold African women in representational stasis as the victims of/bearers of "culture" (female genital cutting becoming a "case study," as outlined above), but also a drift from them. *The Scar* takes as a given the existence of positions that question female genital cutting in its specific cultural contexts in 1960, not just in the 1990s, post-Western feminist intervention or the advent of post-structuralist critique. Like other texts that follow it,[9] it is interested in more than staging dissent to a single act as *the* question of African women's subjectivity.

Instead, the play offers a set of complex questions about the contradictions of cultural change, from the by-now multi-generational spread of Christianity and its cultural rules concerning gender, to so-called "women's culture" or what Miranda Joseph might call "the romance of community" around representations of African women by anti-colonial scholars. It questions compulsory marriage as much as it does compulsory initiation; it asks questions about the conflicts between the push for formal education among both women and men in the decolonized era, and what that might mean for the uneven development of marriageable "types" across gender; it troubles the line between sexual coercion and consent, between commitments to the self and to the individual; it asks us what change and choice mean, structurally, even as they might fail any given individual subject. In other words, the play offers a complex, ambivalent version of African feminism by not representing women as either examples or exceptions, victims or heroines, of the newly decolonized state. Instead, it refuses those poles and those choices, always asking us to contextualize the critical methods available to look "for" African women and African feminist thought in the years to come.

The play begins with a pastoral verse about village life[10] voiced by Ruth, the servant of Mariana, an unmarried woman who runs a group for girls of the village. It soon comes to light that Mariana is harboring girls who choose not to undergo "initiation" or female genital cutting. Both Ruth and Mariana take breaks in the thruline of action in this first brief scene to interact with Erasto, a male servant, who taunts Ruth by saying she has been spoiled by Mariana and that she shouldn't "be too proud; you are only a woman/ And a servant, too!" (7). This crude articulation of ambient gender and class restrictions lets the audience know exactly what is already being defied by both the life (unmarried) and work (teaching young, poor, and rural girls to choose against circumcision, but also to claim public agency) of Mariana.

This echo of work or labor and its relationship to the structure of gender roles (rather than to individual women) recurs throughout, as when, in this opening exchange, Mariana rebuffs Erasto's argument about having too much work by imploring him to: "Look at the women, Erasto;/ They have done their duties for years and years silently;/And they are still working without a break;/ Learn from them;/ Then your hands and fingers will never fail you!" (9–10). This significant pronouncement is important not just as critique but as pretext for the dismissal of the groupthink of village women around circumcision to come. Mariana, and hence the play, recontextualizes the history of women in the village—not as sites and signs of culture, but as valuable intellectual, political, economic, and social laborers themselves. As such, her pending refusal and sharp critique of consolidating gender identity and cultural/community value around a single act stands in concert with her labor to deconstruct bodily "initiation" as the limits of women's representational and political work.

Indeed, almost immediately after this opening exchange, a string of interactions reveals various gender transgressions for women—eating too eagerly in public, speaking in mixed groups, being able to marry those men who are now educated via colonial schooling, being able to marry post one's own "over"-education as a woman. Far from educating and organizing girls around strictly the question of initiation, it's clear that critique lies with the entire institutionalization of sex/gender difference for the play. Not just Ruth and Mariana voice such questioning. One young girl, Nini, remarks: "Perhaps we should wait until marriage becomes/ Something better than a living grave!" (12). Such harsh critique for a banal institution such as marriage is far more controversial than a stance for or against circumcision, in its way—and offers a parallel metaphorization to the simile offered later for circumcision, which is "empty as a cave." Gendered constructs, this play offers, are small, empty spaces filled up by cultural scripts, enclosures that circumscribe the lives and choices of African women, and the very questions that are asked about them—delineating the capacity and boundaries of their representation and their ability to be represented.

Such bleak critiques of available roles for women come not just from those opposing their binds, but from village women who implore Mariana, "Don't put into their heads privileges denied them/ By god" (14). The women assert their past experience in marriage and childbirth, their roles as wives and mothers—the very and only roles that qualify them as members of the community by patriarchal standards. But the response from Mariana is swift and cutting on reliance on personal and individual experience, or even collective history, as a rationale for regulating gendered behavior: "You are women; you are not gods" (15). To make decisions based on ideals of women's community that cannot be altered is to deny the shifts in circumcision practices that had happened even in the recent history of the play. In 1920s and 30s Kenya, Christian missionaries attempted to outlaw the practice of circumcision at the same time and, one could argue, as a means of controlling, it sought to displace Kikuyu property and marriage rites. In anthropological terms, this created a "reactance," or an entrenchment of a "tradition" that was not necessarily, as an act, the most central or defining feature of a culture previous to it being threatening by an external force (Zabus 2007).

This simplistic definition of the Kikuyu's ideological battles with British colonialism and Western missionary activism is by no means a full accounting of anti-colonial organizing around female genital cutting and other claims on women's bodies as the site of cultural definition and meaning. The prize the play won and Njau's subsequent appearance at one of the most historic literary festivals in African history recognizes her questioning as valuable. Njau's own description of the play from the festival, as documented in the "Africa Abroad" radio program, suggests the plot as one of thwarted political desire more than it foregrounds female genital cutting: "Well, it mainly concerns really two people. There is a—my central figure is a woman—a woman leader in a village today, and she's trying to do all she can to help the young girls, you know, to wake up and then she's all right and she's quite successful until her past is revealed by a pastor and she finds she can't continue with her work" (HRC Ep. 9, 6.16.62). The foundational East African literary journal *Transition* published the play in 1963, while a critic on "Africa Abroad" critiques it as "a rather indifferent piece of playwrighting" (HRC Ep. 36 2.5.63)—no outrage here at a question that has yet to fully define African women's political identity, but rather will be belatedly said to characterize it fully in political discourse. The play's dramatization of and ambivalence toward the emerging structures of feeling around African women and female genital cutting again anticipate key responses to the investments of rights groups and Western feminist groups in the 1990s and early aughts in what becomes the "field" of female genital cutting studies—a field that overdetermined and still to some degree over-determines representational possibilities for African women in the feminist human rights imagination. "This is not the land of your birth" Mariana flatly states. The static sign of "African Women" is "empty as a cave," a symbolic battle that marks representational failure rather than remedy, as one cannot separate the colonial and the Kikuyu. To point that out is the common work of African studies and feminist thought, for this play and for this essay's recentering of it as a "shift text"—and drift text—of decolonization—one that already contained critiques that are usually attributed much later to African feminist and human rights studies.

The Scar's "ambivalence" about various status quos, and the price for violating them, even in micro-moments like eating in public and transgressing gender-appropriate expectations, extends to a call to practice critical questioning as initiation. In other words, *The Scar* argues that ambivalent critique is the work that African feminism can offer, and that critique always exceeds the state's boundaries for redress and remedy of the quotidian disciplining of women's bodies. To revisit Mariana's pronouncement to the group of women dissuading her from dissuading girls from initiation: "A 'physical operation' is as empty as a cave;/ It is meaningless./ They must go through a different initiation that will/ Make no man or even women like you shake them" (14). Here the play again anticipates our contemporary negotiations between ritual and rights, as maintaining initiation ceremonies without cutting is a major method of African feminist and humanitarian/NGO intervention in female genital cutting in our contemporary moment. Arguing for a mutable "tradition" that emphasizes preparation for the world as it is, the play emphasizes culture as work, or labor, that shifts with the specifics of the "job" to be had, not just the job/act to be done. As mentioned above, the play's dialogue insists on two constants: work and—ironically—change (16): "my work is my life; it must be preserved" (24), Mariana says, even as Mariana is not, in her role as "leader," preserved. Ruth instead, is instructed to "Take care of this house, Ruth./ And let the people who come here / see what we have labored for" (32). Mariana leaves her individual work after being outed as a woman who had a child out of wedlock, but as the whole social structure of gender difference lives on in the play and beyond, she implores her servant to continue to build feminist infrastructure in the wake of her own story coming to a teleologically inevitable end. Here, "drift," or immanent critique and recognition of both individual ambivalence and ambivalent consequences to transgressing various and even conflicting normative gender discourses, is not a hindrance to "practice," but a practice itself that is sustainable and valuable, beyond personal choice, and beyond petitioning the state, for long-term institutional building.

The Scar is then recognizably "feminist," in 1960 but perhaps even more in our own moment. The play is a catalog of gendered limits from the church, from static definitions of "tradition"/cultural identity, from limits yoked to women's bodies and sexuality, especially in a postcolonial context. It does not engage in obvious anti-colonial critique, but clearly exists in a world of growing access to education and one that has long been influenced by the presence of Christianity alongside Kikuyu cultural practice. The play remains resolutely in present and future tenses, as it exhibits no patience with and little understanding for shaping obedient, past-oriented subjects, and few laments for the presence or absence of Western institutions except to suggest that both Christian and "local" values place undue burdens on women's bodies, sexuality, and subjecthood.[11] But though the main action of the play is not ambivalent about the practice of female genital cutting, it does refuse "for or against" as a plotline, staging instead the failures of such a binary representational frame. Feminist drift, then, becomes the necessary labor to endure the disciplinary protocols of various institutional models for rights—outlined in the new "initiation" model mentioned above. *The Scar* argues for the feminist value of maintaining a critical distance, an ambivalence, toward the coerced belonging and ideology for *or* against the state. There is only doing and being in the world as it is for *The Scar*, not as it was, in the time of the play, for feminist practice.

The play then is also a very early articulation (at a moment full of decolonized hope) for a feminist vision, one that is imagined as the narratives of human rights and aid are shaping narratives of Africa, but are not yet fully solidified. *The Scar* is knowing about the trap of debates around African women's bodies and sexuality that steer conversation toward two opposing poles as the only site of their significance. It recognizes that institutional support for women must continue, even as individual choice must and cannot be the limit of political identity for African women. The play stages a disappearing heroine so that it can put in relief the fiction of heroism and individualism. Like Ama Ata Aidoo, Bessie Head, Assia Djebar, and Mariama Ba, in the generation immediately following her own, Njau recognizes no answer, remedy, or conclusion to the question of this representational bind. Instead of looking for either triumphant or tragic heroines (though it is billed as a tragedy), it suggests we might look to the performance of ambivalence as a particularly feminist narrative out of African expressive culture of the decolonial period, one that doesn't fetishize individual choice as politics, nor group identity as a romantic political formation over time and over history. In fact, the tragedy the play seems to suggest is the absence of constant questioning, the inability to "wander" both physically and politically, and the lack of transmutation of a critical and thoughtful ambivalence to those being ushered into an impossibly complex world, where origins and origin stories are already too entangled, and perhaps often beside the point. The drift isn't indecision or uncertainty, it is a claim to too much knowledge, too many affiliations that one cannot remain attached, wholly, to all of them, or to the idea/ideal of secure attachment itself, even to the decolonized state.

If that sounds like what the twenty-first century has come to analyze and value about a certain set of post-1980 postmodern African women's texts, and about contemporary critiques of human rights, then it's time to think about those texts together, as a politics and aesthetics of African feminist thought that values difference, non-fatal failure, and contradiction—that values ambivalence as generative, as much as we do in our readings (e.g., Stratton 1994; Andrade 2010; Goyal 2010). In locating this at the shift of the comparative moment for the continent—the moment of independence, the moment of Africa's emergence on the world stage as potential power player, the moment where discourses of colonialism existed alongside other modes of narrativizing Africa's relationship to the West as no longer its dependent, but now characterized as its financial and ethical advisee—this drift could be characterized as the "postcolonial condition" for and as African feminist thought, one that recognizes the impossibility of "representation" at home or abroad in the designations and definitions offered up by the state and through its critique. Contemporary African, feminist, and human rights studies have been bound to each other for quite some time—part of the discourse of decolonization, and its limits. "Drift" allows for ways of understanding African feminist thought that offer room for an ambivalence that does not resolve political-ethical dilemmas but sees "African Women" as more than the sum and objects of the "right" side of a teleological history from the very start of the postcolonial era, even before official decolonization. This drift, when recentered as the "mark" of this historical shift, claims African feminism as fundamental to institution building around human rights but also to the constant dissent and critique that pre- and proceeded it. *The Scar* imagines critical distance as part of institutionality and institutional change—including being a part of the "nation"—rather than assuming participation as either resistance or capitulation. As such, the play offers its readers an early questioning of the geopolitical boundaries of the state *and* what has become the classic human rights critique of its limit—claiming ambivalence as a critical tool rather than an obstruction in the work of feminist human rights.

Notes

1. The author's name has changes of spelling across time and texts, including Rebeka and Rebekah.
2. Njau identifies as Kikuyu, and Kikuyu is her first language. She is part of the boom in secondary and college educated Kenyans starting from the 1920s and 1930s, who were part of a new middle class.
3. Of course, not all or even many of these works were to make it out of this short period of circulation, especially those outside of the genre that became the most circulated for writers inside but especially outside of the Africa: the novel. And few of the emergent writers whose works were widely circulated and anthologized were women, especially as cultural nationalist politics came to define the African novel abroad—which, as the designation suggests, privileged a set of traditionally represented "political" issues, of which "women's issues" were considered minor (see Florence Stratton [1994], and critic Susan Andrade [2010] on reading domestic novels as national allegory).
4. Wole Soyinka was even a possible judge for the contest, according to the transcripts from "Africa Abroad" at the Harry Ransom Center.
5. Articles on female genital cutting populate popular collections, and are written by prominent feminists (Mikell 1997; Nnaemeka 2005; Abusharaf 2006; Ogundipe-Leslie 1994; Zabus 2007; Cole et al. 2007). Rehistoricizing African gender systems or going back in history to rehistoricize African women undergirds what I'm arguing here, but also pushes my analysis toward rehistoricizing a particular kind of critique that we associate with post-structuralist Western feminism as already existing in and through this historical moment in African history.
6. Mohanty's critique is pre-dated by Spivak's foundational "Can the Subaltern Speak?" on how to read sati beyond both imperialist and masculine nationalist modes, and echoed and extended in several transnational feminist anthologies of the era, most prominently in *Between Woman and Nation* (1999) and its call for "immanent critique" as method and as goal.
7. There is a long debate about these controversial terms, and what's at stake in terms of cultural hierarchies, representing violence, etc. This is also part of what is now a tradition in Women's and Gender Studies of agonizing over terminology and attempting to "remedy" structural problems with representational solutions.
8. Along with coverage of Middle Eastern and Muslim women across regions, recent stories and studies in the un/rights sector on female genital cutting activism still define the parameters of African Gender Studies,

with the new inclusion of Queer African studies taking some of its place with similarly drawn debates about what is or is not "African" about gender and sexuality as a constant or static truth of historical, religious, and cultural interpretation. See Njau's novels, *Ripples in the Pool* and *Sacred Seed*, and their claims to early representations of queer desire and conflict borne of the limits of gendered discourse regulating African women's bodies and sexuality.

9. Ama Ata Aidoo's early drama *Anowa* (1970), Flora Nwapa's *Efuru* (1966), Mariama Ba's *Scarlet Song* ([1981] 1986), and a range of texts discussed in Asaah and Levin (2009).
10. This was later published as a poem under the pseudonym Mariana Gashe, after the character in the play.
11. Unlike, say, the ambivalence staged in Ngugi's novel on female genital cutting, or even in his play *I Will Marry When I Want.*

Works Cited

Abusharaf, Rogaia Mustafa. 2006. *Female Circumcision Multicultural Perspectives.* Philadelphia: University of Pennsylvania Press.

———. 2002. *Wanderings: Sudanese Migrants and Exiles in North America.* Ithaca: Cornell University Press.

Achebe, Chinua. 1959. *Things Fall Apart.* New York: Astor-Honor.

Aidoo, Ama Ata. 1970. *Anowa.* Washington, DC: Three Continents Press.

Andrade, Susan Z. 2010. *The Nation Writ Small African Fictions and Feminisms, 1958–1988.* Durham: Duke University Press.

Asaah, Augustine H., and Tobe Levin. 2009. *Empathy and Rage: Female Genital Mutilation in African Literature.* Accra, Ghana: Co-published with the Centre for Intellectual Renewal.

Bâ, Mariama. 1986. *Scarlet Song.* Harlow, Essex, England: Longman.

Bunch, Charlotte. 2001. "Women's Rights Are Human Rights." *Lola Press* (16, November 1): 52. http://search.proquest.com/docview/237235064/.

Burke, Roland. 2010. *Decolonization and the Evolution of International Human Rights.* Philadelphia: University of Pennsylvania Press.

Cervenak, Sarah Jane. 2014. *Wandering: Philosophical Performances of Racial and Sexual Freedom.* Durham: Duke University Press.

Cole, Catherine M., Takyiwaa Manuh, and Stephan Miescher. 2007. *Africa After Gender?* Bloomington: Indiana University Press.

Engle, Karen. 1992. "International Human Rights and Feminism: When Discourses Meet." *Michigan Journal of International Law* 13 (3, April 1). http://search.proquest.com/docview/1311476859/.

Goyal, Yogita. 2010. *Romance, Diaspora, and Black Atlantic Literature.* Cambridge, UK: Cambridge University Press.

Grewal, Inderpal. 2005. *Transnational America Feminisms, Diasporas, Neoliberalisms*. Durham: Duke University Press.

Hartman, Saidiya. 2019. *Wayward Lives*. New York: Norton.

Jensen, Steven L. B. 2016. *The Making of International Human Rights: The 1960s, Decolonization, and the Reconstruction of Global Values*. New York: Cambridge University Press.

Joseph, Miranda. 2002. *Against the Romance of Community*. Minneapolis: University of Minnesota Press. https://doi.org/10.5749/j.ctttt4ng.

Levenstein, Lisa. 2018. "A Social Movement for a Global Age: U.S. Feminism and the Beijing Women's Conference of 1995." *Journal of American History* 105 (2, September): 336–365. https://doi.org/10.1093/jahist/jay147.

Lyotard, Jean-François. 1984. *Driftworks*, trans. Roger McKeon. New York: Semiotexte.

Mikell, Gwendolyn. 1997. *African Feminism: The Politics of Survival in Sub-Saharan Africa*. Philadelphia: University of Pennsylvania Press. https://doi.org/10.9783/9780812200775.

Moallem, Minoo. 2005. *Between Warrior Brother and Veiled Sister: Islamic Fundamentalism and the Politics of Patriarchy in Iran*. Berkeley: University of California Press.

Mohanty, Chandra Talpade. 1991. Under Western Eyes. In *Third World Women and the Politics of Feminism*, ed. Chandra Talpade Mohanty, Ann Russo, and Lourdes Torres. Bloomington: Indiana University Press.

Ngũgĩ wa Thiong'o. 1980. *Ngaahika ndeenda, ithaako ria ngerekano = I Will Marry When I Want*. Nairobi: Heinemann Educational Books.

———. 1965. *The River Between*. London: Heinemann.

Njau, Rebeka. 1978. *Ripples in the Pool*. Heinemann.

———. 1963. "The Scar." *Transition* (8, March 1): 23–28. https://doi.org/10.2307/2934731.

Nnaemeka, Obioma. 2005. *Female Circumcision and the Politics of Knowledge: African Women in Imperialist Discourses*. Westport: Praeger.

Nwapa, Flora. 1966. *Efuru*. London: Heinemann.

Ogundipe-Leslie, Molara. 1994. *Re-creating Ourselves: African Women and Critical Transformations*. Trenton: Africa World Press.

Oyěwùmí, Oyèrónkẹ́. 1997. *The Invention of Women Making an African Sense of Western Gender Discourses*. Minneapolis: University of Minnesota Press.

Sembène, Ousmane. 1973. *Xala; Roman*. Paris: Présence africaine.

———. 1975. *Xala*. Senegal: Films sans frontières Firm [distridutor].

Spivak, Gayatri Chakravorty. 1988. "Can the Subaltern Speak?" *Die Philosophin* 14 (27): 42–58.

Stratton, Florence. 1994. *Contemporary African Literature and the Politics of Gender*. London: Routledge.

Walker, Alice. 1998. *Possessing the Secret of Joy*. New York: Washington Square Press.

Walker, Alice, and Pratibha Parmar. 1996. *Warrior Marks: Female Genital Mutilation and the Sexual Blinding of Women*. 1st Harvest ed. San Diego: Harcourt Brace.

Zabus, Chantal J. 2007. *Between Rites and Rights: Excision in Women's Experiential Texts and Human Contexts*. Stanford: Stanford University Press.

CHAPTER 3

Decolonizing Knowledge in Nnedi Okorafor's *Binti* Trilogy

Emily S. Davis

"For Africans, homegrown science fiction can be a will to power. What if? It's a powerful question."
Nnedi Okorafor

In its call for participants for the 2019 Decoloniality Summer School at the University of South Africa, the organizers list a set of questions that provide a useful shorthand for the overarching concerns of this essay. They ask, "How was the modern world constituted and who is producing knowledge? What institutions and disciplines legitimize it? What is knowledge for and who benefits from it?" (UNISA). In the essay that follows I take these questions about what Anibal Quijano terms "the coloniality of knowledge" as the jumping-off point for considering the more specific question of the role of knowledge production in decolonizing human rights. How does centering a decolonial approach to knowledge production inflect our reading of the production of human rights as a

E. S. Davis (✉)
University of Delaware, Newark, DE, USA
e-mail: edavis@udel.edu

A. S. Moore and S. Pinto (eds.), *Writing Beyond the State*,
Palgrave Studies in Literature, Culture and Human Rights,
https://doi.org/10.1007/978-3-030-34456-6_3

body of knowledge, as well as its future possibilities? How do indigenous and other forms of marginalized knowledges transform not only Eurocentric assumptions about the subject of human rights but also the role of an institution like the university, which has traditionally functioned to legitimize certain forms of knowledge and modes of knowledge production while erasing others? In other words, how does a decolonial approach to knowledge work force us to consider not just *what* we know but *how* and *where* we know, what methods and epistemologies we employ to produce knowledge and within and through what institutions beyond the state do we produce and disseminate knowledge?

Decolonial thought is mostly closely associated with a tradition of Latin American intellectuals like Anibal Quijano, Walter Mignolo, and Nelson Maldonado-Torres, who write to expose European deployment of the intellectual apparatus of Western modernity/rationalism as a means by which to consolidate colonialist political projects. Decolonial thought works from the assumption that colonialism is above all a "colonization of the imagination," as Quijano puts it, "a systematic repression [of] the modes of knowing, of producing knowledge, of producing perspectives, images and systems of images, symbols, modes of signification, [of] the resources, patterns, and instruments of formalized and objectivized expression, intellectual or visual" (Quijano 2007, 169). Mignolo claims that although they followed different intellectual and geographical trajectories (Mignolo 2011, xxvi), decolonial and postcolonial thought share a common interest in what Ngugi wa Thiong'o famously called "decolonizing the mind" (1986). In the early 1970s, Steve Biko's work on Black consciousness had already led him to conclude that "the most potent weapon in the hands of the colonizer is the mind of the oppressed" (Biko 2002, 92). In recent years, there has been increasing interest among South African intellectuals in decolonial thought, particularly in the wake of the #RhodesMustFall and #FeesMustFall student organizing campaigns. Sabelo Ndlovu-Gatsheni, who published the book *Epistemic Freedom in Africa: Deprovincialization and Decolonization* in 2018, is a founder of the Africa Decolonial Research Newtork (ADERN) at UNISA, which sponsors the Decolonial Summer School whose questions I quote at the beginning of this essay. At its heart, a decolonial approach to knowledge invites us to consider other genealogies, other ways of knowing that are not bound up in the colonial project of modernity and its resulting contemporary framework of neoliberal globalization.

If decolonial thought urges knowledge workers to think otherwise, so too do some forms of speculative fiction ask literature readers to imagine worlds beyond our own. In her essay in this volume, Hanna Musiol explores the potential of particularly non-Euroamerican speculative fiction to provide "models of re-imagining politics, violence, human-nonhuman relations, and justice" and to "offer new ways of knowing the present and of imagining politics" (Musiol 2020, 265–289). Self-described Naijamerican science fiction writer Nnedi Okorafor's *Binti* trilogy (2015–2018) presents an especially generative set of texts through which to think through questions of decoloniality, knowledge, and educational institutions here not through protesting the state for better institutions but through the imaginative act of creating, in fantasy fiction, different universities altogether. For one thing, its multi-text narrative centers around the university as a crucial institution for producing and legitimizing (or failing to legitimize) decolonial knowledge. Just as importantly, it frames knowledge production as a process that occurs both within and beyond the university; knowledge does not spring from the individual genius of the unitary educated subject but rather emerges through the interdependent, collaborative, and at times fractious interactions of multiple, diverse agents. Finally, Okorafor's grounding of her work within a deeply Afrocentric vision of science fiction activates different intellectual genealogies of and epistemologies for the concepts of knowledge and education that are not limited by current Eurocentric frames or educational institutions. As Okorafor says in the 2017 TED talk quoted in the epigraph, African science fiction's "What if?" is a question about power. Knowledge production and the institutions intended to support it are key sites for learning, imagining, and enabling post-sovereign, decolonial visions of human rights, even as they have been sites of imperial imagination and world-making (Said 1978).

The *Binti* trilogy as a whole follows the process through which Binti, a member of the marginalized Himba people on Earth, leaves home to attend the prestigious intergalactic Oomza University (Book 1), leaves the university to return home and renegotiate her relationship with her family and the multiple racial groups to which she is related (Book 2), and returns to the university having restored and cemented her relationships with both her original and expanded chosen family (Book 3). A catalyzing event for the series as a whole occurs in the first book, when Binti claims the authority to broker a peace agreement between the dominant Khoush from her planet and the Meduse species, whom the Khoush have written off as mindless terrorists. The grievance between the two species stems from the fact that Khoush scholars associated with the prestigious intergalactic Oomza University have, under mysterious circumstances, removed the stinger of the Meduse chief from its body and stolen it. For the Meduse, an octopus-like species, the stinger acts as their main weapon and form of self-defense. They seek to recover the stinger, which is being housed and studied in the university museum. Binti aims to end the perpetual war between the two species by demanding the Khoush return the stinger and make formal amends. In order to act as an ambassador for the Meduse, Binti allows herself to be physically transformed such that she is no longer clearly a unitary, autonomous Himba subject but rather partially Meduse as well; her dreadlocks transform into blue "okuoko" or tentacles characteristic of the Meduse, marking her as multispecies, or "more than human."[1]

This transformation is an important move in the series, because it positions her to demand the stinger as part of her own intellectual and cultural heritage rather than acting purely as an outsider in the situation. As a Himba who is partially Meduse, she simultaneously becomes an agent for collective rights claims and for rights grounded in specific cultural identity, putting into play key cultural and educational rights claims even as she offers an alternative model for understanding and deploying those rights. This physical transformation is the first of many: in the second book, Binti learns that she is also, through her father, part of the Enyi Zinariya, the "Desert People" maligned by the Himba. The Enyi Zinariya have been genetically transmitting an alien technology-based second sight through several generations. After she seeks out her father's people in the desert, her paternal grandmother activates that technology, allowing her to communicate across large distances with other members of the Enyi Zinariya. The last book of the trilogy sees her become "more than human" in yet a third sense when she merges with a "living ship" called New Fish, from which she will always have to remain within 100 miles proximity.

It is telling, then, that the space of Oomza University is the space in which this continuously multiplying, knowledge-seeking being feels most at home. Indeed, the space of Oomza University is a key site for the imaginative work of posthuman rights in *Binti*. In the trilogy as a whole, it is knowledge work that makes possible new forms of solidarity, new technological innovations, and new social imaginaries. This knowledge work is structured as a collective process, in which economic and intellectual benefits must be shared among species, and the range of species themselves expand the boundaries of collectivity past the human to include animal and plant collaborators. Yet, while crucial knowledge work takes place in part at Oomza University, the institution of the university is insufficient on its own. Binti's educational needs exceed the available institutional frameworks, leading her to sources of indigenous and alien knowledge that are then brought back to and transform the university.

US Racism and the Genealogy of Educational and Cultural Rights at the UN

By telling the story of Binti's search for and production of knowledge, Okorafor calls attention to the vital role of some of the most historically fraught and politically volatile parts of the contemporary human rights agenda: economic, social, and cultural rights. In *Binti*'s intergalactic science fiction universe, demands for educational and cultural rights are for the most part respected, and their enforcement is surprisingly robust. The alternate universe that enables this strong rights framework draws from present-day indigenous claims of cultural sovereignty and demands for redress, as well as demands for meaningful and transformative inclusion in educational institutions such as the university. In so doing, the trilogy offers a tantalizing vision of a lifeworld in which those demands may be met and knowledge work is respected as a process that occurs both within and beyond the university.

In our own world, unfortunately, from the earliest discussions leading up to the founding of the UN and the drafting of key human rights documents like the Universal Declaration of Human Rights (UDHR), economic, social, and cultural rights have been a source of contention not just between larger and smaller states, but between majoritarian and minoritarian cultures within states as well. While the UDHR was ratified in 1948, it passed in large part because the domestic jurisdiction clause allowed member states to circumvent these so-called positive rights and to focus more narrowly on civil and political rights (so-called negative rights). To understand the international implications of this hesitancy to assert the right to knowledge production and dissemination we must take a momentary detour through the role of a contemporary imperial superpower, the United States, in controlling the epistemological shape of the international human rights framework, especially in the Cold War struggles around positive rights.

It is not surprising that the United States was one of the most vocal opponents of calling attention to cultural and economic rights in the human rights framework. Eleanor Roosevelt and John Foster Dulles, among other US delegates, worried that the South-controlled Congress, including Texas Senator Tom Connally, would refuse to support any human rights language that made the United States vulnerable to prosecution for Jim Crow racism. At the time of the San Francisco conference in 1945 where delegates negotiated the language of the document, the US Congress had already failed to pass anti-lynching legislation three times. Connally bluntly refused to consider any mention of the word *educational* in a UN Charter because he was strongly "opposed to any plan to provide educ[ation] irrespective of race" (Anderson 2003, 45). The United States was overwhelmingly interested in maintaining white supremacy in the face of international public opinion against Jim Crow, but entangled with the contemporary moment was the clear history of US violence around Native education and ambivalence about indigenous claims with regard to the ownership and uses of cultural knowledge as well.[2]

The desire to insulate the United States from potential human rights prosecution led the US delegation to propose the insertion of a "domestic jurisdiction clause" into the UN Charter, which states that "nothing in the Charter shall authorize … intervention in matters which are essentially within the domestic jurisdiction of the State concerned" (cited in Anderson 2003, 48). With this protection from prosecution in place, the UDHR drafters were able to include some basic language about economic, social, and cultural rights in Aricles 22–27. But, perhaps more than any other decision, the domestic jurisdiction clause preserved the coloniality of the human rights regime, limiting the efficacy of the new UN to intervene in rights abuses and making states the arbiters of human rights within their borders. This move not only strengthened the state's position, but also underscored the soft power of institutions like the university and the museum to act as arbiters beyond the reach of international human rights conventions.

As this unsavory history demonstrates, the United States as an imperial superpower has a long record of hostility to the role of positive rights in a larger human rights agenda. Thus it is not surprising that when, after a decades-long struggle, the UN did adopt a separate document, the International Covenant on Economic, Social and Cultural Rights (ICESCR 1966), the United States was one of only four countries that failed to ratify. The Covenant asserts the right to housing, physical and mental healthcare, food, and a humane standard of living. Most germane to my discussion, however, are Articles 13 and 15. Article 13 includes general provisions regarding "the right of everyone to education" to "enable all persons to participate effectively in a free society, promote understanding, tolerance and friendship among all nations and all racial, ethnic or religious groups, and further the activities of the United Nations for the maintenance of peace." Article 15 sets forth individual rights "to take part in cultural life," "to enjoy the benefits of scientific progress and its applications," and "to benefit from the protection of the moral and material interests resulting from any scientific, literary or artistic production of which he [sic] is the author." Later documents reinforce and nuance this more general set of rights regarding culture and knowledge. For instance, Article 17 of the 1981 African Banjul Charter reiterates that "every individual shall have the right to education," while the 2007 UN Declaration of the Rights of Indigenous Peoples (UNDRIP) asserts that "Indigenous peoples have the right to the dignity and diversity of their cultures, traditions, histories and aspirations which shall be appropriately reflected in education and public information." Crucially, Article 12 of the UNDRIP focuses not only on the context of learning, but also the context of teaching, including indigenous sovereignty with regard to cultural knowledge and objects: "Indigenous peoples have the right to manifest, practice, develop and teach their spiritual and religious traditions, customs and ceremonies; … the right to the use and control of their ceremonial objects; and the right to the repatriation of their human remains."[3] Although these instruments remain tied to the UN's system of nation-states, they gesture toward other forms of sovereignty and alliance.

UNDRIP's Article 12 and the focus on cultural expression are particularly salient for *Binti*. As I describe above, the catalyst for the longstanding conflict between the Meduse and the Khoush is the theft of the Meduse chief's stinger, which is being housed at Oomza University and used for weapons research. The situation evokes any number of real-life cases in which artifacts acquired through colonial violence and domination continue to sit in Western museums all over the world in the name of "knowledge and education," often without acknowledgment of the ownership claims of those who have been dispossessed by the theft of their cultural and intellectual heritage. One particularly notorious case of the intersection of cultural imperialism and scientified racism is the fate of the nineteenth-century Khoisan woman Sarah Baartman, whose body was dissected by famed French naturalist George Cuvier. Her brain and genitals were dissected and displayed in jars, alongside her skeleton, at the Musée de l'Homme in Paris until 1974. It was only a coordinated campaign by South African activists and government officials from the newly independent South Africa that finally managed to repatriate her body in 2002 and reunite her with the ancestors through a traditional Khoisan burial in South Africa.[4]

The recent film *Black Panther* (2018) hones in on this history of colonial exploitation through a scene in which Killmonger (Michael B. Jordan) taunts the white woman "expert" at the museum for her patronizing interaction with a visitor of color, as well as for not understanding the African "artifacts" she is charged with curating in their embodied cultural context.[5] Lise Ragbir, a gallery director at the University of Texas Austin, notes how "ongoing debates about representation, repatriation, and cultural appropriation—all cannily encapsulated in Killmonger's memorable visit to the Museum of Great Britain in *Black Panther*—affirm that a great deal of work is still needed to make our museums truly welcoming and diverse" (Ragbir 2018). Cultural knowledge, in these cases, is taken from the bodies and artifacts of people who do not benefit from, and are often harmed by, that process. In *Black Panther*, the museum curator's failure to understand either her patron or her Wakandan artifact leads to her demise, but in many educational institutions the legacy of stolen and maligned cultural knowledge remains largely unaddressed, much less subject to processes of restorative justice or punishment in any form.

Oomza University and the Work of Decolonizing Knowledge

In *Binti*, as in these other examples, educational and cultural institutions operate in clear violation of Article 15 of the ICESCR as well as Article 12 of the UNDRIP. In the novel's speculative future, as in the Afrofuturist world of *Black Panther*, there are both critiques of the limits of these types of treaties and possibilities for imagining other outcomes beyond the human rights legal regime. One of the Meduse recounts their grievance to Binti, explaining that "In your university, in one of its museums, placed on display like a piece of rare meat is the stinger of our chief. … We know of the attack and mutilation of our chief, but we do not how it got there. We do not care. We will land on Oomza Uni and take it back" (Okorafor 56). Not only has an essential part of Meduse culture, and of a Meduse body, been stolen, but the university is benefitting scientifically and potentially economically from that cultural theft. The goal is to profit politically from the theft as well, since it is implied that the weapons produced through this research are meant to be deployed against the Meduse themselves. Thus, the university has not only failed to properly respect the "moral and material interests resulting from" the stinger but has in fact threatened the culture from which this knowledge is being appropriated.

In order to redress this grotesque bodily and cultural violation, Binti agrees to help present the Meduse's case to the university leadership alongside the chief. In their (the Meduse are not gendered in human terms) presentation of the grievance to the university leadership, the chief asserts the cultural rights of the Meduse, claiming "If you do not give it to us willingly, we have the right to take back what was stolen from us without provocation" (76). Even though Binti has just arrived at the university, she shows a tremendous faith that justice can be achieved in this institutional space, thinking "I was sure they would agree. These professors were educated beyond anything I could imagine. Thoughtful. Insightful. United. Individual" (76). In a book about today's corporate university, this would be the beginning of a narrative arc about her eventual loss of faith and growing cynicism about the potential of the university to escape the limitations of the exploitative and racist power structures of late capitalism in which it is embedded. But Binti's narrative provides other ways of imagining and inhabiting the university. Thus, in this fictional world, she offers a model of the university realized in practices that truly honor diverse knowledges and claims for authority, as well as access to education. The representative of these thoughtful, highly educated professors steps forward and delivers a formal apology to the Meduse chief, proclaiming:

> On behalf of all the people of Oomza Uni and on behalf of Oomza University, I apologize for the actions of a group of our own in taking the stinger from you, Chief Meduse. The scholars who did this will be found, expelled, and exiled. Museum specimen of such prestige are highly prized at our university, however such things must only be acquired with permission from the people to whom they belong. Oomza protocol is based on honor, respect, wisdom, and knowledge. We will return it to you immediately. (78)

Okorafor offers us here a speculative future in which it is possible to enact restorative justice practices in the institutions responsible for producing knowledge. In other words, she performs deeply valuable political work by presenting, in detail, the practice and recognition of cultural and educational rights, as well as the necessary measures to restore justice when these rights have been violated. In her presentation of the Meduse's grievance to the university leadership, Binti schools us in the inadequacy of arguments based on intellectual autonomy and objective knowledge, demonstrating the harm caused by failures to acknowledge interdependence.

But Okorafor's speculative world is not simply, or simplistically, utopian. Neither Binti nor the Meduse are immune to the seductions of knowledge as a means of seeking epistemological or racial superiority. The trilogy presents several examples in which different groups must negotiate claims about the appropriate uses of cultural knowledge and reject attempts to dismiss or appropriate that knowledge. For instance, Binti's exceptional mathematical knowledge is firmly grounded in her identity as a Himba woman.[6] Her hair is braided in complex patterns that represent her family history and identity, which are inextricable from her mathematical genius. The otjize paste, a mix of local clay and oils that she uses to cover her hair and skin, is critical to her sense of who she is and serves as a clear visual marker to everyone around her of her cultural difference and racialized marginalization. Crucially, it is also what allows her to survive the violent confrontation between the Meduse and the Khoush that opens the novella and to connect with a Meduse named Okwu who becomes her close friend. In an early encounter with Okwu, they discover that the otjize paste possesses healing properties for the Meduse. At first, the Meduse demand that Binti hand over the paste. Binti flat out refuses, saying "If your chief knows my people, then he will have told you that taking it from me is like taking my soul" (49). As Binti's relationship with the Meduse develops, two things happen. First, Binti expands her understanding of family as she allows herself to be stung, a process Okorafor has described as her becoming "not other but more" (Okorafor 2017). Once she becomes partially Meduse herself, Binti becomes more invested in healing members of this extended family. Second, the Meduse stop demanding ownership of her cultural knowledge and start appreciating Binti as more than simply the source of a desirable commodity. She becomes a respected negotiator and family member. By the end, Okwu tells Binti that she will still be family even if the new otjize paste she makes on Oomza lacks the same healing properties.[7] While still utopic in its formulation of "family" and cross-cultural appreciation, the text still suggests alternative value systems for the production of knowledge.

Part of the human rights work of the text, then, is rejecting a capitalist model of cultural commodification that treats bodies as always potential objects for sale or theft. The text imagines an encounter where Binti continues to define the significance of the otjize paste and its use as a cultural practice and object. She maintains authority to decide under what conditions and terms it is appropriate to share this cultural knowledge with the Meduse rather than them commodifying it and taking it from her at her cultural expense. Of course, there are many situations in which it is impossible to maintain control of one's knowledge or body, but Binti's speculative world makes it possible to envision that such a moment might occur. Okorafor imagines how the just and mutually beneficial exchange of cultural knowledge might be possible, not because particular groups are idealized as perfect—the Meduse are capable of the same kinds of cultural domination they have suffered—but because diverse groups of committed knowledge workers can abide by a fair set of conventions regarding the production and uses of knowledge. Knowledge workers and the institutions in which they operate can change and respond to collective obligations. As the narrative shows us, the point is not to reject institutions altogether, but rather to move beyond believing that the state is the only viable arbiter of rights and then reclaim educational and cultural institutions from the neoliberal logic of the modern capitalist state.

In the cases of the stinger and the otijze paste, *Binti* allows us to think education beyond capitalism. Oomza University has commodified the chief's stinger as an object of consumption for the university's students. But it has also weaponized the stinger, experimenting with replicating it for weapons manufacturing. Repatriating the stinger re-embeds it within its cultural and physical environment and simultaneously removes the stinger from a capitalist war economy. Similarly, the novella stages a conflict about the appropriate meanings and uses of the otjize paste. For Binti, as a Himba woman, it has essential cultural and use value as a way to connect her to the land and community, as a form of culturally specific beautification, and thus more broadly as a reminder of her home and history. While she is able to prevent it from being stolen and commodified by the Meduse, she does establish parameters within which that knowledge can be shared to benefit all. With her demand to return the stinger, Binti also explicitly rejects a corporate model of education and compels the university community to respect the function of education as an instrument of peace and transcultural connection. Okorafor returns to this vision of the university as a potential alternative space that enables and supports broad cultural and educational interchange time and time again over the course of the trilogy.

Fugitivity and Decolonial Study in the University

Of course, this is not the university many of us know and inhabit in our work. There's already been a great deal of scholarly discussion about the problematic history of institutions like the university and the museum as tools of the colonial project. As Said famously described, the Orientalists as academically trained "experts" were central to imperial domination via the production of discourse about the "Oriental" other (Said 1978). More recent work, like Claudia Rankine's brilliant multimodal text *Citizen*, details how alienating the university is for faculty and students of color, women, and others who must confront endless micro- and macroaggressions with complaining even as they are asked to peform "diversity work" for the institution. Sara Ahmed eloquently traces the familiar and maddening process of being named a problem for naming the problems of racism and sexism within the institution:

> Even to describe something as sexist and racist here and now can get you into trouble. You point to structures; they say it is in your head. What you describe as material is dismissed as mental. . . And think of what is required: the political labor necessary of having to insist that what we are describing is not just what we are feeling or thinking. (2017, 6)

Ahmed succinctly frames the central paradox of critiquing the university from the inside, where "a feminist movement depends on our ability to keep insisting on something: the ongoing existence of the very things we wish to bring to an end" (6). This is exhausting work. In *The Undercommons*, Stefano Harney and Fred Moten describe the intellectual space of minority subjects made to carry this burden of invisible labor for the university as the "undercommons" and characterize their collective affect as "wary of critique, weary of it" (Harney and Moten 2013, 38) For these knowledge workers, "it cannot be denied that the university is a place of refuge, and it cannoted be accepted that the university is a place of englightenment. In the face of these conditions one can only sneak into the university and steal what one can … to be in but not of – this is the path of the subversive intellectual in the modern university" (26). To steal what you need, Jack Halberstam explains in his introduction to *The Undercommons*, requires "study" rather than the neoliberal consumer model of "learning": "Moten and Harney propose that we prepare now for what will come by entering into *study*. Study, a mode of thinking with others separate from the thinking that the institution requires of you, prepares us to be embedded in what Harney calls 'the with and for' and allows you to spend less time antagonized and antagonizing" (11). You have to find ways to study, to get what you (in an emphatically plural sense) need, in spite of the university's corporatized demands for an anemic mode of "learning."[8]

While Okorafor acknowledges the limitations of the university, especially in its colonialist, racist history, she also offers an alternative model to the corporate/professional university which Moten and Harney critique. Binti does not position her work as for or against the university, a stance that Harney and Moten claim is a useless expenditure of energy; she is also not actively thwarted in her study by the institution. Binti pursues the knowledge and community she needs with a clear sense of the "with and for" in mind—a model of the "study" that Harney and Moten call for. In the process, Okorafor reclaims and reasserts the potential of the university as a site for demands for cultural and educational rights. In *Binti*'s universe, the university is not beyond the reach of the state, but it is not equivalent to the state either. Moreover, its power structure is easier to permeate than the state, more capable of becoming multiply-other in the way she herself does over the course of the trilogy.

The *Binti* trilogy then reimagines the place of the university as a site of decolonial knowledge production in two ways. First, it expands the notion of education beyond the limits of the university institutional space. In the second novella, Binti goes home to reconnect with her family and community and, in the process, learns more from the indigenous Enyi Zinariya people about her edan or talisman and her history than she could at the university. By pursuing her own indigenous *study* (in the Harney/Moten sense of the term), she acquires life-changing knowledge of herself and her worlds. The edan is an interesting case in that the university lacks the knowledge to help her with it. She learns in the second book of the trilogy, *Binti: Home*, that she needs the indigenous knowledge she herself once maligned, which turns out to be not insular but of cosmic significance. As it happens, it is the maligned Enyi Zinariya people who have been in contact with aliens for years and who have made alien communication platforms part of their own DNA. After her initiation into the Enyi Zinariya, Binti feels the expansiveness of her self: "I was Himba, a master harmonizer. Then I was also Meduse, anger vibrating in my *okuoko*. Now I was also Enyi Zinariya, of the Desert People gifted with alien technology. I was worlds" (Okorafor 2017, 116). The indigenous is often read as local or parochial, but indigenous knowing in this instance reverberates to the very edges of the universe. Binti's course of study breaks down barriers between indigenous and foreign knowledge, and is also deeply grounded in the environment such that even animals and plants produce knowledge and are not just waiting to be discovered and interpreted by people. Education brings her to Oomza, but it also constantly sends her elsewhere looking for answers. Given the marginalization of the Himba it is important that knowledge from her family, even the most maligned and indigenous parts like her father's desert relatives, is equally important to whatever she gets at university. Oomza is part of a larger constellation of knowledge production, and Okorafor writes the institution as situating itself as such by suggesting Binti seek answers at home and supporting her in a broader, un-sovereign educational journey.

In essence, Okorafor imagines Harney and Moten's fugitive practice of study in a way that is consistent with a decolonial approach to education. Binti feels empowered to occupy that space fully when she is there and is respected for her intelligence and skills. Oomza University, like our contemporary neoliberal institutions, can clearly operate as a site of racist violence, but it is also an institutional space that can be mobilized to work against such violence. Binti holds Oomza University accountable as a place where you learn from each other; you do not take from each other. She asserts her cultural and educational rights and, in doing so, models a mode of sharing knowledge and resources for mutual interest that inscribes the university as the appropriate and necessary site for these kind of battles about cultural authority to take place; thus, it is also a site where changing practices have a major effect.

Second, the trilogy refuses the assimilation model of inclusion in the university and instead posits a transformative model, wherein the institution is fundamentally changed by the new perspectives and forms of knowledge that are brought into it by its students and faculty. By becoming more herself and bringing in members of other species who have never been affiliated with the university, Binti transforms the institution (Okorafor 2018). Binti is, in a very real sense, exactly the kind of "space invader" Nirmal Puwer describes in her aptly titled work on race and gender difference in cultural institutions, *Space Invaders: Race, Gender and Bodies Out of Place* (2004). Ahmed draws upon Puwer's concept of someone who "enters[s] spaces that are not intended for them" and argues that "we can be space invaders in the academy" (Ahmed 2017, 9). Binti comes, and she brings all her friends with (and in) her. Thus, what is offered here is not exactly the maroon space of the undercommons but an occupation and transformation of institutional educational space where their alienness is not sacrificed but retained as a critical source for knowledge production.

By presenting this portrait of the university and its place in (re)claiming educational and cultural rights, the *Binti* trilogy decolonizes not only educational institutions but also the human rights language used to describe their significance. To borrow from Crystal Parikh, it "sanction[s] lifeworlds and forms of 'good life' other than that endorsed by (neo)liberalism" (Parikh 2017, 5). What we get in *Binti* is not the individual rights-bearing citizen that Harney and Moten rightly critique, but something more akin to Rosa Linda Fregoso's vision of human rights, where "rights register as collectivist rather than individualist, embodied not abstract, contingent rather than certain, interdependent and interconnected instead of autonomous and unencumbered" (Fregoso 2014, 587). Not only is Binti as a character made collective, she presents the case for reparation for the Meduse by connecting their case to her own prior experience of marginalization, refusing to treat rights abuses as individual acts perpetrated against particular bodies without calling out the systems of discrimination and disempowerment in which they are embedded. In my capacity as a diversity worker on my university faculty senate's "Diversity and Inclusion" committee a few years ago, I attended a workshop on "institutionalizing diversity" that illustrated the ways in which a failure to think about structures of institutionality replicates the same limitations over and over again. The presenter showed us an image that looked down upon a vast grid of cubicle-style boxes, all connected by their walls. Inside each box were the words "individual case." The point was that the continual representation of cases in which faculty of color were denied tenure, or pursued claims of discrimination against their academic departments, as individual problems obscures the obvious institutional patterns visible in the larger image. This is, of course, the case for affirmative action in a nutshell. Okorafor's characterization of Binti does not just reject this individualist ideology, she renders it irrelevant. Binti's very person embodies the intersectionality and assemblage, the vast interconnectivity, of her intellectual network, as a "harmonizer," one who is especially skilled at recognizing and accessing the sophisticated mathematical patterns of interconnection in the universe. In this idealized vision, elitist white notions of pure individual autonomy are directly contradicted by the profound, collective indigenous scientific knowledge she brings to the university.

Indigeneity and the Subject of Knowledge Production

Okorafor's trilogy not only displaces individualist notions of human rights grievance but also foregrounds indigeneity as a powerful space from which to imagine post-sovereign approaches to human and posthuman rights. As Fregoso points out, indigenous thinkers like the Zapatistas present us with an "understanding of rights as existing in their exercise, prior to and irrespective of their legalization, [which] means that human rights can be envisioned outside the logics of abstract universality embedded in or guaranteed by state law" (594). From this indigenous, decolonial perspective, humans are part of a larger pluriversal network that bridges the human and the natural world, the living and the dead.

> In the refusal to separate 'nature' from 'culture,' or to consider 'nature' in Western/European terms as an entity outside the human, there to be known and possessed, Indigeneity affirms the integral nature of all things—it is anchored first and foremost in an epistemology that affirms the agential capabilities of the living earth, a universal kinship with land as sacred and rights bearing, together with other (nonhuman) species beings in the material world and ancestors in the spirit world. (599)

One could expand Fregoso's vision to include *Binti*'s alien nonhuman species as well. Within this expansive framework, posthuman rights emerge from the collective, creative process of thinking concepts like duty, solidarity, and shared vulnerability rather than remaining constrained by what Samera Esmeir calls the "juridical humanity" to which Western human rights discourse owes its dominant conception of the human (referenced in Fregoso 2014, 589). The *Binti* trilogy calls attention to the knowledge work entailed in thinking those key concepts beyond state sovereignty and in centering education, including relevant institutions like the university and the museum, as a key vector in the imaginative work of creating new lifeworlds. In so doing, Okorafor offers a scenario in which damaging modes of thinking can be acknowledged, redressed, and ultimately moved beyond.

As Okorafor says in the 2017 TED talk entitled "Sci-Fi Stories That Imagine a Future Africa," part of what had turned her off from so-called "classic" Western science fiction was its deep colonialist roots, the xenophobic impulse to identify and conquer behind its quest narratives. Instead, she explains, "Binti leaves to seek education *from* extraterrestrials. She goes out as she is, looking the way she looks, carrying her cultures, being who she is." She goes out motivated by curiosity rather than a need to dominate, and in the process writes Africans into the future. As Okorafor puts it, "like Udide the spider artist, African science fiction's blood runs deep, and it's old, and it's ready to come forth; and when it does, imagine the new technologies, ideas, and sociopolitical changes it'll inspire. For Africans, homegrown science fiction can be a will to power. What if? It's a powerful question." The "what if" that frames Okorafor's talk resonates deeply with decolonial formulations of human rights by locating its vision of African futures firmly in an intellectual and cultural genealogy emerging from African pasts. Its "blood runs deep," and its articulation wills into being a realization of its own Afrocentric visions rather than ones derived from or imposed by a Eurocentric epistemology. Okorafor's "what if" evokes other questions: What if we think human rights through institutions like the university as a utopic site of decolonizing knowledge? What if indigenous knowledges and forms of sociality might offer pathways for articulating demands for justice and the forms of reparation that they would entail? What if the university and the museum can actively support the creation of transformative modes of thriving, sociality, and just community rather than functioning primarily to (re)produce neoliberal capitalist citizenship? As Amal El-Mohtar rightly notes, Okorafor's text, with its "future in which people of color move unfettered through the stars, befriend aliens, make peace between warring factions," feels distant from our current political reality (El-Mohtar 2017). But this distance opens a space for representing, for imagining a "what if," and for willing to power a decolonial vision of knowledge work.

Acknowledgments My deep thanks to Samantha Pinto and Alexandra Moore for organizing this collection, as well as to Samantha Pinto, Eve Dunbar, and Anne Gulick for the incredibly generative ACLA seminar in which I began to develop this essay. It was Anne who really got me thinking about the potential of the university in *Binti*. I also owe profound debts of gratitude to Andrea Fontenot for talking me through the joyous and intellectually perilous process of transforming a jumble of related thoughts into a coherent essay, and to Nadine at Easton's Nook retreat for nourishment of many kinds. This is feminist community at its best.

Notes

1. The phrase "more than human" most directly cites the 1953 novel of the same name by US science fiction writer Theodore Sturgeon, which won an International Fantasy Award in 1954 and was nominated for a "Retro Hugo" award in 2004.
2. The Indian Arts and Crafts Act of 1935 was ostensibly passed to "promote the economic welfare" of Native Americans "through the development of Indian arts and crafts and the expansion of the market for the products of Indian art and craftsmanship," but has suffered from a chronic lack of government enforcement for claims regarding cultural theft including, most recently, a case against Pendleton Woolen Mills, which sells hundreds of blankets described as "Native American" or "Native American inspired." Pendleton paid a small fine after a 2014 case but continues to offer its products under the same labels (Galanda 2016). According to the National Congress of American Indians web site, the Native American Graves Protection and Repatriation Act (NAGPRA), which was only enacted in 1990 with the aim "to establish the rights of Indian tribes and their lineal descendants to obtain repatriation of certain human remains, funerary objects, sacred objects, and objects of cultural patrimony from federal agencies and museums," has similarly met with a lack of enforcement at the federal level. For a more in-depth scholarly placement of NAGPRA within an international human rights framework see Barker (2013).
3. The African Charter on Human and People's Rights, popularly known as the Banjul Charter, can be accessed at http://www.achpr.org/instruments/achpr/#a17. UNDRIP is accessible via the UN's web site at http://www.un.org/esa/socdev/unpfii/documents/DRIPS_en.pdf.
4. Many have written about Sarah Baartman's story. For an incisive discussion of Baartman's experience, the colonial history of the museum as purveyor of scientific racism, and the continuing resonance of Baartman's story for

the Black diaspora, see Gordon-Chipembere (2011). On the ethical questions surrounding museum acquisition of human remains, including Sarah Baartman's, see Cassman et al. (2007).

5. The scene sparked a heated discussion in the fields of Art History and Museum Studies, much of it centered around the Brooklyn Museum's recent hire of a white curator for its African art collection. See Sit (2018).
6. While the Himba are an indigenous community in Namibia, Okorafor specified in a tweet from August 1, 2018 that she is imagining a distant future Himba people rather than any static, anthropological model of cultural authenticity.
7. Binti manages to maintain epistemological control over the otjize paste in this situation, but it does not hold a purely emancipatory meaning throughout the series. For example, when Binti first returns home from Oomza University and encounters a former love interest while not wearing her otjize paste, he shames her for her failure to embody proper Himba womanhood. Binti must constantly engage in the process of decolonizing cultural knowledge not only with alien species, then, but also at home.
8. Chris Newfield (2016) offers a compelling history of the neoliberalization of the US university over the past few decades.

Works Cited

African Commission on Human and Peoples' Rights [Banjul Charter]. 1981. "African Charter on Human and People's Rights." Adopted June 27, 1981. http://www.achpr.org/instruments/achpr/#a17.

Ahmed, Sara. 2017. *Living a Feminist Life*. Durham: Duke University Press.

Anderson, Carol. 2003. *Eyes Off the Prize: The United Nations and the African American Struggle for Human Rights, 1944–1955*. Cambridge: Cambridge University Press.

Barker, Joanne. 2013. "The Recognition of NAGPRA: A Human Rights Promise Deferred." In *Recognition, Sovereignty Struggles, and Indigenous Rights in the United States*, edited by Amy. E. Den Ouden and Jean M. O'Brien, 95–114. Chapel Hill: University of North Carolina Press.

Biko, Steve. 1978, 2002. "Black Consciousness and the Quest for a True Humanity." In *I Write What I Like*, 87–98. Chicago: University of Chicago Press.

Black Panther. 2018. Dir. Ryan Coogler. Marvel Studios, Walt Disney Pictures.

Cassman, Vicki, Nancy Odegard, and Joseph Powell, eds. 2007. *Human Remains: Guide for Museums and Academic Institutions*. Lanham, MD: Alta Mira Press.

El-Mohtar, Amal. 2017. "A Spacefarer's Next Great Adventure Begins at 'Home.'" *NPR Books*, February 4. https://www.npr.org/2017/02/04/512042817/a-spacefarers-next-great-adventure-begins-at-home.

Esmeir, Samera. 2012. *Juridical Humanity: A Colonial History*. Stanford: Stanford University Press.

Fregoso, Rosa-Linda. 2014. "For a Pluriversal Declaration of Human Rights." *American Quarterly* 66 (3): 583–608.

Galanda, Gabriel S. 2016. "Reinvigorating the Indian Arts and Crafts Act." *Indian Country Today*, May 12, 2016. https://newsmaven.io/indiancountrytoday/archive/reinvigorating-the-indian-arts-and-crafts-act-iEwKbhah10-lfHAmcGxAAQ/.

Gordon-Chipembere, Natasha, ed. 2011. *Representation and Black Womanhood: The Legacy of Sarah Baartman*. New York, NY: Palgrave.

Harney, Stefano, and Fred Moten. 2013. *The Undercommons: Fugitive Planning and Black Study*. Introduction by Jack Halberstam. New York: Minor Composition.

Mignolo, Walter D. 2011. *The Darker Side of Western Modernity: Global Futures, Decolonial Options*. Durham: Duke University Press.

Musiol, Hanna. 2020. "Toxicity, Speculation, and Rights: Political Imagination in Mixmedia, Literary, and Cinematic Futurescapes." In *Writing Beyond the State*, edited by Alexandra S. Moore and Samantha Pinto, 265–289. New York: Palgrave Macmillan.

National Congress of American Indians. n.d. "Cultural Protection and NAGPRA." Accessed August 8, 2018. http://www.ncai.org/policy-issues/community-and-culture/cultural-protection-and-nagpra.

Ndlovu-Gatsheni, Sabelo. 2018. *Epistemic Freedom in Africa: Deprovincialization and Decolonization*. New York: Routledge.

Newfield, Chris. 2016. *The Great Mistake: How We Wrecked Public Universities*. Baltimore: Johns Hopkins.

Ngugi wa Thiong'o. 1986. *Decolonizing the Mind: The Politics of Language in African Literature*. Oxford, UK: James Currey.

Okorafor, Nnedi. 2015. *Binti*. New York, NY: Tor.

Okorafor, Nnedi. 2017. "Sci-Fi Stories That Imagine a Future Africa." Filmed August 2017. TEDGlobal video, 9:21. https://www.ted.com/talks/nnedi_okorafor_sci_fi_stories_that_imagine_a_future_africa.

Okorafor, Nnedi. 2017. *Binti: Home*. New York, NY: Tor.

Okorafor, Nnedi. 2018. *Binti: The Night Masquerade*. New York, NY: Tor.

Parikh, Crystal. 2017. *Writing Human Rights: The Political Imaginaries of Writers of Color*. Minneapolis: University of Minnesota Press.

Puwar, Nirmal. 2004. *Space Invaders: Race, Gender and Bodies Out of Place*. Oxford: Berg Publishers.

Quijano, Anibal. 2007. "Coloniality and Modernity/Rationality." *Cultural Studies* 21 (2–3): 168–178.

Ragbir, Lise. 2018. "What Black Panther Gets Right About the Politics of Museums." *Hyperallergic*, March 20, 2018. https://hyperallergic.com/433650/black-panther-museum-politics/.

Rankine, Claudia. 2014. *Citizen: An American Lyric*. Minneapolis, MN: Greywolf Press.

Said, Edward. 1978. Introduction to *Orientalism*, 1–30. New York, NY: Vintage.

Sit, Ryan. 2018. "Museum Appoints White Woman as African Art Curator, Sparks Outrage." *Newsweek*, March 29, 2018.

Sturgeon, Theodore. 1953. *More Than Human*. New York, NY: Ballantine Books.

UNISA. "2019 Decoloniality Summer School." https://www.unisa.ac.za/sites/corporate/default/Colleges/Human-Sciences/News-&-events/Events/2019-Decoloniality-Summer-School-?fbclid=IwAR25zWvhp52SfS1d61jYa1nWWdPsN4JNZMSZ0o0L57sLIsdNJTgYA5CMVV4.

United Nations. 1948. "The Universal Declaration of Human Rights." Adopted December 10, 1948. http://www.un.org/en/universal-declaration-human-rights/.

United Nations. 1966. "The International Covenant on Economic, Social and Cultural Rights." Adopted December 16, 1966. https://www.ohchr.org/Documents/ProfessionalInterest/cescr.pdf.

United Nations. 2007. "United Nations Declaration on the Rights of Indigenous People." Adopted September 13, 2007. http://www.un.org/esa/socdev/unpfii/documents/DRIPS_en.pdf.

CHAPTER 4

Feeling Right: Taste, Style, and Affect in Human Rights Work

Greg A. Mullins

On September 30, 1991, a group of activists engaged the services of an aerial advertising company to fly a banner drawing attention to torture in Mexico. The banner flew over the Stanford University campus and focused on Frost Amphitheater, where it would be visible to the crowd of about 7000 assembled to hear Mexican President Carlos Salinas de Gortari offer his keynote address celebrating Stanford's centennial (Ellison; *Stanford News Service* 1991). Jack Healey, Executive Director of Amnesty International USA (abbreviated in this essay as AIUSA), drew attention to this event in December of the same year, in two pages of a fifty-page draft vision statement he circulated for staff and board discussion.[1] The look and feel of AIUSA today owes a great deal to the strategic planning that followed this discussion.[2] Referencing the aerial banner, Healey wrote: "Some Amnesty members and public officials in the audience were amazed and delighted. Others were amazed and

G. A. Mullins (✉)
The Evergreen State College, Olympia, WA, USA
e-mail: mullinsg@evergreen.edu

A. S. Moore and S. Pinto (eds.), *Writing Beyond the State*,
Palgrave Studies in Literature, Culture and Human Rights,
https://doi.org/10.1007/978-3-030-34456-6_4

appalled. It was a matter of taste" (AIUSA National Office Records Series IV.1.4 Box 263 Folder 14).

Spoken as a rhetorical move, the phrase "a matter of taste" is often deployed to deflect conflict, as is the analogous phrase "everyone has a right to an opinion." Both phrases tend to stop dialogue in its tracks by consigning the topic at hand to a holding area for conflict-avoidant heterogeneity, and to smooth social relationships by tacitly agreeing to disagree. This essay pushes this dialogue forward, to some extent by drawing attention to underlying conflicts, but mostly by taking "taste" seriously, on its own merits. It attends to "taste" and its cousin "style" by way of opening a fresh understanding of some features of human rights work. The style of a human rights action (in the example, flying an aerial banner) and the tastes of human rights activists (favoring or disfavoring this style) speak to a historical shift underway at AIUSA during Jack Healey's leadership. This essay considers that shift: away from the grass-roots and toward professionalization, away from Prisoners of Conscience and toward a broad human rights agenda, and away from letter writing and toward media activism in the broadest sense, including the popular music concerts AIUSA produced during the 1980s. Better understanding taste and style during a discrete period in the history of one human rights organization opens a broader horizon for analysis in two directions: the role of style in human rights projects at large, and the affect of human rights that is traceable, in part, by attending to taste and style.

The 1991 action at Stanford's Frost Amphitheater is not a watershed moment in the history of human rights activism. In many respects it is quite ordinary. I focus on it here because the event, and responses to it, condense aspects of human rights work that merit unpacking. That unpacking entails a journey that begins with Amnesty International's founding thirty years earlier and takes us through a period of extravagant popular music concert tours in the 1980s. In brief, Amnesty International's advocacy for Prisoners of Conscience of the 1960s and 1970s was founded on twined notions of sovereignty: the self-sovereign subject of rights, whose rights were to be guaranteed by the sovereign nation-state. Over time Amnesty International, along with other actors, expanded definitions of human rights and of human rights activism. To be sure this expansion was pursued through law and through state and intergovernmental apparatuses for whom sovereignty is a defining feature, and called into question the absolute sovereignty of states defined by the Peace of Westphalia in 1648. At the same time, AIUSA expanded through savvy engagements with media, entertainment, and mass culture, flowing across boundaries that describe the liberal subject and the nation-state. Attending to style and taste opens our understanding of human rights culture in development; attending to affect clarifies the tactics and routes through which human rights projects establish themselves. In this essay, I draw on material from the archive of AIUSA and offer a glimpse into the historical development of a leading human rights organization. My larger aim, however, is better to understand how style, taste, and affect promote or even accomplish post-sovereign human rights, activated "beyond the state."

Setting the Stage: Feeling Right

AIUSA is a national section of Amnesty International. This essay describes actors and an organization based in the United States and working globally, within a frame that recognizes national sovereignty and that also, over time, calls into question the centrality of the nation-state. Among the many forces that might drive attachment to nation, or detachment from it, and attachment to the lives of distant others or detachment from them are registers of affect. Sentimentality is an especially forceful affective mode of attachment to nation, easily stirred by anthems and flags. The capacity to feel sympathy for the suffering of distant others is, arguably, a necessary precondition for the rise of human rights frameworks in modernity.[3] Close attention to taste and style, understood as modes of aesthetic engagement, sheds light on the structures of feelings produced in and through human rights narrative and advocacy. These structures help some people, such as advocates, "feel right."

Amnesty International, founded in May 1961 with the name Appeal for Amnesty, was formed using and has since replicated a triangular structure of affect. Its original work was to issue appeals (1) by the international public, (2) to states, (3) on behalf of political prisoners.[4] Cast in the idiom of melodrama this structure maps to the roles of (1) hero, (2) villain, and (3) victim. Melodrama is so frequently maligned that I hasten to add that I am not criticizing Amnesty International's founder Peter Benenson, his associates, or generations of Amnesty International and AIUSA members, staff, or leaders for leveraging melodramatic structures and forms to advance their work, nor am I impugning their own affective relation to human rights work. I am merely pointing out that a great deal of political work is accomplished through melodramatic forms that mobilize affect and, at times, mobilize action. Elizabeth R. Anker argues that melodrama is a political genre and, with reference to the United States, "a genre of national political discourse" (Anker, 2). I argue that human rights activism in the United States bears a relation to the national political discourse Anker so persuasively describes, but also engages a transnational discourse of hero, victim, and villain.

Anker defines the conventions of melodrama as a form that "portrays dramatic events through moral polarities of good and evil, overwhelmed victims, heightened affects of pain and suffering, grand gestures, astonishing feats of heroism, and the redemption of virtue" (Anker, 2). As a theatrical form, melodrama originated in late eighteenth-century revolutionary France, and flourished there and in the post-revolutionary United States. If tragedy had been a genre resonant with aristocratic society, melodrama arose during the "age of rights" as a genre of the people. It is in this sense a democratic theatrical and media form, with local expressions found globally from Nollywood to *telenovelas*.[5] On the political stage, so to speak, melodrama offers distinct roles, a readily recognizable narrative structure, and moral clarity. Behind the scenes, a great deal of human rights work is laborious, morally confusing, and politically hazardous; its affective registers take people in many directions, including grief, sadness, anger, and melancholy. On stage, as it were, as a mode of *representing* human rights work, melodrama aligns human rights advocacy with heroism, virtue, and "feeling right."

Dramatis Personae: Ginetta Sagan and Jack Healey

Barbara Keys, in *Reclaiming American Virtue: The Human Rights Revolution of the 1970s*, argues that the meteoric rise of AIUSA in the 1970s was fueled in part by a collective urge to feel virtuous in the aftermath of the war in Vietnam. In her account, use of the language of human rights in the United States flipped from a domestic focus in the 1960s to an international focus in the 1970s; following the devastation of the war against Vietnam and the violent assault on civil rights at home, both liberals and conservatives found moral purpose in international human rights advocacy, the liberals with an eye on Latin American dictatorships and the conservatives more concerned with Communist authoritarianism. Taken as a whole, AIUSA members leaned to the left and emerged from anti-war and social movement activism. At the same time, Amnesty International and AIUSA officially adhered to a non-partisan policy and strategy of advocating for the release of Prisoners of Conscience: people jailed on the basis of their beliefs or expression of their beliefs, whether those beliefs tilted left, right, or toward the unorthodox. With a mission focus on civil liberties, Amnesty International could credibly claim that it pursued a moral, rather than a political, intervention to alleviate human suffering.[6]

The moral project of Amnesty International was championed by Ginetta Sagan, one of the figures most responsible for the rapid growth of AIUSA on the west coast of the United States. Born in Italy, Sagan was a member of the resistance to Mussolini's fascist regime. Arrested and tortured, she narrowly escaped execution. After the war she emigrated to the United States and became active with AIUSA in Washington DC; in 1968 she settled in the suburbs near Palo Alto and Stanford University. She founded the first west coast chapter of AIUSA, and helped launch an AIUSA office, with staff, in San Francisco.

Charismatic, driven since childhood to resist totalitarianism, and an impassioned advocate for civil and political rights, Ginetta Sagan was an exceptionally effective organizer and fundraiser. Her vision and energy made it possible to open the San Francisco office, which operated quasi-independently from AIUSA's headquarters in New York. Rank and file membership in Northern California was eclectic, but drew especially from middle-class circles of students, teachers, librarians, and mainstream Protestant and Catholic peace activists, who were themselves part of a wider Bay Area activist ecosystem fed by civil rights and anti-war energies. Sagan operated from a suburban base in the communities surrounding Stanford University, and her charisma and life story inspired those around her. She didn't work from a template. As an example of her entrepreneurial spirit, in 1971 Sagan organized a Joan Baez and Melina Mercouri concert at U.C. Berkeley's Greek Theater to protest the military dictatorship in Greece and raise consciousness about human rights broadly. The event was a grand success, notable for the scale of the undertaking at a time when local AIUSA groups were more likely to raise funds by selling cookies and T-shirts. Within the context of this essay, it is also notable for being the first of a string of cultural events in amphitheaters and stadiums, each of which self-consciously stages its particular theatricality: (1) through folk music resonating with a Bay Area audience in 1971; (2) through pop/rock music appealing to a youthful global audience in the 1980s; and (3) through aerial protest at Stanford University's Centennial Convocation in 1991.

Jack Healey is responsible for the pop/rock concerts of the 1980s. During the years of his tenure (1981–1993) Executive Director Jack Healey presided over a generational shift at AIUSA. If, as Kenneth Cmiel suggests, AIUSA's early style "felt and looked like earlier antiwar organizing" with "AI staffers paid a pittance and scruffily dressed, cross[ing] the country with beat-up cars and shoestring budgets to recruit primarily on college campuses" (Cmiel, 1240), by the closing years of the twentieth-century AIUSA was a professional NGO sporting a correspondingly professional style in its public face (media campaigns, action events, and fundraising) and in its behind-the-scenes advocacy. In the words of one activist member based in Northern California, in the 1970s and early 1980s AIUSA members were, generally speaking, "a relatively staid, stable, secure, non-risk taking bunch of mostly soft spoken middle class white people," but by the early 1990s Jack Healey had led AIUSA to become "a more multicultural, younger, more activist, and more progressive organization" (AIUSA National Office Records IV.1.7 Box 10 Folder 2).[7] Leno Rose-Avila corroborates this view, recalling that Healey recruited him and other self-described "Black and Latino radicals" to AIUSA staff positions as part of a successful strategy to diversify the organization (Rose-Avila 2018).[8] In the early 1980s, Healey noticed the aging and cautious membership as well as the increasing costs of doing AIUSA's work, and in response to both pressures he championed what would become his signature initiative during his twelve years as Executive Director: celebrity endorsements and media-saturated music concerts.[9] Especially visible in these endeavors were Peter Gabriel and Sting.[10]

In the 1970s Amnesty International extended its founding mission into new areas of work: advocacy for fair trial procedures and abolition of torture. By the end of the twentieth-century Amnesty International had expanded its mission to advance the full range of human rights. Sagan advocated that as AIUSA grew, it should retain a focus on Prisoners of Conscience, a grassroots style of work emphasizing letter-writing campaigns from local groups who "adopted" prisoners, and a tone of writing that was polite, diplomatic, and restrained. This style was closely aligned with Benenson's founding vision. In the 1970s, the instruction pamphlets distributed to local groups described this style and tone as a tactic essential to successful advocacy. Healey championed a more public style and more vigorous tone for AIUSA, not neglecting the tactic of funneling letters from an international public to prisoners and officials who could secure their release but also mobilizing that public through media and the arts. Sagan and Healey stand in here as figures of signature styles. Sagan's reserved and dignified style reflected the tactics invented by Amnesty International's central office, the International Secretariat in London. Healey encouraged a youthful, energized, loud, media-savvy, "celebrity" style to grow the organization. The strategy underwriting style in both cases taps a sentimental affective structure in which the heroes feel right (at times, even righteous) and cast shame on the villains.[11] To be clear, these varieties of style, and their associated affective structures, are not mere byproducts of charismatic leadership. Nor are they mere vehicles for tactics identified in two stages of the life cycle of an organization. As we will see more fully below, these styles generate human rights work.

Scene One, Frost Amphitheater

Stanford University celebrated its first century in 1991, with a string of events culminating in three days of festivity featuring keynote speakers Canadian Prime Minister Brian Mulroney on September 29, Mexican President Carlos Salinas de Gortari on September 30, and California Governor Pete Wilson on October 1.[12] Contexts for the distinctly international cast of the celebration include negotiations ongoing at that time to create the North American Free Trade Agreement (NAFTA) and Stanford's efforts to position itself as a leading global university. Invitations to Mulroney and Salinas de Gortari created an opportunity for off-stage conversations among senior leaders in government, industry, and education. On stage, the speakers explicitly linked the push for free trade with the advantages of free exchange of ideas through research and education, positioning Stanford as an engine in the global information and knowledge economy (*Stanford News Service* 1991). As it turned out, spotlighting NAFTA generated blowback for Stanford. Allegations that the Mexican state security apparatus pushed for NAFTA by suppressing democracy and dissent, including arrest and torture of people opposed to the treaty, fueled protest inside and outside Frost Amphitheater on September 30.

Protests against Salinas de Gortari were organized or endorsed by the PRD (Partido de la Revolución Democrática, Estado de California), Bay Area labor groups, and MEChA-Bay Area. We don't know who flew the aerial banner over Frost Amphitheater, or whether AIUSA members participated in any way. We do know that torture in Mexico was a priority area for research within the context of Amnesty International's global campaign against torture, and that attentive Bay Area members would likely have been aware of research in this area (Amnesty International, "Mexico: Torture with Impunity").[13]

The events at Stanford connect with AIUSA's main office in New York City in the context with which this chapter opened, Executive Director Jack Healey's early draft of a vision document. Healey traveled to Northern California in the fall of 1991 to meet with Group 19, the Amnesty International Group founded by Ginetta Sagan. Presumably he learned about the aerial banner at that time, and he referenced it in a draft vision document written in December 1991 and quoted above. "Some Amnesty members and public officials in the audience were amazed and delighted," wrote Healey. "Others were amazed and appalled. It was a matter of taste" (AIUSA National Office Records Series IV.1.4 Box 263 Folder 14).

Healy's vision for AIUSA's next decade went forward, but the reference to taste was dropped after staff members pushed back. A summary of a conference call with staff includes the remarks, "The 'taste' section was generally thought to be innappropriate [sic] for a vision paper and people felt it should be removed. There was considerable speculation about what prompted such a section to be included and in the end caused more confusion about its intent than a sense of vision. It seems to fly in the face of 'One movement; many voices'" (AIUSA National Office Records Series IV.1.4 Box 263 Folder 14). Prior to 1985 Amnesty International's official slogan had been "one movement, one voice." Healey and other AIUSA national leaders pushed to alter that slogan to "one movement, many voices" as part of a wider strategy to promote diversity and flexibility in the organization (Hopgood 2006, Chapter 5). Implicit in the push back from staff members was the suspicion that Healey's invocation of "taste" might decenter AIUSA even more, to many movements with many voices.

Scene Two: Stadium Concerts

By 1991 Jack Healey had extensive experience managing cacophony, not only among staff, board, and members but also as executive producer of a string of popular music concerts. The concerts signaled a new understanding of human rights activism through their very style (Henke 1988, 71). Attending a concert and purchasing a T-shirt were expressed as acts of activism in and of themselves. If Peter Benenson's original "Appeal to Amnesty" in 1961 was solemn to the point of being pious, the rock concerts were brash in their sentimentality. The emotions of the crowd are evident in the 2013 DVD compilation of video produced at the concerts and ancillary events, as cameras pan across attendees dancing, cheering, crying, and shouting (Amnesty International, *Released: The Human Rights Concerts, 1986–1998*).[14] The 1986 concert tour concluded in Giants Stadium, with Joan Baez and Aaron Neville singing an electrifying rendition of "Amazing Grace." The 1990 An Embrace of Hope Concert concluded with twenty Chilean women on stage, images of their disappeared sons and husbands attached to their clothing, solemnly dancing Chile's national dance style the Cueca while Sting sang "They Dance Alone."

The concerts were organized around several aims: to appeal to the next generation of membership, to increase the total membership (both activist members and donors), and to draw attention to human rights violations around the world. Membership and donations increased substantially, and AIUSA became more attractive to a younger generation.[15] However, in tight relationship with this expansion came a newly vitalized understanding that global human rights work as such could be not only supported by but could be *characterized* by the affect of the crowd assembled before the celebrity spectacle.[16]

The third of the three grand concert efforts organized under Healey's watch was An Embrace of Hope, held in Santiago de Chile in October 1990. This was an especially poignant event for many reasons, including that it marked the end of a dictatorship that had been formative to the development of the US national section of Amnesty International. One year later, in late 1991, the AIUSA board asked Healey to develop a draft vision statement for the coming decades. This is the document mentioned above, in which certain issues are addressed in relation to the "taste" of doing human rights work. Skipping forward a year, to September 19, 1992, Healey circulates yet another document—one that came to be called the "arrows paper" because it included a schematic designation of old ways of doing AIUSA's work with arrows pointing toward new ways of doing that work. If the 1991 vision paper generated some sparks from staff, the 1992 arrows paper turned sparks to fire. The title of this document is "Funding Amnesty's Human Rights Work: Issues for the IEC Discussion." (The IEC, or International Executive Committee, was the governing board for Amnesty International as a global organization, charged to set policy for the movement as a whole.) Polemically, Healey writes, "The movement has evolved…. There are new human rights issues

– we haven't been as successful in mobilizing the world on human rights work beyond the POC [Prisoner of Conscience]. We can't be stuck in the human rights world of an era which has passed – the people who fund us aren't interested" (Healey, "Funding Amnesty's Human Rights Work: Issues for the IEC Discussion," 19 September 1992, Page one of eleven, AIUSA National Office Records Series I.4 Box 14 Folder 11).

In these words we hear the voice of an executive director speaking frankly about the relationship between money and program. The analysis expressed in the arrows paper wasn't a departure for Healey. It effectively summarized the directions in which he had been leading AIUSA for a decade. It envisioned a globally diverse membership inclusive of young and less affluent people, and called for human rights work pursued through media-savvy campaigns organized around a broad array of themes. The 1980s rock music concerts had been doing this work not as an ancillary function of the organization but as a defining mode of political engagement in and through popular culture and representation as spectacle, including through the crowd's affect generated at these concerts.

Throughout his tenure at AIUSA, Healey had pushed the organization to seek a younger and more racially and socioeconomically diverse membership. This concern dovetailed with IEC discussions about the organization globally, and with a camp that wished to see Amnesty become more truly international in its membership, with active national sections on all continents (Hopgood). The push toward becoming a global mass movement was resisted, actively, from many quarters, including from those members, like Ginetta Sagan, who wished to retain the "moral clarity" of Amnesty's adoption and letter-writing tactics from the 1960s.

In late 1992 Ginetta Sagan wrote a strongly worded letter to Jack Healey in response to his arrows paper expressing her disagreement with the direction he was pushing not only AIUSA but also the global movement via the IEC. She critiqued Healey's polemical thesis that programing follows money; especially remarkable is the energy her letter devoted to her perception that "Much of the conflict that breeds human rights violations around the world occurs in situations of profound moral ambiguity." She continued:

> Amnesty owes its success to the notion of the prisoner of conscience, a concept of such crystalline moral clarity that it created a concern around which huge numbers of people could rally. There were clearly identifiable

> good guys and bad guys, and it was easy to weigh in on the side of the angels.
>
> Over the past decade, the world has become a much more complicated place. Besides prisoners of conscience, many human rights crises now seem to involve victims of circumstance. (Ginetta Sagan to Jack Healey, December 6, 1992. Page two and three of seven. AIUSA National Office Records Series I.4 Box 14 Folder 11)

As examples of these victims of circumstance Sagan names "groups of people assaulted by tribal bandits, ethnic gangs, or warring factions" who "are people who happen to be in the wrong place at the wrong time." These stand in contrast to the individual who suffers "as a result of specific actions taken by a brutal regime." Sagan argued on both moral and pragmatic terms. In moral terms, at least within a liberal frame of morality, the individual who stands up to a dictator and faces prison, torture, or death is clearly a victim, likely to capture the attention and sympathy of heroic Western liberal subjects. In pragmatic terms, the prisoner of conscience can be released, and alleviation of suffering can be measured when the prison door swings open. The distant and racialized other, who experiences violence under the banner of "tribe" and "gang," remains morally inscrutable to Sagan. In its first decades, Amnesty promoted its successes in terms of who, and how many, were released from prison. Sagan argued that Amnesty should stay true to this course.

As for the victims of circumstance, Sagan asked rhetorically, "Can Amnesty really hope to free people from racism, homophobia, religious persecution, ethnic hatreds, and tribal animosities?" (Sagan to Healey, December 6, 1992). It is not the case that Sagan entirely lacked a structural analysis of the conditions that led to atrocities such as political violence and torture. However, she strongly preferred an Amnesty International that leveraged moral outrage at individual circumstances, and that worked to alleviate specific cases of suffering rather than working for systemic change. A tremendous advantage of this approach was that one could proceed as if the context did not matter—that it was sufficient for Amnesty International adoption groups scattered around the globe to know (or believe) that a person had been imprisoned on account of conscience.[17] Adoption groups could pin their efforts on the so-called "universal" knowledge of decontextualized political violence.

Sagan was speaking to a longstanding tension between members who gravitated to adoption groups and those who gravitated to action groups.[18] Activism based on structural analysis and hope for structural change can be dated at least as far back as 1972, when Amnesty International's first global campaign against torture was initiated. In the first decade of Amnesty International thousands of people who had been adopted as Prisoners of Conscience had been released. However, many Amnesty members were concerned with the uncounted thousands who languished in prison, often suffering torture. The 1972 campaign to abolish torture was launched to address systemic suffering and to prevent it in future. This campaign grew naturally out of the liberal narrative that had defined the Prisoner of Conscience as the exemplary victim deserving of amnesty (out of which, of course, the very name of the organization arose). However, it also represented the first wedge of a mission expansion that would eventually take AIUSA and Amnesty International globally toward structural analysis and activism for systemic change. It is in this context that I wish to return to the remarks Jack Healey made about the variety of "tastes" human rights advocates are capable of expressing.

In addition to the example of positive and negative responses to the aerial banner at Stanford, Healey's draft vision offered these examples: "We also face issues of musical taste. Leonard Bernstein has contributed significantly to the Amnesty movement. So has Peter Gabriel. So has Joan Baez." Healey continued, "In fact, Joan Baez and one of AIUSA's foremost guiding spirits, Ginetta Sagan, showed the entire movement what effective fundraising means through the concerts they organized in the early 1970s" ("Vision Paper—Draft as of December 27, 1991." Page 7. AIUSA National Office Records Series I.4 Box 14 Folder 10).

This sly backhanded compliment stole Sagan's moral high ground, so to speak, and claimed continuity across time of AIUSA endeavors to pursue human rights work as theater, as spectacle, as sound and as image played out before a crowd. In the "taste" section of his vision paper, Healey deploys tropes of "multi-cultural identity," "diversity," "tolerance," and "mosaic" by way of signaling a vision for Amnesty's future that is also a retrospective look at his accomplishments in the 1980s. In referencing the aerial banner at the 1991 Stanford centennial, as well as the classical, rock, and folk celebrities who support AIUSA, Healey advanced the argument that "AIUSA can legitimately claim to be moving toward a multi-cultural identity only if we tolerate diverse tastes" ("Vision Paper"). By the early 1990s, the tropes of multiculturalism were widely available, both in progressive and mainstream usage, and as tropes they came to have denotations and connotations thickly connected in a web of discourse. Let's call that a discourse of cultural politics. As deployed in Healey's vision paper, the tropes of multiculturalism staked out a position quite familiar in liberal activist circles in the United States. In the early 1990s, the tropes especially evoked difference across race, ethnicity, class, gender, and sexual orientation; globally, they evoked difference across the global north and global south dependent upon racism and imperialism. Calls within AIUSA for expanded membership had focused on these and related categories throughout the 1980s, and Healey's remarks in this document tapped into that ongoing conversation.

Notably, the particular variety of cultural politics that Healey's vision statement traded in connected identity, relative positions of power, and the breadth of possible strategies, tactics, and specific actions that Amnesty International activists might deploy:

> No member has to like the way particular Amnesty groups organize a demonstration or raise funds, the ads staff place in newspapers, or articles written by Co-group members. But every member should recognize that we're a movement with diverse tastes that must be tolerated if expression of those tastes furthers Amnesty's work. More activism and more human rights protection is the litmus test. ("Vision Paper—Draft as of December 27, 1991")

This litmus test—"more activism, more human rights protection"—begs the question of who gets to decide the standard against which "more" is measured, let alone the definitions of activism, of human rights themselves, and of who counts as human. To cloak these questions under the mantle of "taste" opens a Kantian moment. In the *Critique of Judgment* Kant strives to locate "universal" good taste in the discernment of the disinterested spectator. Healey would at first glance appear to be anti-Kantian, insofar as he mobilizes "taste" as a concept that understands variety to be irreducible to a single commonality: "diverse tastes must be tolerated." However, he also, implicitly, plants himself (or if not himself, some abstracted body) in the shoes of Kant's disinterested spectator, as someone who can see clearly what human rights are, and can measure the increase of human rights activism and protection. This person has good taste, against which the taste of everyone else is measured.

Healey's deployment of the tropes of multiculturalism hinged on a move quite common in mainstream, white, late twentieth-century liberalism. Difference is celebrated, but its potential cacophony and radical critique is contained within a liberal narrative that reproduces normative structures of power. The echoes of Immanuel Kant in Healey's vision paper simultaneously speak to why he might have turned to the language of "taste" and why that language was so quickly eliminated in the drafts that went forward to the general membership. The language of multiculturalism did, by the way, go forward in subsequent drafts and discussions. The language of taste, however, had the potential to open a quagmire of dissent. For Kantians, "taste" is radically singular and universal. As such, one might aspire to good taste in human rights work consistent with the universal claims of human rights frameworks. Pierre Bourdieu, in contrast, locates taste in a field of social relations (*Distinction*, 1984). For Bourdieuians, "taste" is radically contingent and contextual. As such, speaking of the tastefulness of human rights work erodes universal claims, including those on "moral clarity," to use Ginetta Sagan's phrase.

Ostensibly, Healey's argument calls for diverse approaches to Amnesty's human rights work, locally, nationally, and globally. Substantively, his argument calls for more of the kinds of work he championed so successfully in twelve years as executive director: organize splashy media-saturated events that tap into popular culture, leverage mass communication technologies, and foster a sense of belonging among people who need share little more than a *feeling* that Amnesty is a good organization doing good work. Controversially, his argument implies that AIUSA has already bid farewell to its past as a grassroots civil liberties organization, and that it has become and will continue to be a professionally led, information-age, post-populist human rights movement that does its work in and through representation. These are the key terms of the cultural politics that fuel Healey's musings on taste: image, audio, spectacle, press release, radio, television, video, film, concert tour, celebrity endorsement.

When, in offering examples of "taste" in human rights work, Healey celebrated Ginetta Sagan as a "guiding spirit" who exemplified "what effective fundraising means" in her partnership with Joan Baez, his remarks carried some sting. "Taste" in this case means not only whether someone does or does not like folk music. It also signals the entry of a category of aesthetic appreciation into human rights work. Or even more precisely, it openly acknowledges a set of relationships, structures, and forces of meaning-making that are usually ignored or disavowed in human rights politics. Healey's words—perhaps dashed off quickly in a draft document, and all the more intriguing for their roughness—suggest that aesthetic appreciation is precisely the route we need to follow to understand what usually goes unspoken about the forms, structures, and relationships that actually create the work of an organization such as AIUSA. Sharon Sliwinski shifted the foundations of human rights scholarship by unveiling the extent to which aesthetic judgment underwrites an ethics of action on behalf of distant others: the exercise of that judgment makes possible the recognition of the distant other's humanity (Sliwinski 2011). I press human rights studies even further, and argue that aesthetic choices (or, in many cases, aesthetic necessities) drive human rights projects, perhaps consciously but more likely unconsciously. Thinking about taste is a route toward understanding the style of AIUSA. The scandal of Healey's backhanded compliment to Sagan and Baez was the implication that AIUSA's work was already about style in the 1970s, even before he came on board and started promoting rock concerts. In fact, at some level that work was nothing *but* style. All the research in London, all the research on the ground, all the communications between London, New York, and local groups, all the media coverage, and all the garage sales and bake sales and folk music concerts to pay for this work collectively produced a tone, a texture, and a feeling among the membership. Ginetta Sagan's vaunted "moral clarity" was an effect of style and a practice of style.

Susan Sontag is helpful in interpreting the weight of style on human rights politics here. She writes, "Awareness of style as a problematic and isolable element in a work of art has emerged in the audience for art only at certain historical moments – as a front behind which other issues, ultimately ethical and political, are being debated" (Sontag 1966, 18). When someone criticizes the style of a work of art, one is ultimately criticizing the ethics and politics that produced that style. In her critique of Healey's arrows paper and his vision for the 1990s and beyond, Ginetta Sagan took exception to what we can best understand as Healey's taste and his style, and hence as his ethics and his politics. Healey wrote in his arrows paper, "AI's work must produce blasts at oppressors rather than documents to be studied" ("Funding Amnesty's Human Rights Work: Issues for the IEC Discussion." 19 September 1992. Page two of eleven. AIUSA National Office Records Series I.4 Box 14 Folder 11). Sagan in turn wrote to him:

> There is a problem with the notion of being 'in the face of governments.' The very idea of being in someone's face has all the wrong connotations for Amnesty. It advocates an approach that is negative, nasty, gratuitous, shrill, mocking, arrogant, and showy. This is not the sort of approach that translates into a principled appeal for moral and financial support. (Letter from Ginetta Sagan to Jack Healey, December 6, 1992. Page three of seven. AIUSA National Office Records Series I.4 Box 14 Folder 11)

We don't know whether Ginetta Sagan attended Salinas de Gortari's keynote at Stanford's Centennial celebration. But her critique of Jack Healey's activist aesthetic might well have been spoken by those AIUSA members who were "amazed and appalled" at the sight that day of the aerial banner protesting torture under the presidency of Salinas de Gortari. Many among the older generation of west coast activists preferred, as did many among the older generation of mainly British staff and volunteers in London's International Secretariat, an understated and dignified style, expressed as a writing style in letters written on behalf of prisoners of conscience.[19] In contrast, the activists at Stanford were brash. They leveraged shame, or at least went through the motions that one might assume would shame a head of state and his host, Stanford University.

Conclusion

In conclusion, a brief return to the two central characters of this essay: Jack Healey would presumably be delighted with the brazen style of the aerial protest. After all, he spent the better part of a decade promoting human rights activism as spectacle, as media, as representation. Ginetta Sagan would presumably be appalled by it. Not only was it "mocking, arrogant, and showy" in style, but it also arose from a structural analysis and tactical toolbox she disagreed with. Furthermore, it represented human rights work *as representation*. As Susan Sontag helpfully reminds us, "every style embodies an epistemological decision, an interpretation of how and what we perceive" and "Every style is a means of insisting on something" (Sontag, 35). In other words, style directs knowing. It isn't merely the case that the style of human rights changes as the work changes, but that the style changes the work. In fact, the style is the work.

Once we appreciate what is gained by approaching human rights work as representation, and the style of that work as the work itself, we are better prepared to grasp and make sense of human rights affect. The example provided by Amnesty International's pop/rock music tours helps underscore how and why human rights affect exceeds the emotional life of the individual liberal subject of rights, and indeed calls into question the boundaries, coherence, and self-sovereignty of that subject. The pulse of the crowd overtakes the individual and creates an inevitability of political feeling beyond one's control. Audiences in the sixteen countries in which Amnesty International produced music concerts in the 1980s expressed rapture, elation, and hope as well as exhaustion, grief, and sorrow, moved by the music as well as by the crowd.[20] Press conferences before the concerts would highlight local and global human rights violations, but no nation-state was identified from the stage as an abuser of human rights, and neither was any representative from a state allowed to stand on the stage. As theater, as performance, as pop/rock ritual, Amnesty International's concerts in the 1980s carved out a space of mass culture and mass feeling that exalted human rights and snubbed state authority. To be sure the assertion of distance from state authority had been a founding principle of the organization since 1961, but Jack Healey's concerts materialized that assertion in ways that light a path for the essays in this volume. A human rights movement that moves crowds through music, pop culture, and affect not only challenges the authority of a state to abuse those within its borders; it challenges the very coherence of nation-state sovereignty, and insists that all manner of human rights work is performed.

Notes

1. Subheadings within this paper: growth, change, taste, daily work, financial resources, managing growth, international cooperation, concluding thoughts. AIUSA National Office Records Series IV.1.4 Box 263 Folder 14. See also I.4 Box 14 Folder 10.
2. A Membership Development Task Force was charged to consider the discussions that emerged in late 1991 and early 1992, and to draft a discussion paper entitled "Vision 2000" for circulation and comment at volunteer leadership meetings of the June 1992 Annual General Meeting. See the first page of the "Vision 2000" discussion paper. AIUSA National Office Records Series I.4 Box 14 Folder 10.
3. This argument is developed by Lynn Hunt and expanded by Sharon Sliwinski in relation to aesthetic engagement with human rights. The literature on affect and nation is vast. Lauren Berlant's work on sentiment is especially influential. On affect and tactic see Thomas Keenan. For affect

and genre an excellent starting point is James Dawes. Lilie Chouliaraki critiques humanitarianism rather than human rights as such, but her work inspires much of my thinking in this essay.

4. The name changed to Amnesty International in 1962. On Amnesty International's founding and Peter Benenson's role, see Stephen Hopgood.
5. I'm grateful to Cael Keegan for introducing me to critical studies of melodrama and persuading me that melodrama underwrites and permeates affective domains of political engagement in the United States.
6. I concur with Keys that AIUSA's work has always been political, both in the sense of petitioning, lobbying, and networking within the state apparatus as well as the broad sense of intervening in structures and representations of power. AIUSA's work from the outset had been pursued through letter-writing campaigns, lobbying efforts in Washington DC, and educational efforts both locally and among public officials.
7. Contribution to discussion forum igc:aicg.general authored by Tom Gill, Southern African Co-Group, February 13, 1993, regarding "Topic: Comments on the 'Arrows' Paper." AIUSA National Office Records I.4 Box 14 Folder 11.

   See also a survey of membership in 1987 with a tally indicating that 55% of responding local groups had an entirely white membership. Memo from Susannah Sirkin to the Task Force on Cultural Diversification dated January 29, 1987. AIUSA National Office Records IV.1.7 Box 10 Folder 2.
8. Leno Rose-Avila also confirms that the concerts were part of Jack Healey's vision of moving the organization toward youth and diversity, and that they succeeded.
9. Tours: A Conspiracy of Hope (six concerts in the United States, June 1986); Human Rights Now! (twenty concerts in fifteen countries on five continents, September–October 1988) and An Embrace of Hope (Santiago, October 1990).
10. A Conspiracy of Hope also featured Bryan Adams, Joan Baez, Jackson Browne, Ruben Blades, Miles Davis, Peter Gabriel, the Neville Brothers, Lou Reed, Carlos Santana, Peter Townshend, U2, Fela, and Third World. Headline artists for Human Rights Now! were Sting, Bruce Springsteen & The E Street Band, Peter Gabriel, Tracy Chapman, and Youssou N'Dour. Additional celebrities participated in various countries. See http://www.humanrightsconcerts.com/background.html. Web accessed October 1, 2018.
11. On the question of whether the tactic of shame works in practice see Cohen, 2001.
12. All three received front-page coverage in *The Stanford Daily*, September 30, September 31, and October 2, 1991. President Bush was represented

by Health and Human Services Secretary Louis Sullivan (*The Stanford Daily,* October 2, page 14).

13. Amnesty International's global campaigns against torture began in 1972, extending the founding work on Prisoners of Conscience and advancing a structural analysis of state violence and the tactics needed to counter it. See the 54-page report published in September 1991, Amnesty International, "Mexico: Torture with Impunity."
14. In addition to A Conspiracy of Hope (1986); Human Rights Now! (1988) and An Embrace of Hope (1990) the compilation includes The Struggle Continues... (1998).
15. Leno Rose-Avila confirms that membership soared during and after the concerts. He was Southern Regional Director of AIUSA at the time of Conspiracy of Hope in 1986, and concert attendees "lit up my phone for hours. All I could do was take numbers and call people back later." Rose-Avila further notes, "If you look at the board and staff today, you will see leaders who joined at this time and were inspired through the concerts." Some concert attendees became active in local groups. Many became dues-paying members.
16. For the Human Rights Now! tour (1988) Rose-Avila was Media Director and also became Head of Security. Responding to a question about the audiences Rose-Avila recalls the enthusiasm of the youth. He notes: "if people *feel* the message they will join the movement."
17. "Whose side does one take in the struggle between Ossentians [sic] and Ingush in Vlaikavkaz [sic]? These are people and places most people have never heard of before. How does one protest the murder of nuns in Liberia? Anarchy does not allow us easily to fix guilt. How does one choose among the warring clans in Somalia or the ethnic factions in Bosnia-Herzegovina? In a world filled with such moral ambiguity, an organization such as Amnesty must help people comprehend the underlying forces at work, not turn a moral gatling [sic] gun on a distant horizon filled with the blurry forms of real or perceived enemies." Sagan to Healey, December 6, 1992, AIUSA National Office Records Series I.4 Box 14 Folder 11.
18. Adoption groups focused on writing letters regarding Prisoners of Conscience as identified by the International Secretariat. Action groups conducted and shared research, and promoted a range of advocacy actions.
19. See Hopgood's *Keepers of the Flame* for the tone and feel of the work environment at the International Secretariat in London.
20. Establishing historical evidence of the feelings of other people is an endeavor fraught with hazards. I rely on video footage of the crowds captured at the time and subsequently edited into six DVDs in *Released: The Human Rights Concerts, 1986–1998,* 2013, corroborated by James Henke's reporting in *Human Rights Now!* and a personal interview with

Leno Rose-Avila, Media Director for the Human Rights Now! tour. The organizers, celebrity musicians, and technical crew were also left awash with powerful emotions; to stand in the crowd was, in the words of AIUSA's Leno Rose-Avila, "a great feeling."

Works Cited

AIUSA archival sources cited in this paper are held in the Amnesty International of the USA, Inc.: National Office Records collection at the Rare Book and Manuscript Library, Columbia University Library; citations are abbreviated AIUSA National Office Records.

AIUSA National Office Records Series IV. I.4 Box 14 Folder 10 and 11.

AIUSA National Office Records Series IV.1.4 Box 263 Folder 14.

AIUSA National Office Records Series IV.1.7 Box 10 Folder 2.

Amnesty International Human Rights Concerts. http://www.humanrightsconcerts.com/background.html. Web accessed October 1, 2018.

Amnesty International. 1991. "Mexico: Torture with Impunity," September (AI Index: AMR 41/04/91).

_____. 2013. *Released: The Human Rights Concerts, 1986–1998.*

Anker, Elizabeth R. 2014. *Orgies of Feeling: Melodrama and the Politics of Freedom.* Durham: Duke University Press.

Berlant, Lauren. 2008. *The Female Complaint: The Unfinished Business of Sentimentality in American Culture.* Durham: Duke University Press.

Bourdieu, Pierre. 1984. *Distinction: A Social Critique of the Judgment of Taste.* Cambridge: Harvard University Press.

Chouliaraki, Lilie. 2013. *The Ironic Spectator: Solidarity in the Age of Post-Humanitarianism.* Cambridge: Polity.

Cohen, Stanley. 2001. *States of Denial: Knowing About Atrocities and Suffering.* Cambridge: Polity.

Cmiel, Kenneth. 1999. "The Emergence of Human Rights Politics in the United States." *The Journal of American History* 86 (3, December): 1231–1250.

Dawes, James. 2016. "Human Rights, Literature, and Empathy." In *The Routledge Companion to Literature and Human Rights*, edited by Sophia A. McClennen and Alexandra Schultheis Moore, 427–432, 430–431. London and New York: Routledge.

Ellison, Katherine. 1991. "Salinas Receives Mixed Reviews: Mexican Leader Cheered, Jeered in Bay Area." *San Jose Mercury News.* Front Section, 1 October. Web accessed via newsbank.com archive, March 13, 2014.

Henke, James. 1988. *Human Rights Now! The Official Book of the Concerts for the Human Rights Foundation World Tour.* Topsfield, MA: Salem House Publishing.

Hopgood, Steven. 2006. *Keepers of the Flame: Understanding Amnesty International.* Ithaca and London: Cornell University Press.

Hunt, Lynn. 2008. *Inventing Human Rights.* New York: Norton.

Kant, Immanuel. [1790] 2007. *Critique of Judgement.* Oxford: Oxford University Press.

Keenan, Thomas. 2004. "Mobilizing Shame." *South Atlantic Quarterly* 103 (2/3, Spring/Summer): 435–449.

Keys, Barbara. 2014. *Reclaiming American Virtue: The Human Rights Revolution of the 1970s.* Cambridge and London: Harvard University Press.

Rose-Avila, Leno. 2018. Telephone interview with the author, October 24.

Sliwinski, Sharon. 2011. *Human Rights in Camera.* Chicago: University of Chicago Press.

Sontag, Susan. 1966. "On Style." In *Against Interpretation and Other Essays.* New York: Picador/FSG.

Stanford News Service. 1991. "Salinas: World Change Requires Education Changes; 40 Protest Appearance." September 9. Web Accessed March 13, 2014.

The Stanford Daily. 1991. Vol. 200 No. 6, September 30; Vol. 200 No. 7, September 31; and Vol. 200 No. 8, October 2.

CHAPTER 5

Inside the "Empathy Machine": Virtual Reality and Humanitarian Campaigning

Kerry Bystrom and Ramona Mosse

In December 2015, politicians, economists, journalists, and others attending the World Economic Forum in Davos experienced an unusual film premiere: *Clouds Over Sidra*, the first film in the United Nations Virtual Reality (UNVR) series. The film, which depicts in 360° a day in the life of a twelve-year-old Syrian girl in the Za'atri refugee camp in Jordan, was meant to mobilize concern and commitment to the Syrian refugee crisis. As UNVR touts the film on its website, "[this] is the first ever film shot in virtual reality for the UN, using the medium to generate greater empathy and new perspectives on people living in conditions of great vulnerability. Its powerful capacity allows anyone on a global scale to experience life within a refugee camp and has the ability to inspire a message of hope among not only the millions displaced but also those motivated to act."[1] Co-creator Chris Milk, from the Hollywood studio

K. Bystrom (✉)
Bard College Berlin, Berlin, Germany
e-mail: k.bystrom@berlin.bard.edu

R. Mosse
Goethe University, Frankfurt, Germany

A. S. Moore and S. Pinto (eds.), *Writing Beyond the State*,
Palgrave Studies in Literature, Culture and Human Rights,
https://doi.org/10.1007/978-3-030-34456-6_5

Vrse which partnered with the UN and Samsung on the film, shares in the hopes attached to this film and the medium of virtual reality (VR) more generally. For Milk the "true power" of VR is as follows:

> It connects humans to other humans in a profound way that I've never seen before in any other form of media. And it can change people's perception of each other. And that is how I think virtual reality has the potential to actually change the world. So, it's a machine, but through this machine, we become more compassionate, we become more empathetic, and we become more connected, and ultimately we become more human. (2015; cited also in Bailenson 2018, location 1064)

VR is, Milk claims, "the ultimate empathy machine."

Measuring the impact of a film or a medium on the development of empathy is—while avidly underway, as we will see below—a tricky business. However, the United Nations seems to be convinced of its effectiveness. On its website, UNVR notes that *Clouds Over Sidra* has been translated into 15 languages, is being mobilized to raise awareness at civil society events, and has been shown in 40 countries as part of UNICEF fundraisers, at which VR is "twice as effective" in raising donations as traditional fundraising techniques.[2] Since filming *Clouds Over Sidra*, UNVR has developed 20 additional films on issues ranging from migration to Ebola, desertification, and the plight of groups like the Roma.[3] Other organizations such as Amnesty International, CARE, Doctors Without Borders, and Oxfam, often similarly foregrounding empathy, have followed suit in including VR and other immersive media techniques into their education, advocacy, and fundraising projects.[4] Doctors Without Borders medical team leader Donna Canali, who served as a tour guide in a 2017 traveling exhibition called "Forced From Home"[5] which uses VR among other immersive techniques to publicize refugee experiences, describes her goal for the exhibition: "What I would most like people to get out of this is empathy… they're [refugees and internally displaced people are] not so different than us" (cited in Kerr 2017, n.p.).

In this chapter, we will critically explore the turn to VR in human rights and humanitarian campaigning, and specifically the contention that VR and allied immersive technologies enable the creation of helpful connections between "distant others" in the form of increased empathy.[6] What should we make of the increasing use of VR and its close alignment to the rhetoric of empathy creation? To what extent should we celebrate this new "empathy machine"? Through a close analysis of two artworks that respond to the Syrian "refugee crisis" using VR and allied immersive technologies—the VR film *Clouds Over Sidra* and Irish photographer Richard Mosse's video installation *Incoming* (2017)—as well as a short excursion into theories of virtuality, we will ultimately suggest that VR as a "post-human" technology may most progressively enter into the humanitarian field precisely by decentering the sovereign subject and upending the politics of empathy described here in our opening paragraphs. In this view, immersion, understood as a fluid existence-beside-and-through rather than the standing-in-the-shoes-of usually associated with empathy, becomes the key word for imagining a post-sovereign political agency that crosses national borders to bring relief to suffering people and support human rights claims.

Yet as we have already seen, VR productions are already operating within what Wendy S. Hesford defines as the hegemonic Euro-American "human rights spectacle" and in this setting are being used to reinscribe rather than trouble the "mobilization of empathy" long understood to be at the heart of humanitarian (if not always human rights) campaigns.[7] The concept highlights the extent to which diverse narrative, performative, and visual economies can come together with national, transnational, and post-national institutions as well as political and legal frameworks to project certain imaginaries of human rights and humanitarian work; as well as how artworks, narratives, and performances created and mobilized by the UN and NGOs may assist individuals in need or may further narrow the ends of specific nations or other interest groups (Hesford 2011, 7). Scholars in both critical human rights and performance studies have persuasively argued that empathy—at least on its own—can be something of a trap when it comes to creating true solidarity with others: first, because of its focus on the emotional or affective rather than the historical, political, or structural dimensions of relationships between spectators and distant others; second, because of its tendency to narrow from the collective to the individual; and third, because of the way the feelings of connection with an individual it creates can obscure the real differences between spectator and sufferer that are often responsible for the human rights violations in need of redress.[8] Yet as part of the human rights spectacle, VR technology, and in its use in *Clouds Over Sidra* specifically, is portrayed as a revolution in humanitarian assistance because it is the *most* effective means to create empathy, intensifying its working by creating total presence and bringing the spectator fully inside the experience of a distant other.

VR's immersive capacities are thus, we contend, fundamentally ambiguous. They combine a capacity to decenter the sovereign human subject with a tendency toward totalizing the powers of technology. The following section explores both the heightened sense of connection and the ethical vulnerabilities created through the use of VR technology in *Clouds Over Sidra*. This discussion not only gives a sense of how the technology shapes perception and empathy but also reveals the need for an immersive, post-sovereign politics that moves beyond the rhetoric of empathy to encompass a permeation or perforation of the self in changing relations of both proximity and distance. We describe this politics via performative definitions of virtuality before then, in turn, offering Mosse's installation *Incoming* as a work where immersive technologies are used "otherwise" in a way that may help conjure this politics into being.

Clouds Over Sidra

In 2011, a group of young Syrians inspired by the "Arab Spring" rose up against the dictator Bashar al-Assad to establish democracy and put an end to the regime's extensive surveillance on ordinary citizens and underground network of prisons for dissidents, among other injustices. As Alexander Betts and Paul Collier chart in their overview of the Syrian war and its impacts on human mobility, the hope of the revolution quickly dissipated as Assad, with the support of allies and the inaction of the larger international community, clamped down on protesters and began attacking the wider civilian population itself (Betts and Collier 2017, 71–72). Cities from Aleppo to Ghouta were bombed almost to their foundations. The Syrian Revolutionary Army fractured, ethnic tensions came to the fore and wide swaths of the country saw fighting between the regime, democratic revolutionaries, and Islamist groups including ISIS (Betts and Collier 2017, 72–73). Over 10 million people were forced to flee their homes. Most of the over 4 million who crossed international borders and became refugees made it only as far as the neighboring countries of Jordan, Lebanon, and Turkey where they chose between camps or an informal existence, while about a million Syrians braved crossings to Europe, which for a time between 2015–2016 seemed to offer hospitality (Betts and Collier 2017, 2–3, 73–88).

For a variety of reasons including intractability in the UN Security Council and the Eurocentrism of the Western media, this situation was identified as a "refugee crisis" and was largely—especially in the countries where the bulk of displaced Syrians were living—handed over to UNHCR. Betts and Collier argue that the UN agency had neither conceptually adequate plans nor sufficient funds to manage the situation. Speaking to the latter, they note how the agency's normal model of petitioning the international community for "emergency funds" failed as the Syrian war stretched on and donating to support Syrian refugees fell out of fashion; in spring 2015 "just 35% of the UN's 3.5 bn Syrian regional response plan was funded" (Betts and Collier 2017, 76). Much of the slack had to be picked up by hosting governments who themselves were growing desperate with regards to modes of supporting the new refugee populations (Betts and Collier 2017). This is the context in which *Clouds Over Sidra* was made.

Standing in the middle of a desert: that is how you enter Christopher Milk and Gabo Arora's short (8:46) VR film Clouds Over Sidra. *Once you put on the VR goggles and headphones, you find yourself surrounded by red sand that the twelve-year-old narrator of the film, Sidra, has crossed on her way from Deraa in Syria to the camp in Jordan. Directly transplanted into the Za'atri refugee camp, you are able to follow Sidra around the camp, apparently acknowledged and greeted by her and the other children roaming between the tents and containers. You find yourself inside of the UNHCR container where Sidra lives with her family, watching the girl on her makeshift couch as her brothers and sisters play on the floor. You later step into a classroom, peek inside a tent where young men are playing video games, pause beside a football pitch full of enthusiastic girl players, and then return to the family for dinner. Sidra's engaging narration ties these different spaces together. She can be humorous, as when she comments on the young men in the computer cluster with: "I don't understand computer games ... or boys." She points to the benefits of being in the camp for girls when she notes: "here in Za'atri girls can play football too, that makes us happy." Yet she also poignantly phrases the challenges and dilemmas of being in the temporary zone of a refugee camp when she explains in the final lines of the film: "A year and a half is long enough. I'm not going to be here forever and I'm not going to be twelve forever. My teacher says the clouds over the camp also came from Syria. Someday the clouds and me are going to turn around and go home."*

The story Sidra tells is more description of daily routines than an act of storytelling. It highlights the fact that experiencing what it is like to be Sidra lies at the heart of this endeavor. The viewer is always at the center of the action and cannot passively sit back to watch; there is a constant need to look up, down, or behind, each movement further immersing you into Sidra's reality. The peculiarity of one's position, as one that suggests such proximity, becomes most strikingly apparent in the closing montage.

Here, the scene places you in the midst of a group of children running towards you (Fig. 5.1). And as the VR user lowers their gaze to look at the children, they realize the paradoxical nature of their position: placed in the center of the video as the holder of the gaze but at the same time utterly invisible, and literally without a body in VR. In an odd transformation, the children crowding in ever more closely *merge* with the viewer, at least in terms of physical positioning.

The sense of physical immersion enhances Sidra's testimony and generates much of the film's affective power. Jeremy Bailenson, founding director of the Virtual Human Interaction Lab at Stanford University, has identified this persuasive quality of immersion as "presence" (2018,

Fig. 5.1 *Clouds Over Sidra*, kids at play (film still) (By permission of Chris Milk)

loc 261)—or what we might call "co-presence" with Sidra. *Clouds Over Sidra* is shown through a VR headset device and its interactive capacities with the VR environment remain limited to exploring the space visually (in contrast to actual interaction with the world through controllers that allow one to manipulate and change the environment). The focus lies on generating a spatial and emotional communality with the people in the film. It also underscores the potency of Sidra's final plea to be allowed to return home. Anecdotally, this co-presence has powerful effects. Bailenson describes seeing fellow spectators weeping at the film festival where he first encountered *Clouds Over Sidra* (2018, loc 1050).

Researchers have coded such feelings as empathy and located them within the possibilities of the VR medium itself. In a study of Australian undergraduates, half of whom where shown *Clouds Over Sidra* in VR format and half whom were shown it in a modified two-dimensional documentary format, Nicola Schutte and Emma Stilinovic found that participants in virtual reality had "significantly greater" amounts of "engagement" and "empathy" for Sidra in a series of follow-up questions after the film, and conclude that "the higher level of engagement experienced in the virtual reality condition was a path to the greater empathy experienced in reaction to this condition" (2017, 710). We may wish to question what exactly "empathy" means in this context and how long-lasting it is, but this study does suggest that the VR dimension in particular made an impression on the study subjects. The donation statistics cited by the UN and relayed above also suggest that the medium helps to convert feeling (empathy) into action (donation).

Importantly, such results are achieved without turning to some of the more insidious techniques developed in the literary, performance, and photographic media to "mobilize empathy," culminating perhaps in the dehumanizing photography used in mid-twentieth-century Oxfam or Save the Children appeals (see Benthall 1993, 179). In the UNVR film, the VR medium overrides the necessity for stylistic or formal innovations designed to create shock or pity. As Bailenson argues, "these reactions weren't produced by a dramatic score, or clever editing ... Viewers of *Clouds Over Sidra* are confronted simply with a series of ordinary moments—people baking bread, families laughing together, children at play or in school. The major difference is that the immersive video made us briefly feel as if we were there with them" (2018, loc 1050, 1064). *Clouds Over Sidra* is a far cry from depictions of often sensationalized suffering.

At the same time, *Clouds Over Sidra* engages in a number of problematic rhetorics long associated with humanitarian campaigning. One of these is the emphasis on the child, and particularly the female child, refugee. Sharon Stephens (1995) has noted how children are used in political campaigns to symbolize the future. Childhood innocence in particular makes these figures easy to identify with and adopt a paternalistic attitude toward (Suski 2009). Women are also traditionally seen as figures in need of care in the humanitarian imaginary, so the female child doubles the call for care (Hesford 2011). The film may thus inadvertently infantilize the broader population of Syrian refugees for whom Sidra is meant to stand—an act which can also be a way of shoring up the "better" or "savior" identity of the humanitarian, as Teju Cole is the latest in a line of critical theorists to point out in his comments on the "white savior industrial complex."[9]

Further, as the film doubles down on the needs of refugee children, it also performs the potentially dubious operation of decontextualization that Richard A. Wilson and Richard D. Brown note often occurs when narratives (and visual iconographies) of innocent suffering are constructed for humanitarian campaigns (2009, 19–20, 25). Specific information regarding the numbers and situation of Syrian refugees in Jordan or more generally is left out. As with most of the coverage of the "refugee crisis," the dynamics of war that produce refugees are ignored and refugees themselves rather than the political context of the war are presented as the problem.[10] However, without such information, it becomes difficult to make any connection to the people in the film beyond "mere humanity." In a classic essay on the ways refugees tend to be dehistoricized and depoliticized in both professional and public discourse, Liisa Malkki argues that a sense of connection based on this "mere humanity"—the chance to "wal[k] in the shoes of another" as Bailenson puts it (2018, loc 1038)—can only be thin in contrast to an understanding of the actual historical, political, and economic links as well as disjunctures between people (Malkki 1996; see also Bystrom 2014, 16).

In terms of its medium, however, *Clouds Over Sidra* poses the crucial question of whether VR technology is just a new tool to create an already classic empathic response or whether it more fundamentally reframes the relation of knowledge, ethics, and agency. Does the appeal of such presence-based spectacles speak to empathy alone, is it part of a solipsistic desire for an experience machine that ultimately foregrounds the consumption of ever new immersive environments, or does it afford another experience altogether? The discourses on VR remain ambiguous because empathy and immersion are often used interchangeably as enablers of knowledge.

As we have already suggested in our introductory section, it may be that the most radical potential of VR lies not in its intensification of empathy but rather in distinguishing immersion more clearly from empathy in its ability to model a different concept of subjectivity altogether. This becomes apparent in the most interesting and underdeveloped scene in *Clouds Over Sidra*: the final one of children crowding around the user who remains both at the center of the film, experiencing the VR as having entered the environment of the refugee camp, while also remaining utterly invisible with the children crowding into the space where the user's body should be. Here, we gain a glimpse of a potential posthuman fusion of self and machine, propagating an entirely relational sense of self. The user has entered the frame perceptually, while they physically remain in a different space. VR thus creates an out-of-body experience that offers the potential of remaking how subjectivity is experienced, as part of a perpetual flow and transition between states and bodies rather than a stable self based in identity. In other words, VR supplements the Western subject with a proliferation of virtual selves that are capable of taking a variety of shapes and forms. As it is, this reframing of subjectivity remains momentary and insubstantial and somehow at odds with the film's main emphasis of amplifying a single story to personalize the refugee crisis and to generate empathy. VR's potential as a technology that could change our social and political perception becomes subsumed by a reliance on empathy as the established narrative trope within human rights campaigns. To reiterate Bailenson's description of immersion in *Clouds Over Sidra*, what is striking is VR's capacity to make us feel "as if we were there with them" (2018, loc 1050, 1064). Herein lies also the crucial distinction between immersion and empathy: "being there with them" is deceptively close but not necessarily the same as "feeling with someone." By offering a theoretical excursion on virtuality and immersion, we will explore further how *Clouds Over Sidra* can reframe notions of empathy and sovereign subjectivity, thus raising the question of what is at stake in the medium of VR technology.

Framing Immersion and Empathy in Virtual Reality

In October 2017, the *Guardian* ran an article under the headline "Empathy—the latest gadget Silicon Valley wants to sell you." It framed empathy as a crucial term within the tech industry: "Empathy is a word that suffuses the tech industry. The ability of an engineer or a designer to put themselves in someone else's shoes is widely considered critical ... But with VR, empathy is not just a design value - it's a sales strategy" (Tarnoff 2017, n.p.). This sales strategy is deeply embedded in a fundamental problem that digital technology in its social media dimension has been facing. That is to say, social media has been widely associated with affecting a drop in empathy. A long-term study of the University of Michigan from 2010 concludes that "one likely contributor to declining empathy is the rising prominence of personal technology and media used in daily life" (Konrath et al. 2010, 188). The study's findings support the contention that social media technology promotes the proliferation of so-called echo chambers, keeping the user in a state of perpetual confirmation bias and lowering their ability to accept, acknowledge, or engage with different perspectives or "distant others."

The discourses on VR within the tech industry respond to these criticisms by foregrounding the heightened empathic effect that the presence and proximity of VR affords. Chris Milk's earlier conclusion that VR makes us "more human" emphasizes just these aspects of VR. Likewise Aaron Koblin, co-founder of Vrse, argues that the sense of vulnerability that the VR user experiences in facing a new and essentially overwhelming environment, effectively leads them to become more open to the vulnerability of others, enabling an empathic connection and the potential of permanent transformation.[11] Koblin and Milk's arguments can be read as a direct response to the deficiencies of social media and their instrumentalization of self and others by offering a new dimension of social sensibility and human interconnectivity. It is, in other words, the newest technological answer to technology's problems.

Such optimism about VR is grounded in the particular experience it can generate: that of (almost) total presence and immersiveness. Immersion is a slippery term. One of the challenges in defining immersion lies in its varied usage across a range of disciplines from video gaming (Nilsson et al. 2016) to education (Johnson and Levine 2008) or theater and performance (Machon 2013). Similarly, the precise distinction between immersion and empathy remains tenuous and is worth investigating more deeply in order to understand how subjectivity becomes framed in this context.

VR technology's origins intertwine computing and film technologies. In 1962 Morton Heilig patented his "Sensorama Simulator," which provided a multisensory surround film experience in an "arcade-style theatre cabinet,"[12] which now counts as one of the earliest VR machines. Three years later, Ivan Sutherland published the foundational essay "The Ultimate Display," in which he described the potential of computing technology to render a complete alternate reality. Later, Sutherland would develop one of the first head-mounted VR sets. He describes the VR as follows:

> The ultimate display would, of course, be a room within which the computer can control the existence of matter. A chair displayed in such a room would be good enough to sit in ... and a bullet displayed in such a room would be fatal. With appropriate programming, such a display could literally be the Wonderland into which Alice walked. (Sutherland 1965, 506)

Reality and display merge here to the extent that they become indistinguishable. Sutherland's reference to *Alice in Wonderland* makes explicit the curious intertwining of technological innovation and the fantasies upon which fiction and artistic production have built. Total immersion into an alternate world is what the sensorama and the ultimate display promise. Immersion, as Janet Murray defined it in an early study on digital environments, offers the promise of entering an alternate world: "We seek the same feeling from a psychologically immersive experience that we do from a plunge in the ocean or swimming pool: the sensation of being surrounded by a completely other reality" (1998, 98).

In VR, this sense of plunging into a new reality becomes manifest in the most direct terms, for VR may elicit strong physiological responses in addition to providing mental stimuli. As a recent study on VR's ability to change user behavior when users are confronted with a virtual copy of themselves suggests: "virtual selves have the power to stoke a physiological response that may also serve as an impetus for physical behaviors" (Fox et al. 2012, 71). In other words, the actions of the virtual selves created physiological responses and a body memory capable of influencing future behavior in the user. In this sense, VR realizes a commonly shared desire of the arts to overcome the gap between reality and representation in favor of total presence.

This idea of a total presence lies also at the core of avant-garde theater maker and theorist Antonin Artaud's *The Theatre and Its Double* (1938), credited with coining the term "virtual reality": his avant-garde reconceptualization of theater itself envisages a highly immersive and participatory "realité virtuèlle" that eradicates any distinction between stage and auditorium and fuses their reality levels (Bay-Cheng 2015, 687–688). Virtuality also has a varied history that precedes the development of VR technology itself. In *The Virtual Window*, Anne Friedberg (2006) draws an evocative history of art in relationship to digital technology by theorizing the status of the frame itself from perspectival paintings to the screen windows that a PC computer provides. Similarly, Oliver Grau creates a history of virtual art that goes back to the Roman period, in which he traces the development of immersive painting strategies such a *trompe l'oeil* and the panorama, which "developed into a presentation apparatus that shut out the outside world completely and made the image absolute" (Grau 2003, 59).

Both Grau and Friedberg foreground the question of distance and proximity implicit in the notion of perspective. In the case of the panorama, the "absolute image" manages to abolish the distance between viewer and artwork much like the VR headset will do in a more complete manner given its expanded technological means. That is to say, the aesthetic strategies employed lead to a cognitive shift for the viewer, in which reflection from a distance is replaced by immersion close-up. Grau goes on to define immersion as "a passage from one mental state to another … characterized by diminishing critical distance to what is shown and increasing emotional involvement in what is happening" (2003, 13). In this definition we find both the *potential of* and *problem with* immersion that make for its ambiguity: the intensity of its affective involvement also suggests a loss of control in terms of rational judgment, be it moral or critical. In other words, knowledge (produced by reflection) is replaced by an immersive experience. The question that the discourses on learning through immersion raise is whether such a privileged connection between reflection and knowledge is not itself outmoded.

The shift from critical reflection to emotional involvement that Grau traces here in his definition of immersion connects to long-standing debates about the workings of aesthetic reception and the cultural dimensions of human rights and humanitarian campaigns that traditionally have circulated around empathy. Speaking for the importance of this concept in the latter field, Lynn Hunt identifies artistically induced empathy as a precondition for the emergence of human rights (2007, 26–29). She notes that in eighteenth-century Europe wildly popular novels like Samuel Richardson's *Pamela* (1740) and Jean-Jacques Rousseau's *Julie* (1761) encouraged readers to enter into the inner lives and feelings of female characters who were not previously seen as having complex interiority or a recognizable desire for autonomy. Through this imaginative leap, readers were able to recognize themselves in these characters, developing a habit of empathy that could then be activated to blur social boundaries in the real world (Hunt 2007, 41–48). The habit of empathy was further developed in response to tales and images of torture circulating in this same period (Hunt 2007, 32). Once others could be easily imaginable as people "like us" desiring and deserving of individual autonomy and bodily security, something like the "rights of man" proclaimed in the French Declaration of the Rights of Man and Citizen (1789) became possible (Hunt 2007, 30–32). In short, Hunt argues that "reading accounts of torture or epistolary novels had physical effects that translated into brain changes and came back out as new concepts about the organization of social and political life. New kinds of reading (and listening and viewing) created new individual experiences (empathy) which in turn made possible new social and political concepts (human rights)" (2007, 33–34).

In contemporary media discourses, immersion has become fused with or replaced empathy as the primary concept for describing the affective dimension of digital media. Hunt's thesis not only reminds us that empathy is seen as crucial to the birth of human rights in many influential accounts—and that media other than VR played a crucial role in creating both empathy and at least the hegemonic modern conception of human rights rooted in the French, British, and US-American traditions—but also leads us toward a potentially useful distinction between empathy and immersion. While empathy is subject-focused and describes the ability to emotionally or cognitively put oneself into the place of another (see Lanzoni 2012, 287; Krasner 2006, 174), immersion is environmental, i.e. becoming surrounded by or suffused into a different space or atmosphere. In that sense, the mental movement implied in each is different. While empathy seems to propel the self outward into another person, immersion comes to permeate the self from the outside in. This differentiates the concept of subjectivity implied in each of these terms and may lay out the post-sovereign potential in VR immersion. Unlike empathy, which asserts human similarity but retains the idea of a stable and sovereign self, immersion's impetus to suffuse and permeate subjectivity makes porous the borders between self and environment as a set of fluid relations and changing positions.

The fluidity implicit in immersion is apparent in Janet Murray's framing of immersion through the metaphor of water and in immersion's history in music and sound studies. Ross Brown connects the "liquefying of the sonic environment" with an increasingly noisy soundscape rather than music (2010, 1). In such an immersive space, the fluidity of the environment extends to the audience and challenges the distinction between inside and outside, matter and self, potentially contributing to a posthuman version of selfhood built around interconnection. As Judith Halberstam and Ira Livingston argue in their sonic definition of the posthuman: "The posthuman does not reduce difference-from-others to difference-from-self, but rather emerges in the pattern of resonance and interference between the two" (1995, 10). In this regard, VR technologies may open up an example of how a posthuman condition might be experienced and sensed in practice, rather than just thought conceptually.

On another level, the notion of liquidity also implies a sense of proximity that links immersion and empathy in the current VR discourses employed by Chris Milk and others. This usage takes us back to critiques of empathy in diverse modernist aesthetics and critical human rights discourses, which position empathy as an outmoded affective response as likely to cause harm as to remedy it. To return to the theater, which with Artaud had conjured up the possibility of virtuality as a reality: Bertolt Brecht disbanded the Aristotelian categories of fear and pity, or of an empathic response to staged action, because of its lacking critical and ultimately political dimension. Brecht instead privileged the distanced observer, always able to disentangle themselves from suffering, and foregrounded the potential of manipulation in the empathic act:

> Whoever empathises with someone, and does so completely, relinquishes criticism both of the object of their empathy and of themselves. Instead of awakening, they sleepwalk. Instead of doing something, they let something be done with them. [...] They have only the illusion that they are living, in reality they are vegetating. They are, so to speak, passively lived. (2003, 201)

Brecht's evaluation of empathy casts it as a passive state where one "vegetates" because one is dominated by forces outside of one's own frame of judgment. The sense of giving up one's critical capacities recurs in Oliver Grau's earlier framing of immersion, where immersive interaction leads to a reduction of one's critical faculties. Effectively, Brecht points out a narrowing that occurs through the moment of empathic identification and that undoes the opportunity for investigating how the illusions the spectators live under are created. In Brecht's view the empathic spectator lacks the ability to understand the intermedial forms that condition the empathic response sparked by immersion (or in Brecht's case, its precursor, illusion). Critical human rights scholars have pointed in similar directions, suggesting pitfalls including over-identification and the blocking out of context (be it historical, political, economic, or other) that together comprise the traps of empathy already outlined in our introductory section (see inter alia Chouliaraki and Orgad 2011; Hesford 2011; Malkki 1996; Wilson and Brown 2009). These all suggest a need to think beyond the "empathy machine" model.

Dismantling the Empathy Machine: Richard Mosse's *Incoming*

The previous section suggests that focusing so strongly on empathy can cause us to overlook key elements necessary to address the root causes of the problems that humanitarian and human rights campaigns seek to redress, and which cannot ethically be left out of consideration. It simultaneously speaks to an ambiguity at the heart of the VR medium: its apparent increase in empathic involvement based on the immersive experience of being plunged perceptually, not just imaginatively, into another environment also implies a totality of the technology, since the freedom of gazing around the virtual world comes with being unable to disentangle oneself from the medium. In other words, any sense of framing the aesthetic alterity of the experience becomes impossible. Herein lies the particular vulnerability that the user of the VR experience is prone to and that entails potential ethical conflicts.

Mosse's installation *Incoming* (2017) responds to this vulnerability as it blurs the line between humanitarian campaign and cultural performance. While not an example of VR technology, the exhibition employs advanced camera technology in order to explore digital technology's general ability to render immersive experiences. More specifically, Mosse employs a thermal camera to record scenes of mass movement, screened in wrap-around format, combined with an immersive soundscape to create an immersive installation piece. The camera Mosse employs visualizes its images through the heat patterns they create and is able to shoot from a 30 km distance, so that the subjects of film and photo stills never realize that they have been in the eye of a camera lens. *Incoming*, then, similarly to the VR goggles, can provide the effect of absolute proximity but alternately offers large-scale surveys of landscapes, patterns, and networks of refugee existence that open up only at a distance. The immersive practices employed switch between distance and proximity, creating a layered experience for the viewer that ultimately offers something other than a narrowed focus on saving individuals in moments of crisis. Instead of working as an empathy machine, the installation creates an experience both estranging and affective of structures and patterns of destruction and migration. It thus creates a powerful alternative to the use of immersive technologies within the "human rights spectacle," helping us see how they might be bent toward different ends.

Sitting in the dark, cavernous room, you are surrounded by three massive white screens that arc slightly around the viewing benches. Simultaneously, a soundscape extends all around you, thus enhancing the immersion of the piece. As the performance begins and the screens light up with a dispersed film collage, it is hard to get a handle on where to focus. The three screens each show separate unworldly black-and-white scenes. The pace is slowed down, adding a ghostly quality which simultaneously is reminiscent of dance, as these bodies move through deserts, cross the seas, and line up along the stark geometric lines of the refugee camps.

The most striking and hypnotic quality of these images lies in the strange luminosity of bodies and faces paired with a curious blurring of their individual features. As light and dark shift, their bodies glow from the emanating heat, while their faces turn into either bleached or darkened masks with eerie holes where eyes would have been. From the blast of the missile launches to the chilly glow of the corpses, it is a world of heat and cold, their otherwise invisible traces forged into haunting images.

Filmed in Europe, the Middle East and Africa between 2014–2016, and with cinematographer Trevor Tweeten and composer Ben Frost, Mosse's immersive 50′ 32″ HD film installation documents two large movements of people (Fig. 5.2). The first is that from Syria, Iraq, Afghanistan and elsewhere in the Middle East to Germany though Turkey,

Fig. 5.2 Detail from *Moria in Snow*, Lesbos, Greece, 2017. Digital C on metallic paper, 35.5″ × 120″. From *The Castle* by Richard Mosse, published by Mack Books, 2018 (Image courtesy of the artist and Jack Shainman Gallery)

the Aegean Sea in Greece, and the Balkans. The second moves from sub-Saharan Africa through the desert to Libya, then across the Mediterranean and ultimately to Calais with the hope of making it onwards to the United Kingdom. As Mosse notes:

> I used a military grade camera designed for battlefield situational awareness and long-range border surveillance in an attempt to confront the viewer with the ways in which our governments represent–and therefore regard–the refugee. We wanted to use the technology against its intended purpose to create an immersive, humanist art form, allowing the viewer to meditate on the profoundly difficult and frequently tragic journeys of refugees.[13]

If Mosse's desire to raise awareness about the plight of Syrian (and other) refugees syncs with that of Chris Milk and Gabo Arora's, then his choice of technology and the meta-critique of both technology and war within his installation creates a distinctly different film experience. As noted above, *Clouds Over Sidra* works largely by harnessing the total presence of VR to enhance the notion of "walking in her shoes"—or at least next to Sidra. It aims to draw us into the frame, to immerse the viewer in another world and to forget the means by which this immersion is achieved. The VR immersion is such that it has physiological, not only mental, effects. *Incoming*, in turn, absorbs through the alternating scales and the strangeness of its luminous textures, which remain radically alien. The images create a constant dance between proximity and distance, both in how to relate to the images in general, and, more specifically, through the range the camera can navigate between the detailed close-up from afar and the panning out beyond what is normally possible to create a large-scale picture where individuals become unrecognizable and massive economies of violence and depersonalized scrambles for refuge take center stage. The desired result, as we will see, is not empathy, or at least not the kind of empathy that Milk and Arora attempt to call up.

Mosse's thermal camera is able to record at incredibly long range, and does so by capturing only relative heat in monochromatic grayscale. Live human beings touching a dead body leave white (or black) handprints registering the way their body heat lingers on a corpse. In exchange for such range of details, ordinary human features get washed out and individual people become unrecognizable. The camera is "portraying people in zombie form, as monstrous, stripping the individual away from the body and portraying the human as a mere biological trace" (Mosse 2017, n.p.).

Importantly for our argument, Mosse notes: "The usual signals of human empathy are turned on their head. We are left confused, alienated, the world feels suddenly unfamiliar, new" (2017, n.p.). This turn from empathy to alienation recalls Brechtian theory and its insistence that unsettling empathy can open the door to historicized and structural insight that may reveal the conditions of our very imaginings. The installation thus stages the contradictions implicit in the economies of violence that continue to shape the refugee crisis. Such contradiction also undermines the possibility of a unified perspective or stable value system onto the events. In contrast with *Clouds Over Sidra*, the dispersed choreography Mosse charts moves beyond refugees to include the war machine—the fact that each missile carries multiple cameras similar to the one he uses to guide the weapon to its destination (Mosse 2017, n.p.) highlights the question of the role of technology itself in promoting and perpetuating war. It renders visible the camera as a weapon (see also O'Hagan 2017).

Incoming employs immersion effectively to cast new spaces and worlds, highlighting its environmental nature. However, instead of foregrounding the experience of being plunged into the frame exclusively, *Incoming* stresses the transition between frames that is part of the immersive experience (most immediately in the simultaneity of different images on three large scale screens in the installation) to create a play between proximity and distance. Spectators are not inside the machine, they are inside and outside at once: immersed within and overwhelmed at times by the fantastical and piercing three-channel display and surround soundscape, but also reminded of the context of migration and the often disturbing way in which it is represented (indeed, how it unfolds right before their eyes). Through this interplay, the installation avoids the overemphasis on the individual story of the Syrian refugee that threatens to personalize, decontextualize, and ultimately depoliticize the "refugee crisis" as it pushes away the individual object of empathy and opens into a panorama that includes the waging of war itself. At the same time, the focus on the transitionality between multiple worlds and the perceptual frames that are part of the immersiveness of digital technologies in general returns us to the fluidity of selves and the possibility of post-sovereign subjectivity in a human rights context. The oscillation between proximity and distance also amends the notion of how audiences create knowledge, i.e. in the interplay of immersion and reflection rather than by a privileging of the distanced observer alone. In this sense *Incoming* may help create a model for employing immersivity that could contribute to creating an "agonist solidarity" that Lilie Chouliaraki and S. Orgad have explored in their essay on "spatialities of solidarity," thus defining the ethics implicit in a play with proximity and distance (2011, 3). Chouliaraki and Orgad critique the absolute proximity between self and other that empathy implies, and also undermine the currently more prevalent form of an essentially postmodern ironic distance which "treats our actions on suffering as public but keeps judgment on why we should act on such suffering private" (2011, 12). In contrast, they promote an agonistic approach to human rights that relies on both distance and proximity and "enables the co-articulation between judgment and imagination" (2011, 19). It is in this interplay between reflection and immersion, empathy and judgment, that VR and other immersive technologies could make a strong impact if they can harness a way of oscillating between the two.

Conclusion

By engaging with two prominent examples of immersive experiences designed to confront the so-called refugee crisis, we have aimed to evaluate whether Virtual Reality in particular, and immersive technologies in general, radically change how the question of human rights and humanitarian aid is cast in humanitarian campaigns and how it might contribute to exploring the idea of the post-sovereign subject. For our argumentation we combined human rights discourses with analyses of intermediality. *Clouds Over Sidra*, honing in on a 12-year-old girl, provides a rich example of how immersion can become a catalyst for creating empathy with Sidra and the plight of refugees more generally. While the effectiveness of combining immersion with empathy seems to be evident in the rise in donations, there remains a question about whether this example exploits the full potential of VR also to destabilize established notions of Western subjectivity and agency and shed light on the political conditions and technological apparatuses that have led to the "refugee crisis." In contrast, the different aesthetic context of Richard Mosse's *Incoming* allows for a self-conscious exploration of the political role of technology, which has the apparatus that created the immersion always remain part of the reception process of the audiences. Moreover, empathy itself ceases to be the primary driver of his work. Instead, Mosse maintains an interplay between proximity and distance that allows the viewer to alternate between immersive experience and critical reflection rather than opting for one or the other exclusively.

VR technology ultimately is a young technology and its social and political uses are still in flux. The totality of its immersive experience raises not only the potential for increasing audiences' affective responsiveness within the human rights context but also the issue of political misuse and manipulation. At the same time, the current exploration of the complexities of immersivity as such also offers up the posthuman potential of VR technology to redefine human subjectivity and thus offers a novel approach to ethics based on an agonistic relationship between beings rather than a single universal understanding of humanity and human rights. Yet, VR as a medium which is increasingly part of the "human rights spectacle" is in need of moments when the viewer comes out from under the spell of the machine to contribute to the reflection on how its uses might be diversified. Such diversification can occur in the transitional moments between immersive worlds as well as in the moments of permeation between inside and outside. Both ultimately render the recognition that the perceptual shift itself is part of the immersion, offering an alternative post-sovereign ethics and understanding of the relationality between self and others.

Notes

1. More information about the film can be found at the UNVR website: http://unvr.sdgactioncampaign.org/cloudsoversidr.
2. See http://unvr.sdgactioncampaign.org/cloudsoversidra/ and http://unvr.sdgactioncampaign.org/get-involved/donate/.
3. This number is as of August 2018. See http://unvr.sdgactioncampaign.org/vr-films/ for a full list of VR films in the UNVR catalog.
4. See for instance: https://www.amnesty.org.uk/press-releases/amnestys-virtual-reality-themed-360syria-project-wins-prestigious-third-sector-award; https://www.care.org/vr; https://www.oxfam.org.au/media/2017/06/oxfam-innovates-with-virtual-reality-film-on-water-shortages-facing-families-in-kenya/.
5. You can take a virtual tour of the exhibition at the MSF website: http://www.forcedfromhome.com/.
6. Following Wilson and Brown (2009), we would point out that human rights and humanitarianism are different projects, with the former being focused more on rights claims and the latter on creating emotional and moral arguments meant to generate action to stop the suffering of "distant strangers." Nevertheless, as Wilson and Brown also note, there are many sites of overlap between these projects, and drawing on this overlap critical human rights scholarship often treats these categories fluidly with human rights indicating a wider set of discourses into which humanitarianism can fit (see for instance the title of Slaughter [2014]: "The enchantment of human rights; or, What difference does humanitarian indifference make?"). Here we will focus largely on humanitarian campaigns—as indicated in our title and as is appropriate given the focus on Syrian refugees—but bring human rights into the discussion as appropriate to enrich connection with other essays in this volume.
7. Wilson and Brown (2009) define the core of humanitarianism—at least the non-religious strands of humanitarianism beginning in Europe in the eighteenth century—as the "mobilization of empathy" for others and especially for distant strangers perceived as innocent and suffering individuals.
8. We explore many aspects of the "empathy trap" in further detail below, building on the work of scholars including Malkki (1996), Brecht (2003), Wilson and Brown (2009), and Chouliaraki and Orgad (2011). While we

don't return to it below, Slaughter (2014) provides a compelling critique of posing "the problem of humanitarianism" as a "problem of empathy," engaging with Hunt (among others) and listing a series of problems with the empathy model which prefigure our list here (2014, 49–51). Slaughter however argues for replacing empathy not with the kind of fluid and immersive exchange we set out between proximity and distance but with what he terms the "indifference" or distance seen in professional humanitarian workers.

9. For the complete set of Cole's Tweets, see their reproduction in *The Atlantic*: https://www.theatlantic.com/international/archive/2012/03/the-white-savior-industrial-complex/254843/.
10. We thank Muhannad Kaikanni for formulating these points so precisely in his BA thesis at Bard College Berlin (May 2019).
11. See https://www.youtube.com/watch?reload=9&v=vAEjX9S8o2k.
12. "History of Virtual Reality." In *Virtual Reality Society*. https://www.vrs.org.uk/virtual-reality/history.html (accessed August 10, 2018).
13. See http://www.richardmosse.com/projects/incoming.

Works Cited

Bailenson, Jeremy. 2018. *Experience on Demand: What Virtual Reality Is, How It Works, and What It Can Do*. New York: W. W. Norton. Kindle.

Bay-Cheng, Sarah. 2015. "Virtual Realisms: Dramatic Forays into the Future." *Theatre Journal* 67 (4, December): 687–698.

Benthall, Jonathan. 1993. *Disasters, Relief and the Media*. London: I.B. Tauris.

Betts, Alexander, and Paul Collier. 2017. *Refuge: Rethinking Refugee Policy in a Changing World*. New York: Oxford University Press.

Brecht, Bertolt. 2003. *Brecht on Art and Politics*. Edited by Tom Kuhn and Steve Giles. London: Methuen.

Brown, Ross. 2010. *Sound: A Reader in Theatre Practice*. Houndsmills: Palgrave.

Bystrom, Kerry. 2014. "Humanitarianism, Responsibility, Links, Knots." *Interventions* 16 (3): 405–423.

Chouliaraki, Lilie L., and Shani Orgad. 2011. "Mediation, Ethics and Otherness." *International Journal of Cultural Studies* 14 (4): 363–382.

Friedberg, Anne. 2006. *The Virtual Window*. Cambridge: MIT Press.

Fox, Jesse, Jeremy Bailenson, and Tony Ricciardi. 2012. "Physiological Responses to Virtual Selves and Virtual Others." *Journal of Cyber Therapy & Rehabilitation* 5 (1, Spring): 69–72.

Grau, Oliver. 2003. *Virtual Art: From Illusion to Immersion*. Cambridge, MA: MIT Press.

Halberstam, Judith M., and Ira Livingston, ed. 1995. *Posthuman Bodies*. Bloomington: Indiana University Press.

Hesford, Wendy S. 2011. *Spectacular Rhetorics: Human Rights Visions, Recognitions, Feminisms*. Durham: Duke University Press.

Hunt, Lynn. 2007. *Inventing Human Rights*. New York: W. W. Norton.

Johnson, Lawrence F., and Alan Levine. 2008. "Virtual Worlds: Inherently Immersive, Highly Social Learning Spaces." *Theory into Practice* 47 (2, Spring): 161–170.

Kerr, Dara. 2017. "How Tech Helps Tell the Story of Refugees." C-net, October 31. https://www.cnet.com/news/how-tech-helps-tell-the-story-of-refugees-vr-virtual-reality-doctors-without-borders/.

Krasner, David. 2006. "Empathy and Theatre." In *Staging Philosophy: Intersections of Theatre, Performance, and Philosophy*, edited by David Krasner and David Z. Saltz, 173–186. Ann Arbor: University of Michigan Press.

Konrath, Sarah H., Edward H. O'Brien, and Courtney Hsing. 2010. "Dispositional Empathy in American College Students Over Time: A Meta-Analysis." *Personality and Social Psychology Review* 15 (2): 180–198.

Lanzoni, Susan. 2012. "Introduction: Emotion and the Sciences: Varieties of Empathy in Science, Art, and History." *Science in Context* 25 (3): 287–300.

Machon, Josephine. 2013. *Immersive Theatres: Intimacy and Immediacy in Contemporary Performance*. Houndmills: Palgrave.

Malkki, Liisa. 1996. "Speechless Emissaries: Refugees, Humanitarianism, Dehistoricization." *Cultural Anthropology* 11 (3): 377–404.

Milk, Chris. 2015. "How Virtual Reality Can Create the Ultimate Empathy Machine." Filmed March 2015. Video, 10:26. https://www.ted.com/talks/chris_milk_how_virtual_reality_can_create_the_ultimate_empathy_machine#t-551080.

Mosse, Richard. 2017. *Incoming*. London: Mack.

Murray, Janet. 1998. *Hamlet on the Holodeck*. Cambridge, MA: MIT Press.

Nilsson, Niels Christian, Rolf Nordahl, and Stefania Serafin. 2016. "Immersion Revisited: A Review of Existing Definitions of Immersion and Their Relation to Different Theories of Presence." *Human Technology: An Interdisciplinary Journal on Humans and ICT Environments* 12 (2): 108–134.

O'Hagan, Sean. 2017. "Richard Mosse: Incoming Review—Shows the White Hot Misery of the Migrant Crisis." *The Guardian*, February 15. https://www.theguardian.com/artanddesign/2017/feb/15/richard-mosse-incoming-review-barbican-curve-migrant-crisis.

Schutte, Nicola S., and Emma J. Stilinovic. 2017. "Facilitating Empathy Through Virtual Reality." *Motivation and Emotion* 41: 708–712.

Slaughter, Joseph R. 2014. "The Enchantment of Human Rights; or, What Difference Does Humanitarian Indifference Make? *Critical Quarterly* 56 (4): 46–66.

Stephens, Sharon. 1995. *Children and the Politics of Culture*. Princeton: Princeton University Press.

Suski, Laura. 2009. "Children, Suffering and the Humanitarian Appeal." In *Humanitarianism and Suffering: The Mobilization of Empathy*, edited by Wilson and Brown, 202–222. New York: Cambridge University Press.

Sutherland, Ivan. 1965. "The Ultimate Display." In *Proceedings of the IFIP Congress*, 506–508.

Tarnoff, Ben. 2017. "Empathy—The Latest Gadget Silicon Valley Wants to Sell You." *The Guardian*, October 25. https://www.theguardian.com/technology/2017/oct/25/empathy-virtual-reality-facebook-mark-zuckerberg-puerto-rico.

Wilson, Richard Ashby, and Richard D. Brown. 2009. "Introduction." In *Humanitarianism and Suffering: The Mobilization of Empathy*, edited by Wilson and Brown, 1–28. New York: Cambridge University Press.

CHAPTER 6

A Global Critique of Neoliberalism? The Comparative *Humans of New York* and the World

Mukti Lakhi Mangharam

"It's like I'm on eggshells all the time. Nothing but stress" begins one post on the Facebook photoblog *Humans of New York* (henceforth HONY). The post continues to describe the experience of a New Yorker who lives on social security, which leaves him less than $30 a month for food, so that he survives on 59 cent tuna fish cans and is hungry much of the time. The post is accompanied by a photograph of a pair of feet clothed in cheap white trainers, which rest on a concrete pavement lashed with snow and ice. This is all that is visible in the photograph, the man's white shoes and bare white legs against the gray (Fig. 6.1).

HONY is a photography blog that was begun in 2010 and quickly became a worldwide phenomenon. The HONY post above, for instance, has over 116,000 likes, 4595 shares, and 3700 comment responses sharing other personal stories of financial uncertainty, or even telling the pair of legs in question to "get a job." This level of reception, dialogue, and

M. L. Mangharam (✉)
Rutgers University, New Brunswick, NJ, USA
e-mail: mukti.l.m@rutgers.edu

A. S. Moore and S. Pinto (eds.), *Writing Beyond the State*,
Palgrave Studies in Literature, Culture and Human Rights,
https://doi.org/10.1007/978-3-030-34456-6_6

Fig. 6.1 From the HONY Blog. Reprinted with permission of Brandon Stanton (https://www.facebook.com/humansofnewyork/photos/a.102107073196735.4429.102099916530784/1177764265631005/?type=3&theater)

engagement makes HONY unique and difficult to classify. The project is neither simply photojournalism nor a form of social work or fundraising. Yet its unique coupling of photography, short-form narrative, and the medium of social media has resulted in unprecedented popularity and circulation, bringing millions together to raise awareness and empathy about difficult topics like homelessness, mental health, immigration, homosexuality, race, and religion in New York and across the world. By examining these issues, HONY raises the question of a human rights subject that is specific to the American nation state and yet global, for, as the comments on each post testify, HONY is based in New York City but has an international audience, spanning nations from the Global South to the Global North.

This essay asks whether HONY constitutes a post-sovereign form of collective and ethical resistance to the violence that global capitalism visits on the human rights subject across the world. I first explore "neoliberalism" as a particularly virulent mode of global capitalism, before analyzing how HONY, in its coverage of subjects in New York City, functions as a space within which anti-neoliberal discourse circulates through an innovative form of collective storytelling. HONY's stories, I suggest, posit a human rights subject that has a different rationality at its core than the "human" of neoliberalism, for HONY is concerned with collective rather than individual self-interest. Since humans suffer from specific forms of neoliberalism all over the world, I then ask whether HONY's storytelling about the Humans of Iran and Pakistan is also successful in illuminating and critiquing inequality. I turn to HONY's interviews of the inhabitants of countries that often function as a non-Western Orientalized other in mainstream American discourse, asking whether Brandon Stanton, the author and photographer behind the blog, is able to mobilize the same kind of anti-neoliberal sentiments in these locations as he does in New York without flattening out cultural particularities and details. If not, what does this failure say about the limits and possibilities of forming a truly global human rights social movement, through storytelling, against neoliberalism and an increasingly predatory global capitalism? After considering these questions, I end with an exploration of how and why other spin-offs of the blog written from locations in the Global South are more successfully able to fulfill the function of a localized yet simultaneously global resistance against oppressive forms of capitalism.

Neoliberalism and Its Attack on the Human Rights Subject

Wendy Brown defines neoliberalism as a "generalized practice of 'economizing' spheres and activities heretofore governed by other tables of value" (Brown 2015, 21). These other "spheres" have historically underwritten the "universal human" of human rights discourse, and include justice (and its sub-elements, such as liberty, equality, and fairness), individual and popular sovereignty, as well as cultures of democratic citizenship. As a result of the neoliberal "economizing" of these spheres, capabilities tied to physical and mental well-being, creativity, reflection, and invention have also suffered.[1] Neoliberalism, then, picks up on one historic aspect of human rights discourse—the right to exchange labor and buy property—and exaggerates it to the detriment of other facets—including mental well-being and bodily integrity—thus producing a persistent contradiction. As a structural regime, neoliberalism disseminates the model of the market to all domains and activities, turning all rights into commodities available to those who can afford them, and configuring human beings exhaustively as owners of private property and market actors—as homo economicus. The latter is a post-Enlightenment characterization of man as a person who pursues wealth for his own self-interest through rational judgment. The history of the term dates back to the nineteenth century when J.S. Mill first defined the economic actor as possessing a rationality through which he "inevitably does that by which he may obtain the greatest amount of necessaries, conveniences, and luxuries, with the smallest quantity of labor and physical self-denial with which they can be obtained" (Mill 1968, 137). Despite its historical popularity, homo economicus has a fallacy—its individualism—at its core, which proclaims that each person knows his own interest better than government and that the interest of the individual is the interest of all.

This kind of economic rationality, in privileging individualism, is unrestrained by moral precepts regulated by the government, law, or larger social structures, and is purposely blind to inequalities in power, wealth, and income and how they bear down on the fate of individuals and groups. Instead, as Henry Giroux notes, neoliberal cultures are infused with the language of self-help and individual responsibility. As a policy and political project, neoliberalism is wedded to the privatization of public services, the dismantling of the welfare state, the selling off of state functions, the deregulation of financial institutions and corporations, the liberalization of trade in goods and capital investment, and the marketization and commodification of society (Giroux 2014, 1–2). These trends have resulted in what many have called "precarity," which expresses the sense that the state has broken its ideological promise to ameliorate the misery capitalism generates (Polanyi 2001). The state tries to offload as much of the responsibility for maintaining a minimum standard of well-being for its citizens, while corporations simultaneously shift as much of the economic risk to their workers, offering little in the way of benefits, pensions, and security. This results in the widespread condition of temporary, flexible, contingent, casual, and intermittent work in postindustrial societies, brought about by the neoliberal labor market reforms that have strengthened management and weakened the bargaining power of employees since the late 1970s. As we will see in our analysis of HONY's documentary photography and storytelling, this leaves many to suffer.

Significantly, Wendy Brown stresses that the neoliberal phenomena described above are "globally ubiquitous, yet disunified and nonidentical in space and over time" (Brown 2015, 21), manifesting differently according to the specificities and histories of the contexts within which it is put to work. Yet, neoliberalism's global ubiquity is explained by the fact that it is the ideological accompaniment to late stage capitalism, which is a world system. And if neoliberalism is global and ubiquitous, we must consider the ways in which resistance to it may be more effective if it also takes on a global dimension, even as such resistance is grounded in particular experiences and contexts. Following this line of thought, I ask whether a storytelling of the kind that Humans of New York professes—one that assumes a universal humanity that spans the globe, that is not defined by property and entitlement rights, and that privileges physical and mental well-being over all other imperatives—can be one such form of global resistance.

In asking this question, this essay focuses on post-sovereign storytelling like HONY's as constitutive of a rights-bearing subject that can resist neoliberalism. In doing so, it resists the many scholarly critiques of rights as ineffective because they depend on the nation state for enforcement.[2] While acknowledging the failures of the nation state in the age of neoliberalism I hesitate to dismiss the effectiveness of human rights on these grounds because, as many scholars have pointed out, human rights do not only depend on the nation state for their implementation; they also come into being by changing popular consciousness through their articulation in literary and cultural forms.[3] Thus I seek to understand the discursive working of human rights within and beyond the state in cultural texts like HONY, paying attention to how rights are refigured in those texts in ways that critique and even circumvent the nation state. Such an approach does not mean putting the material state-centered institutions of human rights in opposition to discursive articulations of rights. Rather, it is to acknowledge the ways that popular storytelling such as that done by HONY can also constitute human rights in a way that puts pressure on the state to live up to its social responsibilities. In what follows, I investigate the way HONY constitutes discursive pressure to live up to human rights ideals.

HONY as an Anti-neoliberal Public

In 2010, a young self-taught photographer named Brandon Stanton began wandering the streets of New York City, asking strangers if he could take their photograph and posting them in a Facebook album titled "Humans of New York." The original goal of the project was to "take a photographic census of the city, plotting the photos on an interactive map."[4] The project soon turned into a collection of subjects' quotes or short stories published alongside their photos. He logged them on a "Humans of New York" blog, which then began to stake a presence on other forms of social media, including Facebook, Instagram, and Twitter.

While HONY posts appear to be simple, only encompassing a photograph and a caption (like the one above), the content changes drastically from post to post, concerning itself with whichever subject the person being interviewed wishes to talk about. Yet, the posts all have one commonality: they are tailored to reveal some element of a common human condition that unites strangers into collectively identifying with, and responding to, the experiential stories the subject provides. Thus the HONY Facebook page—which contains almost 17 million followers and counting—often earns hundreds of thousands of "likes" on each photo, and thousands of comments on each post from followers worldwide who engage in discussion and create a learning community of acceptance, where judgment is overwhelmingly shot down and empathy is encouraged. Indeed, in post after post, the positive and affirming comments are the ones that get the most likes and rise to the top of the page.

HONY's popularity as an informal, unplanned campaign for a humanism that unites people across socioeconomic, racial, cultural, and now national barriers, puts it in the same category as other human rights campaigns that aim to accumulate massive audiences, circulating stories in order to gain sympathy for victims of rights abuses across the globe. These larger human rights campaigns, however, define themselves explicitly in terms of "rights," are often sponsored by multinational corporations, and center memoirs or novels documenting forms of spectacular violence against these rights, as Starbucks did with Ishmael Beah's *A Long Way Gone*, a memoir about child soldiers in Africa. Unsurprisingly, this kind of mass human rights awakening aimed at the public sphere usually ignores forms of structural everyday violence, using narratives about exoticized difference someplace far off. The emphasis on spectacular violence and difference has itself been criticized as being a particularly neoliberal aesthetic, for it often turns attention away from larger quotidian socioeconomic inequalities. Walter Benn Michaels thus suggests that the mark of neoliberal aesthetic production is a focus entirely "on how we see people," highlighting racial, cultural difference at the expense of, rather than along with, less visible markers of structural economic difference.[5] While HONY does participate in such a highlighting of racial and cultural difference, it does not do so in neglect of economic and structural inequalities in its American posts.

But acknowledging its critique of precarity is not to deny that HONY is also a product of neoliberal capital. As Vinson Cunningham notes, storytelling of the HONY kind is no longer an arrangement of events organized in light of artistic, intellectual, or moral principles but rather a "glossier, less thrilling thing: a burst of pathos, a revelation without a veil to pull away. "Storytelling," in this parlance, is best employed in the service of illuminating business principles, or selling tickets to non-profit galas, or winning contests."[6] There is much about HONY that would support this charge. For one, the only immediate solutions HONY poses in response to social problems are private ones. In the wake of especially poignant stories, such as those surrounding children at underfunded, inner city public schools, HONY sets up donation pages to raise money through private funds. The more privileged readers of HONY thus take over the public responsibilities of the state, reducing a public problem to private and individual acts of charity.

An ethos that is part and parcel of neoliberalism can also be read into HONY's aesthetic photographic form. For, as Susan Sontag suggests, needing to have reality confirmed and experience enhanced by photographs is an aesthetic consumerism to which everyone is now addicted (Sontag 1977, 24). Indeed, many photographs and captions run the risk of existing primarily as a cathartic release for the readers and viewers who consume them. They do so by centering the facial expressions of the photographed subjects, most of them minorities, among stories of drug use, addiction, and incarceration. Such a focus on subjective experience cultivates a feel-good personal connection to the photographed subjects, thereby reinforcing the idea that these are individual problems that can be fixed through private acts of emotional or financial charity. A cathartic function is reinforced by the fact that these posts are themselves story fragments at best, functioning primarily as partial accounts that lead us to believe that we have the complete story. We consume these fragments and keep coming back for more. As such, the fragment undermines the idea of larger structural understandings of the socioeconomic factors responsible for the precarity described.

While acknowledging these realities, I argue that HONY also centers stories of structural economic violence, thereby *registering* precarity, changing public perceptions of the faces of poverty and inequality, and clearing space for social change. In contrast to Susan Sontag's observation about photography as a kind of facile consumerism, and building on Walter Benjamin's argument about photography's capacity to revolutionize the masses' modes of perception, Ariella Azoulay centers what she calls the "civil contract of photography"; photos produce a contract of "partnership and solidarity" that reaches across national boundaries to "universal spectators." This contract entails agreeing to treat photos as witnesses for the people or events represented, thus anchoring spectators in "civic duty towards the photographed person" and enabling individuals to consider the forms of existence they share with others (Azoulay 2012, 16).

More specifically, though, I believe that what makes HONY effective at spreading awareness of growing precarity is what Caroline Levine would call its form's affordances, which refers to whatever a given object (say, a spatula) allows an agent to do, whether that is clean windows, fix a tire, or flip pancakes (Levine 2016, 6). HONY's form allows it to posit a textual message, to emphasize, undermine, or nuance that message through an accompanying photograph, and to allow multiple other viewers to offer their opinions as part of the growing content of the post. This quality is what makes HONY a public. For, as Michael Warner has argued via Jürgen Habermas, publics are text-based enactments of a relation among strangers. Without the idea of texts that can be picked up at different times and in different places by otherwise unrelated people, we would not imagine a public as an entity that embraces all the users of that text, whoever they might be. Through discourse, strangers imagine each other as already belonging to common worlds, so that strangerhood paradoxically becomes the necessary medium of commonality. As Warner puts it, our subjectivity is understood as having resonance with others, even as we also recognize ourselves as strangers to the other members of the public. The readers of HONY are united into a public by a constant imagining of the other as one who belongs to a shared geographic, economic, and mental space. As such, a public is the self-created and self-organized social space created by the reflexive circulation of discourse (Warner 2002, 90). While this shared space is a national one for Benedict Anderson, HONY conceptualizes it as a global one defined by a common humanity. The discursive constitution of a public—a material entity with tangible effects in the world—makes human rights storytelling a particularly powerful vehicle for social change.

In its capacity as a public, HONY spreads awareness of everyday forms of structural economic violence, countering the idea that capitalism is central to democracy, and focusing on the ways that the powerlessness of the person haunts modern capitalism. As such, HONY insists on a radical democratic politics that calls out the economic precarity capitalism creates. As such, HONY posts are decidedly anti-neoliberal because they highlight the structural economic conditions that force people into violence, poverty, and mental illness, eroding individual agency while relying on the illusory neoliberal notion of individual autonomy. As I show in the examples below, many posts also highlight the attrition of social welfare services such as health care and education that were previously theorized as human rights but have now been shifted to privatized corporate endeavors. Others stress the production of mere life or a concern with survival and the erosion of other human capacities as a result. And they do so by bringing the human back into focus as a universalizing category that is deliberately inclusive.

What does this human look like? For one, HONY's humans are possessed of a different kind of rationality than that of homo economicus—for its humans are not defined by an individual self-interest that will magically tally with the interest of all through unrestrained, competitive struggle. Rather, as Warner points out, the development of the social imaginary of publics, as a relation among strangers that is projected from private readings of circulating texts, has created a human within which the faculties of the private reader as rational and critical are elevated into the essential faculties of man:

> If you know and are intimately associated with strangers to whom you are directly related only through the discursive means of reading, opining, arguing, and witnessing, then it might seem natural that other faculties recede from salience at the highest levels of social belonging. (Warner 2002, 116)

Within the rationality of homo economicus, the individual seeks to attain specific goals at a minimal cost. By contrast, the larger social and ethical rationality involved in the enactment of this kind of public relies on argument and critical analysis with other members of the public. A public, then, is based on realizing one's humanity in interaction with others through critical interpersonal discourse, which inextricably links individuals to the collective.

Take the post above as an example of a universalizing anti-neoliberal public within which individual readers and strangers constitute each other as human through their relation with each other. At one level, the post itself orchestrates such an imagined relation independently of the discourse it engenders. The photo deliberately does not show the man's face or upper body. The shoes that are the center of the post function as a metonym for the idea that we could walk in his shoes and occupy his position, reinforcing the idea that neoliberalism is an ubiquitous problem while also creating a public that any viewer can imagine themselves inhabiting. In addition, the text that accompanies this photo also stresses the structural nature of this problem, thereby suggesting that it can affect anybody who happens to occupy the man's subject position:

> It's like I'm on eggshells all the time. Nothing but stress. I get $696 a month from social security. I could get more if I pretend to be bipolar like some people I know, but they make you take medicine to get your disability benefits. I'm not going to sit around like a zombie to get extra money. When I pay my bills, I have $30 left over. I can feed myself with 59-cent cans of tuna. I tried one of those food pantries but they aren't even worth the time ... The bus drivers in the Bronx are cool so they let me ride for free. So that's good. I can get around. But I can't afford for anything to go wrong. Some lady is letting me stay in her place for cheap while she lives with her daughter, so I have a place to live. But it's rent controlled so I'm not even supposed to be there ... Nothing but stress. I never feel safe. Every time there's a knock on the door, I think it's the end.[7]

Avoiding a personal narrative about the individual choices and actions that may have led to his circumstances, this individual immediately places his suffering in a wider context—referring to the paltry sum of social security he receives, the possibility of fraudulently acquiring disability benefits, and the inadequate food pantry system. In doing so, he effectively conveys the precarity of his position and the socially produced nature of that precarity.

The post also constitutes the strangers who read it as anti-neoliberal subjects of an emergent public by encouraging rational discourse among them through its form as a comment blog. While the post does not explain the source of this man's suffering, the comments write the rest of his story through strangers' own experiences, making it clear that a large part of the problem is an economic order in which the number of living-wage jobs keeps decreasing due to a growing trend of corporate mergers and monopolies. These top-rated comments, moreover, generate the most likes, thereby appearing above the ones calling on the subject to "get a job." In doing so, they effectively rewrite the hegemonic meritocracy narrative of American capitalism. One commenter responds:

> All these comments about "getting a job"! You have no idea how old he is or why he collects social security. One day I hope all the unsympathetic people in this world will get to spend just a week in situation they have no easy way to get out of. He may have been a veteran and protected you. He may have been a teacher who taught you. Or maybe he was just in the service or construction industry and his body just doesn't hold up anymore. My point: don't judge what you don't understand! Oh, and STFU.[8]

The comment actively invites the readers to become part of this public by imagining the faceless stranger of the post as the self. The words: "one day I hope all the unsympathetic people in this world will get to spend just a week in situation they have no easy way to get out of" generates a public by adding imaginative possibilities to the writing of the photographed subject's story so that he can appear as a potential version of the readerly self, no longer an isolated stranger but someone who shares a potentially common experience: "He may have been [...] He may have been [...] Or maybe he was just [...]." The photos and captions function as a self-contained text that can nevertheless be changed and appropriated by the countless viewers who encounter the photograph during its participation within an emergent public.

The second comment joins in and expands the anti-neoliberal public further by adding the commenter's own experience, building on the story possibilities imagined by the first commenter. She notes that she has been repeatedly laid off

> due to restructuring. Yet they keep on making construction projects that cost millions of dollars. This is the THIRD job in six years that I've been let go because it's either gone bankrupt, it's been relocated to another state or my position was eliminated. All these three jobs I've been at two years each and this happens. I only want a job that I can retire in. It's

> not that we are lazy or don't want to work. Anxiety comes from things like this happening and it can be debilitating. The good thing is I paid my February rent. Now off to scramble for March rent.[9]

The commenter places herself in a larger community of strangers that the white pair of shoes also belong to, including both within a collective "we." Both strangers can be imagined as suffering precarity from a global system that cuts costs by eliminating or shifting jobs across borders through "free trade" policies, or that downsizes workforces for the sake of maximizing profits.

Another HONY post similarly focuses on the larger structural economic reasons that force those close to retirement age into unsustainable minimum wage jobs. One photo provides a close-up shot of an older man, his face wrinkled into a permanent frown. He notes: "I'm just trying to survive. I don't have any money in the bank. I pick up whatever minimum wage jobs that I can, mainly fast food. At the job program, they tell us that we should never tell an interviewer: 'I need a job.' Instead we're supposed to say: 'I like customer service.'"[10] The post highlights the neoliberal phenomenon of economic conflicts losing centrality in the social and political arenas, so that even job seekers are instructed to conceal the material circumstances underlying their job search, focusing instead on centering their subjective preferences. This is of course also a manifestation of the liberal humanist subject, supposedly possessed of individual agency and able to shape the world in accordance with his or her own inclinations, even though such a world nor such a subject exists any longer and perhaps never did.

Significantly, the comments also create a universal anti-neoliberal human by placing the problem of homelessness in a global context. One commenter from Belgium provides her own experience of being homeless. She describes the state-funded "social networks" that enabled her to escape the cycle of poverty that she found herself in.[11] Thus the comment immediately casts neoliberal suffering as well as its alleviating structures in a comparative framework, portraying homelessness and precarity as rising global problems that can be addressed by governments. Such a comparative form allows American readers to zero in on the ways their government fails them and to contrast ameliorating organizations available to them with state-funded structures in other parts of the world.

Significantly, these anti-neoliberal messages are reflected in the aesthetic form of the posts. What would an anti-neoliberal aesthetic look like?

This is a variation of a question that has been long pondered in Marxist literary theory in relation to capitalism. Lukacs, for instance, characterized social realism, marked by thick seemingly objective description of reality in a third-person narrative voice, as the form best suited to inciting revolutionary action (Lukács 2007, 56). Rancière agrees, denouncing art that elevates formalism over politically agentive content for its "aesthetic neutralization of the social hierarchy" (Rancière 2009, 14). However, as Walter Benn Michaels argues, such critiques of formalism can unwittingly collude with neoliberalism, for in focusing solely on art as a transparent medium of representation that is primarily devoted to making subjects visible, these works just as often overlook material conditions of inequality.[12] In response to these critics, I take a Brechtian position, suggesting that critical realism, photographic or otherwise, is not a mere question of form. Anti-neoliberal messages can be expressed in many ways, whether through direct description, narrative, parable, satire, experimental play, or otherwise.

Indeed, HONY displays a mixture of various kinds of aesthetic strategies in service of its message. Take, for instance, the photograph (Fig. 6.2), and its accompanying caption, which highlights its own status as an aesthetic object in service of a critique of neoliberalism:

> I've got a bit of a jewelry addiction. [...] I go into a sort of trance when I see a piece of jewelry, and I feel like it's going to give me a power or beauty that's not obtainable without it. I saw this gun and thought it would make me feel more 'hip hop.' [...] Now I'm not so sure about it. I've got to stop spending money.[13]

The photograph has no speaking subject within it, just an object, a large gaudy gold necklace pendant in the shape of a gun, held in a white hand. It provides a visual message with the gun supposedly pointed at the person speaking about their jewelry addiction as if to say that the rampant ideology of consumerism is a mode of committing suicide. Discourses of commodity consumption consume and define her entirely, reducing a person to a series of exchangeable identities that can be bought and sold just as the "hip hop" gun is. This post, then, is a critique of consumerism and of the neoliberal self as a secure self-possessed individual whose identity is predetermined, complete, and issues from within. The aesthetic composition of the photograph colludes with this critique. The subject of the

Fig. 6.2 From the HONY Blog. Reprinted with permission of Brandon Stanton

photograph disappears from view even as the intentionality of the photographer is writ large, working to let the readers not just sympathize with the subject but empathize with her and imaginatively occupy the subject's position; we could walk in the shoes above; the gun could be pointed at us. This is an emerging universal humanist subject that is decidedly anti-neoliberal, stubbornly focused on the larger socioeconomic structures that subjugate a multitude of subjects within a resistant and increasingly aware public.

As I note above, capitalism, its profit-driven infrastructures and practices, and its accompanying ideologies of neoliberalism are global fixtures, albeit with context-specific manifestations. It becomes reasonable to consider, therefore, whether HONY's type of storytelling can work to counter neoliberal ideologies in locations other than New York. I ask this question given Brandon Stanton's decision, in the summer of 2015, to shift the focus of his photography from New York to Pakistan and Iran, calling that section of his website "Travel" by way of explanation.

In exploring this transition, the following section asks: Is HONY's anti-neoliberal public sustained when the blog moves to locations demonized by hegemonic forms of US Orientalism?

HONY in Iran and Pakistan—An Example of Global Resistance?

To consider whether HONY's anti-neoliberal human subject is able to incisively critique oppressive economic structures in non-Western regions far from New York, one must first understand the different forms capitalism takes in other areas of the world. How does one craft a collective global struggle against neoliberalism given the particular forms it takes in different places? And do the particularities of cultural contexts overwhelm any similarities and connections between different local capitalisms all over the world? To understand capitalism as a global phenomenon, I draw on the Warwick Research Collective's characterization of the world system as "one, and unequal," which is influenced by the Marxist theory of combined and uneven development. Within this formulation, capitalist modernity is to be understood as governed always by unevenness, the historically determinate "coexistence," in any given place and time, of precapitalist as well as capitalist formations; "of realities from radically different moments of history – handicrafts alongside the great cartels, peasant fields with the Krupp factories or the Ford plant in the distance" (Jameson 1995, 307). In this argument, development does not mark the relationship between some formations (that are "developed") like NYC and others like Mali (that are not or not yet so). Uneven development is not a characteristic of Africa or India only. NYC, Middlesbrough, and even London are among the most unevenly developed cities in the world (WRC 2015, 12).

Seeing Iran and Pakistan within such a frame of a unitary, global but uneven system of capitalism subverts the understanding that these countries' problems with poverty are a result of incomplete capitalist development as opposed to the developed capitalist contexts of the US or Europe. This stagist understanding from neoclassical economic theory holds that features of unevenness, such as income inequality, equalizes as a result of capital diffusion throughout the open market and that "developing" economies will rise above inequality through capitalist expansion and free-market policies.[14] By contrast, the unitary but uneven view of capitalist expansion that I am propounding here following Marxists such as Wallerstein and David Harvey, encourages us to see inequality, poverty, and its effects as a result of the imperialist expansion of capitalism for, as the Warwick Research Collective puts it, "capitalist development does not smooth away but rather produces unevenness, systematically and as a matter of course" (WRC 2015, 12). This unevenness is the result of capitalism's persistent search for competitive advantage and consequently, its movement away from oversaturated economies toward new spaces from which it can extract greater profit (Harvey 1975, 9–21). The result is inequality in different forms in both "developed" Northern and "developing" Southern economies. The latter gain jobs but at a terrible cost, and the former lose them. The effects in both locations include increasing inequality and the erosion of welfare and support.

Yet HONY does not represent such an interlinked global frame; it does not explore the kinds of unevenness that capitalism produces in Iran and Pakistan alongside the kinds of unevenness it produces in New York. I argue that this is because it is primarily interested in countering the Orientalist othering of these locations, with New York and the larger Western world as its primary audience. While Stanton does not explicitly explain his rationale in this manner, the content of his posts suggests that HONY's Iran and Pakistan posts are almost wholly about undoing the demonization of Muslims by neutralizing cultural differences for an American audience. The posts misguidedly carry out the admirable goal of countering Islamophobia by subsuming, even erasing, all differences for the sake of producing a common shared humanity. Take, for instance, Stanton's introductory "thesis statement" to an assumed Euro-American audience at the beginning of his Pakistan section:

> Imagine that the world is never notified about the 99.99% of the time that you are a completely normal, productive, law-abiding citizen. The world only learns about you when things go wrong. Now imagine what the world would think of you. It's not that terrorism, patriarchy, and violence aren't real problems in Pakistan. They exist and the country is battling these issues every single day ... The problem is that so many people seem to only be aware of that extremism ... when those stories are all that we hear, it's so easy to imagine a world that's far scarier than it really is ... And living in fear can be a dangerous thing. Because if we're afraid of each other, we'll never be able to work together to solve our common problems.[15]

Stanton's words here orchestrate a public in their setting up of an imagined relation among American and Pakistani strangers, the latter of whom are characterized as "normal, productive, law-abiding." In order to strengthen this relation, Stanton emphasizes the lives of ordinary Pakistanis rather than the spectacular violent anomalies that are highlighted by the mainstream American media in order to demonize Muslims and their countries of origins. Yet, unfortunately, HONY achieves this goal by choosing photographs that flatten out contextual particularities, and by overdetermining the lens through which these photographs are viewed.

One of the top commenters on this post (Fig. 6.3) writes:

> i think the beautiful thing about this picture is that if you had left out the location, it could've been taken anywhere. and that's what i love about this page - it blurs lines of nationalities and instead shows that we are all essentially the same - humans.[16]

Fig. 6.3 Reprinted by permission of Brandon Stanton (https://www.facebook.com/humansofnewyork/photos/a.102107073196735.4429.102099916530784/1047264865347613/?type=3&theater)

However, these two little Pakistani girls can be mistaken for their American counterparts only because they are light skinned, dressed in Western frocks, and are clearly from well-off families. What makes the evocation of a common humanness possible, then, is the photograph's suppression of social differences or hierarchies within the society these girls inhabit. By contrast, because Stanton's audience takes for granted that New Yorkers are legitimate subjects of human rights, his New York posts can focus on unsavory and systemic problems such as homelessness and inequality, and commenters can chime into a conversation that contains deeper analyses of these issues. While HONY brought divisions and suppressions back into focus, in Pakistan Stanton does the exact opposite.

Even when the Pakistani or Iranian posts focus on subjects of economic hardship, the way in which they frame these questions follows a similar formula of eliding contextual particularities in favor of highlighting the similarities of its subjects to New Yorkers. The following post focuses on a mother–son pair in a small town in Iran:

> Since he was very young, I've tried to show him that we can't always afford the things that we want. When my wallet is full, I show him. When my wallet is empty, I show him. Things have been especially hard lately because my husband has missed a few paychecks. We couldn't get new supplies for school this year. But he told me: 'Don't worry Mom, we'll get them when the wallet is full.' And then the other day he saw that I was upset because we couldn't get all the groceries we needed. So he went into his room and brought me his own savings.[17]

A series of comparable posts and comments in Humans of New York focuses on countering the individualist homo economicus with a rational human formed by and through an interconnected public of strangers that can critically dissect economic ideologies and effects while retaining their particularities. In this Iranian post, however, there is no focus on specifics in case it renders these Iranians too different and thus less human to American readers. Instead the post and the comments it elicits are centered on abstract universal messages like love and family. One of the top comments states: "Money is a certain type of exchangeable resource but love and understanding within family is the greatest resource you can have. With that you will always be wealthy and empowered to get what you need."[18] The subjects in both the above photographs are rendered into static and fixed objects of consumption. Ironically, the attempt to render them human means that they cannot participate in the conversation as full-fledged “humans” constituted through rational discourse within a public’s imagined collective of strangers. Moreover, like the content, the aesthetic form here is simplistic, centering the subjects’ similarities rather than shifting attention to the larger structural forces at work in the production of the photograph and its contents. There are no guns pointed at us here, nor are there fragmented metonymic images of legs or shoes.

This is not to say that Stanton completely eschews focusing on contextual particularities. Rather, the problem seems to be that he does so without exploring the interlinked global capitalist material structures that underpin these contextual particularities, thereby reducing these particularities wholly to problems of culture. For instance, a series of posts from the Pakistan coverage zeroes in on the local problem of bonded labor, even setting up a fundraising page to help bonded individuals pay their debts and climb out of their oppression. The local activist that Stanton interviews writes:

> Bricks are the primary unit of construction across Pakistan… There are 20,000 brick kilns across the country. We estimate that an average of 40 families work on each of these kilns and that each family is required to make 1000 bricks per day. That means 4.5 million people are living in slavery conditions. And so many of these workers are young children…The laws don’t reach the kilns, so the workers live in constant fear of violence and retribution. The kiln owners are so rich and powerful. Their profits represent nearly 3% of Pakistan’s GDP. They put their friends and relatives in the legislature. They bribe and intimidate the police. It is very dangerous to speak out against them. I’ve been attacked and threatened so many times that I no longer fear death.

The oppressive structures of Pakistani serfdom could have been more fruitfully understood if framed as an example of combined and uneven development, for the above story is a perfect illustration of how Pakistan’s existence within a global capitalist system coexists with, and even exacerbates, feudal precapitalist formations such as serfdom. This is because the rich capitalist elite that owns these brick businesses export their price-competitive bricks to countries including the US, Saudi Arabia, UAE, South Africa, Poland, and Japan. Yet, Stanton misses the opportunity to portray this complex network of relationships in depth, and none of his American commenters have the knowledge or the prompting to frame the issue in this way either. The result is that in one of the few posts focusing on socioeconomic particularities, there is no mention of the effects and inequalities of global capitalism. The inequalities within a particular location appear purely as cultural specificities rather than complex linked phenomena within an economic world system. The resulting rather shallow analysis of global precarity only ends up reinforcing Orientalist notions of essential cultural difference and facilitating what Melissa Smyth has called sentimentality in place of action determining empathy, while clearing the way for top-down neoliberal approaches to problems such as poverty alleviation.[19]

Truly Comparative Humans

What then would a truly collective and global form of human rights storytelling look like that registers and resists the particular effects of capitalism in a comparative frame? The answer seems to be provided in another Facebook blog "Humans of Pakistan," one of the many "copies" of the original HONY. Unlike "HONY-Pakistan," "Humans of Pakistan" is permanently based in Pakistan and is run by a Pakistani for a mainly English speaking Pakistani audience. Its readership, then, while comparatively more elite, is also much smaller and more local than that of HONY, consisting of about 500,000 viewers in comparison to HONY's 18 million and growing, although some global northerners routinely show up as commenters. The posts on "Humans of Pakistan" convey a contextually located yet universal human rights subject by portraying the economic trials faced by ordinary Pakistanis as a result of the combination of a unitary yet uneven global capitalism. One post, for instance, focuses on the difficulties of a 13-year-old girl trying to get an education in a mountainous province of Pakistan, Balochistan:

> I am 13 and studying in 5th class. My father is ill so...mother and sister sew clothes to earn money for us. I want to become an English teacher or a doctor when I grow up. But to do that, I need to pass the 6th class, which my school doesn't offer. We can't even go to other schools in the city because it is 5 km away... It makes me sad that I might not be able to study anymore because of this. I request the government to...provide transport so I can study further... I love learning new things, especially speaking in English. I know that I can make my parents proud if only I get the chance to study more. If I can get education, I will be able to support them and my mother will never have to worry.[20]

Since the photograph is of a poor female subject whose voice is not usually heard in mainstream political discourse, the photographer chooses to center her face and expressions. The poignant effect of the photograph and accompanying words is complemented by the angry comments that respond to the post. These are mostly by local Pakistanis who are quick to point out the inadequacy of educational spending in Pakistan and its political corruption rather than eschewing critiques of their own nation in the interests of representing themselves to the West. For instance, one commenter notes the siphoning of public funds by politicians within elite political parties, raging: "May all the looters face the wrath of Allah be they Khaki, civilian or our holy cows the Mullahs." Another agrees, noting that "every individual has right to get education in Pakistan, and this is the responsibility of the state not a single person."[21] Unlike homo economicus, the human evoked here is not an individual whose interests come before and automatically tally with that of the collective. Rather, it is an obligation to the collective, here invoked by the gesture to "the responsibility of the state," that is responsible for ensuring individual welfare.

These comments reflect and denounce a complicated nexus of political and economic policy that has systematically sustained neoliberal policies and aided the production of inequality in Pakistan. As political scientist Tariq Thachil has noted, South Asian governments have largely advocated privatization, interpreting neoliberalism as justifying the "retreat of the state" even in the sphere of social policy provision (Thachil 2009, 481). One of the results has been continuing inadequate spending levels in education. When money is spent, it is on private endeavors that ensure continued patronage flows to elite supporters during reform. Thus, much of the Pakistani educational budget has been devoted toward subsidizing expensive English-medium schools and universities and military cadet colleges for training the country's elites, with the country's vernacular schools suffering as a consequence (Thachil 2009, 477).

Moreover, as reflected in the comment against "our holy cows, the Mullahs," these globally produced neoliberal policies are also the result of local realities such as political ties to religious organizations; the promise of the backing of religious groups provides a political incentive to continue the withdrawal of the state from funding education. As a result of the government's politically motivated and deliberately inadequate educational spending, religious schools have acquired higher enrollments. Thachil notes that in the post-Zia era, corresponding with neoliberal reforms, registered madrassas increased from 2801 in 1988 to 12,153 in 2007. The enrollment in these schools now crosses 1.7 million students, the majority from the poorest communities in Pakistan. The comments on the post by Americans and other global participants, while admittedly few, participate in this deeper understanding of the country's socioeconomic and political realities, producing a truly global collective rights-bearing subject that does not elide particularities but registers them in order to launch a unified critique.

The various local "humans of" blogs have no official connection to HONY, having only adopted and copied HONY's form. Nevertheless, taken together, this collection of blogs speaks to the potential of cultural texts to move beyond the limitations of the nation state toward crafting a more fully realized rights bearing subject. The texts I have examined do so by gesturing to a larger collective and global whole made up of countless particularities. Aesthetic attention to these texts reveals how a context-rich universalism is crucial in combatting a unitary yet local and uneven global capitalism buttressed by neoliberalism's homo economicus. Resistance to an unfettered global capitalism must happen through local publics in which particular strangers are both situated in their own contexts while also being related to each other through rational participation in discourse. Otherwise, we may end up with an essentializing, fixed, and narrowly economically defined human rights subject, encountered through predetermined modes of reading. Together, but not individually, the countless "Humans of" blogs, in New York, Mumbai, Pakistan, Iran, and elsewhere retain an open-ended discursive notion of the rights bearing subject that is formed collectively through the particular lived experiences of individuals. Every person's voice, in this schema, is a particular, unique addition to a universal horizon of humanity. Rather than setting up the particular in opposition to the universal, a collection of such blogs taken as a whole, curated by locals for a local as well as secondary global audience, posits the universal human as an unbounded sum of particulars.

Notes

1. The capability approach is a theoretical framework that entails two core normative claims: first, the claim that the freedom to achieve well-being is of primary moral importance, and second, that freedom to achieve well-being is to be understood in terms of people's capabilities, that is, their real opportunities to do and be what they have reason to value. See Martha Nussbaum, *Women and Human Development: The Capabilities Approach* (Cambridge: Cambridge University Press, 2000).
2. One of the best-known arguments along these lines is Hannah Arendt's in which she argues that the rights of man and the rights of the citizen are deeply imbricated. When a person loses recognition as a citizen by the nation-state, they also lose recognition as a rights-bearing subject. See Hannah Arendt, *The Origins of Totalitarianism* (New York: Harcourt, Brace, and Jovanovich).
3. The most well-known example is, of course, Joseph Slaughter's *Human Rights Inc.: The World Novel, Narrative Form, and International Law*, which points out the ways in which the bildungsroman fleshes out the human rights subject of international law. However, Slaughter also acknowledges the fraught nature of this alliance, for "the human envisioned by human rights is a creature of the law and the state; that is, the human of the law and the human of literature do not fully line up (5)."
4. Brandon Stanton, "Humans of New York: Behind the Lens," May 2013, http://www.huffingtonpost.com/brandon-stanton/humans-of-new-york-behind_b_3210673.html.
5. Walter Benn Michaels, "Neoliberal Aesthetics: Fried, Rancière and the Form of the Photograph," Nonsite.org, January 2011, http://nonsite.org/article/neoliberal-aesthetics-fried-ranciere-and-the-form-of-the-photograph.
6. Vinson Cunningham, "Humans of New York and the Cavalier Consumption of Others," *New Yorker*, November 3, 2015, http://www.newyorker.com/books/page-turner/humans-of-new-york-and-the-cavalier-consumption-of-others.
7. https://www.facebook.com/humansofnewyork/photos/a.102107073196735.4429.102099916530784/1177764265631005/?type=3&theater.
8. https://www.facebook.com/humansofnewyork/photos/a.102107073196735.4429.102099916530784/1177764265631005/?type=3&theater.
9. https://www.facebook.com/humansofnewyork/photos/a.102107073196735.4429.102099916530784/1177764265631005/?type=3&theater.

10. https://www.facebook.com/humansofnewyork/photos/a.102107073196735.4429.102099916530784/1171894682884630/?type=3&theater.
11. https://www.facebook.com/humansofnewyork/photos/a.102107073196735.4429.102099916530784/1177764265631005/?type=3&theater.
12. Walter Benn Michaels, "Neoliberal Aesthetics: Fried, Rancière and the Form of the Photograph," Nonsite.org, January 2011, http://nonsite.org/article/neoliberal-aesthetics-fried-ranciere-and-the-form-of-the-photograph.
13. https://www.facebook.com/humansofnewyork/photos/a.102107073196735.4429.102099916530784/1175762312497867/?type=3&theater.
14. See for instance Rostow, *The Stages of Economic Growth: A Non-Communist Manifesto.*
15. http://www.humansofnewyork.com/post/127078073936/a-final-word-on-pakistan-imagine-that-every-time.
16. https://www.facebook.com/humansofnewyork/photos/a.102107073196735.4429.102099916530784/1047264865347613/?type=3&theater.
17. https://www.facebook.com/humansofnewyork/photos/a.102107073196735.4429.102099916530784/1062528570487909/?type=3&p=10.
18. https://www.facebook.com/humansofnewyork/photos/a.102107073196735.4429.102099916530784/1062528570487909/?type=3&p=10.
19. Melissa Smyth, "On Sentimentality: A Critique of Humans of New York," *Warscapes*, January 16, 2015. http://www.warscapes.com/opinion/sentimentality-critique-humans-new-york.
20. https://www.facebook.com/HofPak/photos/pb.587679261321488.2207520000.1466705639./1018482791574464/?type=3&theater.
21. https://www.facebook.com/HofPak/photos/pb.587679261321488.2207520000.1466705639./1018482791574464/?type=3&theater.

Works Cited

Arendt, Hannah. 1951. *The Origins of Totalitarianism.* New York: Harcourt, Brace, and Jovanovich.

Azoulay, Ariella. 2012. *The Civil Contract of Photography.* Cambridge: MIT Press.

Benn Michaels, Walter. 2011. "Neoliberal Aesthetics: Fried, Rancière and the Form of the Photograph." Nonsite.org, January 2011. http://nonsite.org/article/neoliberal-aesthetics-fried-ranciere-and-the-form-of-the-photograph.

Brown, Wendy. 2015. *Undoing the Demos: Neoliberalism's Stealth Revolution*. Cambridge: MIT Press.
Cunningham, Vinson. 2015. "Humans of New York and the Cavalier Consumption of Others." *The New Yorker*, November 2015. http://www.newyorker.com/books/page-turner/humans-of-new-york-and-the-cavalier-consumption-of-others.
Giroux, Henry A. 2014. *Neoliberalism's War on Higher Education*. Chicago: Haymarket Books.
Harvey, David. 1975. "The Geography of Capitalist Accumulation: A Reconstruction of the Marxian Theory." *Antipode* 7 (2): 9–21.
Jameson, Fredric. 1995. *Postmodernism or the Cultural Logic of Late Capitalism*. Durham: Duke University Press.
Levine, Caroline. 2016. *Forms: Whole, Rhythm, Hierarchy, Network*. Princeton: Princeton University Press.
Lukács, György. 2007. "Realism in the Balance." In *Aesthetics and Politics*. London: Verso.
Mill, John Stuart. [1844] 1968. *Essays on Some Unsettled Questions of Political Economy*. New York: Augustus M. Kelly.
Nussbaum, Martha. 2000. *Women and Human Development: The Capabilities Approach*. Cambridge: Cambridge University Press.
Polanyi, K. 2001. *The Great Transformation: The Political and Economic Origins of Our Time*. Boston: Beacon Press.
Rancière, Jacques. 2009. "Notes on the Photographic Image." *Radical Philosophy* 156 (July/August). https://www.radicalphilosophy.com/article/notes-on-the-photographic-image.
Rostow, Walt W. 1971. *The Stages of Economic Growth: A Non-Communist Manifesto*. Cambridge: Cambridge University Press.
Slaughter, Joseph. 2007. *Human Rights Inc.: The World Novel, Narrative Form, and International Law*. Fordham: Fordham University Press.
Smyth, Melissa. 2015. "On Sentimentality: A Critique of Humans of New York." *Warscapes*, January 2015. http://www.warscapes.com/opinion/sentimentality-critique-humans-new-york.
Sontag, Susan. 1977. *On Photography*. New York: Farrar, Strauss & Giroux.
Stanton, Brandon. 2013. *Humans of New York*. New York: Macmillan.
———. https://www.facebook.com/humansofnewyork/.
———. 2013. "Humans of New York: Behind the Lens." May 2013. http://www.huffingtonpost.com/brandon-stanton/humans-of-new-york-behind_b_3210673.html.
Thachil, Tariq. 2009. "Neoliberalism's Two Faces in Asia: Globalization, Educational Policies, and Religious Schooling in India, Pakistan, and Malaysia." *Comparative Politics* 41 (4, July): 473–494.

Warner, Michael. 2002. *Publics and Counterpublics*. Brooklyn: Zone Books.
Warwick Research Collective. 2015. *Combined and Uneven Development: Towards a New Theory of World Literature*. Liverpool: Liverpool University Press.

CHAPTER 7

A World in "Small Hands"? Globalization as Risk and Rights

Peter Hitchcock

Among the plethora of alternative facts that have emerged from forms of conservative populism in the present is the idea that dyed in the wool neoliberal globalizers are now clamoring to save nations, sovereignty, and citizens from the ravages of neoliberal globalization. While it is true that many a free marketeer has indulged in hand-wringing over the more obvious excesses of pricing inequality and indeed inequality per se, their invisible hands have been busy playing the same old shell (and shell company) games with surplus value and accumulation (obviously, one can include in that list many a generously philanthropic tax-deducting billionaire). Small hands, which here is a metaphor for a general condition of political paradox rather than only a reference to a specific embodiment of such politics, seem to have no problem in parading such contradictions in the contemporary world system, boldly massaging incompatible agendas with all of the subtlety of a backhoe (I am thinking of these hands, for instance, in contrast to those that form the Human Rights Logo). Beyond

P. Hitchcock (✉)
The Graduate Center, Baruch College of the City University of New York, New York, NY, USA

A. S. Moore and S. Pinto (eds.), *Writing Beyond the State*, Palgrave Studies in Literature, Culture and Human Rights,
https://doi.org/10.1007/978-3-030-34456-6_7

the peripatetic boorishness of individual statesmen, a crisis in internationalism is certainly in evidence, and no amount of bluster and distraction will erase the systemic features in play including, most worryingly, the reemergence of aggressive nationalism and authoritarianism. Human rights violations have intensified, with attacks on migrants and migrancy symptomatic of a recalibration of intolerance in state and interstate relations. Opposition to such tendencies takes many forms, and includes a complex genealogy featuring the postcolonial and decolonial heirs of Bandung, NAM, and Third World solidarity who have long pushed for a "New International Economic Order"—codified to some extent in the 1975 UN Charter of Economic Rights and Duties of States—that at once revealed a challenge to neoliberalism even before it became hegemonic. Because of the overdeterminations inherent in state structures, governance, and finance, the question has often been the degree to which globalization merely extends or sublates charter precepts in practice.

There are different and difficult moments in globalization that offer a constitutive ambiguity in the exchange relations of rights and economy, an antinomy of rights over risk versus the right to risk. In part what follows will question the paroxysms of political economy that currently riddle globalization today, but it will think of this specifically in the reconfiguration of incommensurability and/or extensivity between human and economic rights, and in a neoliberal nexus prone to accentuate the limits in both. More than this, however, I want to suggest the positive endgame of such contradictions, a fraught space where the drama of irresolution must itself be grasped as a corresponding right to change. If small hands (states, subjects, or the vigorous opposing thumbs of the world order) could emulate a Venn diagram of the human and of the economic, the overlap here is where rights constitute a reflex of risk management, a risk that is hard to hold but is widespread in contemporary capitalism. Indeed, a new articulation of risk is central to the logic of a globalization which conjoins economic and social relations as if it were the primary or only means of connectivity between the two. And this must, perforce, have deep implications for sovereign possibility (caught between that of the individual and that of the state), forming as it does a *zoe oikonomía* where the fabric of life in human rights appears to fall away.

Why think of these developments in terms of risk? In capitalism, the securitization of risk has a long history, and securities clearly play a key role in bonding or binding accumulation. For instance, life annuities in Eighteenth-century France secured fixed income returns on life itself as an asset. In one opportunistic derivative strategy (known in the literature as the "Thirty Maidens from Geneva"), Swiss bankers bought annuities from the French state on behalf of healthy young women in order to price risk over a longer period than their male counterparts. Creditworthiness is almost literally a sign of (gendered) health in this example, but it also emphasizes that safe returns can be managed by rearticulating the risk in play. Unfortunately, the institutions that manage risk cannot manage all of the conditions that secure its role in accumulation. Thus, the French Revolution subverts the formal agreements made and offers something other than security to the aristocracy that often indulged in them, with the bankers meanwhile being offered largely worthless currency in their stead. Risk pivots on possibility and revolutions defy its quantification. And yet, of course, risk is defined across its systematization; that is, the idea of creditworthiness is not dependent upon the fate of an individual creditor or even their substantive agglomeration. But how can risk be secured in the face of bankruptcy and the collapse of an extant state? The differentiation of risk provides clues to its mediation of quality and quantity, but this means attending to the materialization of its logic within political economy (and history) and not simply to its manifestations in finance per se. There is something of a transformation problem in such differentiation, like that seen between labor, time and money in *Capital* (Volume Three), but here the idea at least is to articulate where the handling of risk is revealed as impossibly enmeshed, and is more than just an allegory of rights management in distress. Can something comparable be said of human rights discourses in general?

At face value, human rights at once address both the small-minded small-hand approach of contemporary populism and the saturation of market priorities at a world scale. Because of the differences among rights discourses, however, there is no single appeal to rights that would undo their contradictory logics. This reaches beyond the normative disputation in rights assessment and further problematizes the unhappy synergy of human rights and capitalism. Why? To be sure, human rights are special rights within rights articulations as a whole, generally pinned to the Universal Declaration of Human Rights of 1948. Yet if the universality of rights is expressed within state-centered reason, what happens when such rights are brought to bear on supra or non-state manifestations of, for instance, economic harm? Would this constitute a state of exception that would call the system of relations as a whole into question? Both De Feyter and Baxi among others have focused attention on the limits of human rights before the borderlessness of globalization, since UN-sponsored rights have often assumed a form of state monopoly over distributive justice and security. One can certainly seek redress against a state or an individual corporation, but how does this case-file approach answer a logic of extraction and circulation within capitalism as a whole?

The dilemma is only surprising if one refuses the common history that ties natural rights philosophy to property rights (a concept of having/owning consonant with a form of divine desire). Even so, there is an enthusiastic discourse proposing that if globalization scales up what is preternaturally exploitative in capitalism it can yet be reined in by human rights that are contingently attuned to its transgressions without simply reproducing a bourgeois or capitalist class outlook as such. Various appeals to fairness can be deployed to ward off predatory global capital, paradoxically by primarily shoring up state regulations and defending a modicum of protectionism for local or "infant" businesses. "Humanizing" global capitalism in this way (Nash, 67) may indeed bolster rights, but legislating excess only works if one can actually recognize it and oversee the processes by which it takes place. An economic historian might regard the move from GATT to the WTO as decisive in the effulgence of globalization, but can human rights activism affect the core principles at stake? There is plenty of evidence that International Finance Institutions are not beyond supporting poverty reduction programs, and NGOs often do this on their behalf (the World Bank has been a locus for such collaboration for many years). Clearly, however, the sovereign rights of some states are more powerful and all-encompassing than others and their interests will be deemed decisive regarding what poverty gets reduced where (beyond and within their borders). The United States, for example, while not strictly a fragile or failed state (as Noam Chomsky once assessed it) nevertheless has enough debt to qualify for structural adjustment, but the market itself, rather than the World Bank, would overdetermine how that might effectively come to pass (one could argue, for instance, that the United States has already been structurally adjusted in its deep relationship to Chinese production capacities). The logic of circulation, however, is not necessarily at stake in an approach to state inequality, and the wealthy and resource-rich may find this level of legislative concern merely bothersome rather than a contravention of their interests.

Whatever the scale, of course, there are many aspects of capitalism that must flaunt risk as a constitutive idea while covering for its negative consequences. State institutions might exude this approach but the question of mandate and outcome is differently arrayed. A government's ability to risk-manage human rights is often taken as a litmus test of its legitimacy. Failure to secure such rights in constitutions, charters, international agreements, and juridical infrastructures is interpreted as a failure to ratify the terms of modernity, and all manner of calamities, from civil strife to the collapse of state sovereignty, are seen to follow. Not surprisingly, this narrative of modernity squandered or betrayed has been met with justifiable incredulity. Within globalization, how do the logical sutures of economic risk management overdetermine or mediate the practical efficacy of rights? This is not to argue that rights discourses are always and only a complement of neoliberal desire, but obviously one is not merely the opposite or the flouting of the other either. The fluidity at stake is something like that between identity and subjectivity in cultural critique, or human being and personhood in rights discourse, and all are dialectically consequential (Jacques Rancière's question, "Who Is the Subject of the Rights of Man?" is directly connected to this provocative admixture of opposites).

For capitalism, rights are a risky business but it is only in the last fifty years that they have been priced, bundled, and circulated as if the voting rights of the shareholder supersedes all other conditions of socialization and polity (the *longue durée* of the corporate commodification of rights in general has, as Joseph Slaughter avers, a much deeper and circuitous history, like that indicated above). The right *to* share is destabilized within a system of rights *by* shares. The point is not about the absence of rights but their pecuniary substantiation which otherwise produces an aura of "rightlessness." Whereas for Hannah Arendt the refugee signifies a specific state of exception, a beyond citizen subjectivity, a state beyond oppression (since rights or rights violation can only be assessed by the state that secures them), the securitization of risk as a right is presented as the property rights of networked statelessness where human rights, if not suspended, face a transformed architecture of exception.

In light of these comments, I want to suggest three dimensions of the political economy of rights that represent a specific critical challenge in globalization as currently construed: the security of securitization, the personhood of corporatism, and the saturating commodification of basic conditions of life. The first among these concerns the limit to security in concepts of securities. Whereas empirical studies about how naughty capitalism is regarding human rights are legion, there is comparatively less work on the epistemological processes of this disjunction and the economic unconscious in which risk must dominate. We know the essence of security in finance is that it is a tradable asset and it is fungible. The universality in the agreement is distinct from what is realizable in the asset's exchange. We may say that such an understanding of security is a semantic happenstance separable from the question of security for human rights, yet few would doubt that the procedures of one have burrowed, rhizomatically, into the civil codes of the other. In a world where food and water security, for instance, are overdetermined by the terms of structural adjustment and debt deliberation, financial securities, or "structured finance," have assumed an ambivalent position in the order of security per se. On the one hand, such securities can collateralize rights, bridging the terms of financial strife by offering entities, including states, the capacity to cover their obligations in the face of demonstrable need. On the other hand, the terms of securitization, the bonds of debt (to borrow from Richard Dienst), are themselves subject to margin calls in which the maintenance of state prerogatives might be considered a second or tertiary market to the premiums in exchange offered by the first. The rational choices for both are not synonymous but consanguine—whatever the guarantees against risk that may exist in the short term, these may not cover the risk over the life of the security, which can be re-collateralized from moment to moment. If a loan permits the distribution of good to proceed it cannot secure the principle of distributable good itself. The rapid expansion of securitization shadows an equally brisk diminution of a constitutive outside to globalization, particularly after the collapse of actually existing socialism in the late Eighties and early Nineties. This intensified a process in which all that was solid did not just become air but was outsourced and/or became algorithmically virtual. Securities can now price borders and their subvention; they can denote any space of capital in the image of its security yet simultaneously mark exceptions to that endeavor.

If the pricing of assets is a floating signifier of the commodity, few could have predicted that the commodification of risk would saturate financialization itself. True, with the end of the Long Boom in the early Seventies, innovations in finance were legion (this saw the emergence of the modern or digital version of the derivative as a speculative instrument) but how might this inflect and affect the relations of money and commodity to the value form? The question is important because the tethering of value signals its social relation (in classical Marxism, at least), whereas the circuits of financialization in globalization render this relation if not irrelevant then obtuse and otherwise inscrutable. There is a basic risk in seeking value or its fraction from trading on an underlying asset, yet the speed through which such risk can be displaced and deferred in algorithmic trading obfuscates the *ratio* of risk and the materialization of the social at any one moment in the circulation of value. The preponderance of notional value in derivative trading seems harmless enough since potential losses are a receding horizon of further contracts, but this technical efficiency masks the social impact it can take, not just by following the money for the trade to its source, but by registering who or what exercises power over the conditions of realization. In globalization the virtualization of risk is the virtualization of rights in general.

The insecurity in financial securities is not just a problem for investment banks, or commercial banks fronting investment with cash reserves (a necromancy curtailed to some degree by Dodd-Frank in the United States and associated adjustments to institutional trading after the crisis of 2007–2008). The old saw about privatizing profit and socializing debt assumes a different valence at a world scale where the distribution of risk means that locatable ledgers large and small are carrying otherwise networked obligations elsewhere. The abject immateriality of finance produces doggedly material effects. Whereas in a Keynesian conception of state, macroeconomic flows of risk might be offered a fail-safe in the form of the state itself as a social bulwark, a kind of federal insurance, neoliberal logic celebrates the state only as a medium, as a point of relay in securitization; unless of course the investment infrastructure of the "free" market is itself at risk, in which case Central Banks can use their relative autonomy to print new balances for the investment community (in effect, globalization is a new symbiosis in state and circulation rather than a break of one from the other). Interestingly, during the aforementioned crisis, dubious instruments like Collateralized Debt Obligations, were repriced as a matter of national security. The state in this instance relays and relayers debt by "retiring" it. The point is not just that the government stepped in to prevent social harm but that it actively used its fiscal and monetary mechanisms to *preserve* the principle of risk in play. This kind of hedging has implications for how human rights and sovereignty are conceived.

Only a cynic would say that financiers knew that assets would return to their rightful owners (the owners of capital) should profligate pricing of debt push credit provisions in general to the precipice. The science of price modeling had long attempted to calculate risk without resort to the fortuitous proclivities of intervention like TARP (the Troubled Asset Relief Program 2008–2013). Black-Scholes option pricing, for instance, was developed around risk neutral strategies that effectively hedged the underlying asset on a continuous basis. Yet the science of derivative pricing found it more difficult to assess risk across bundles of securities premised on ratings over the quality of individual assets per se. As financial products became more complex there was a sense that circulation itself would save the process, allowing time for further drawdowns from commercial bank reserves and the creation of still more contracts to cover more immediate due dates. The Federal Reserve, while calculating in its own way, did not foresee that a risk management strategy based on writing securities rather than actually securing them would see them covering debt and capital requirements in the trillions of dollars. Given critiques of sovereignty, the exercise of a sovereign guarantee via quantitative easing must give one pause about the financial infrastructure of globalization as the supercession of sovereign right. Whenever a central bank crosses borders, it is simultaneously stitching them, for this is but another way to perform the exchange of risk at a global scale.

The differentiation of financial risk from population security or the exercise of human rights in the defense of populations at risk could not be more stark. As LiPuma and others have argued, the Black-Scholes formula must imagine a closed circuit of market exchange without the broader social mediation of risk that might interpellate citizen subjects or indeed populations in general. What happens when the social is reintroduced into pricing assessment? The social is already an abstraction in the calculation, immanent in the ambivalence of price and value. LiPuma makes the basic materialist point that both the institutional development of mathematics and market practices are socially specific. The aura of expertise and the nature of the instantaneously global obfuscate the concrete situatedness of market mechanisms, as if the right price is the only right in play. This vital aspect of globalization LiPuma calls "the objectification of abstract risk" and it is worth wondering the extent to which it is generalizable as a global logic. Put another way, the protocols of financial risk management are embedded by globalization as a justifiable risk of being a global citizen or world subject, and no universal declaration was necessary to make this so. Of course, in the finance industry itself there are many metonymic versions of such subjectivation, like the value-at-risk function deployed to assess international bank capital requirements in the Basel Accord of 1996. In a portfolio society, the subject of rights is overdetermined by risk and return; indeed, anywhere that products and services are underwritten by capital outlays—we might say the subject is constantly "credited," irrespective of volition, consciousness, or personal identification. To be sure, this is not the subsumption of natural law into property law, whose imbrication is as old as divine freedom itself. No, from this perspective human rights in the era of securitization present civil society as a market index, as contingent upon terms that are not reducible to state mandate or simply bound to state-derived obligations. On one level, there is a tendency to wish that capital would revert to its default divisions, so that finance, for instance, could be safely quarantined as the "merely speculative" and the human subject of rights could be reassessed in its autonomy. From another perspective, however, there is a utopian desire regarding the spread of financialization, that its saturation will accelerate the collapse of the system that sustains it, and that the commodification of human rights is a mediatory moment in such catastrophe. In the latter scenario, it is not enough that securitization produces insecurity: it is that it presages a collapse of security functions specific to capital in general. If the value of the human has been circumscribed by the value forms of capital and labor then the value of rights must surely be transformed by their prospective eclipse? Unfortunately, such questions are held in abeyance by other features of globalization in the current conjuncture. There is, for instance, a way back into capitalism's distributive dysfunctions, especially where it deigns to divide political from economic obligations. This is what I would call its second nature, its profligate personhood.

If financialization within globalization produces a subject for capital circulation, then the question of corporate equal rights before the law further accentuates how this subject can be cathected to capital demands. True, while corporate personhood is not new, the United States in particular has made a virtue of this ruse of rights representation. Roscoe Conkling, for one, argued in 1882 that the 14th Amendment on equal protection should extend to corporations, and more recently the Citizens United decision of 2010 affirmed the First Amendment rights of corporations to engage in political speech (by speaking freely through indirect campaign contributions, for instance). In the latter case, the Supreme Court majority opinion took the position that the government should not interfere in the "marketplace of ideas"—a telling phrase that links corporate personhood to commodity relations in general. In a dissenting opinion, Justice Stevens argued that corporate independent expenditures are not an embodiment of the First Amendment, which protects individual self-expression, self-realization, and the communication of ideas. Rather, corporate spending should be viewed as a business transaction, as an investment based on profitability. At this level, the right to free speech is merely a fig leaf for the exercise of raw monetary power, where equal protection fosters "personhood" of unequal capacities. Legal personhood has become controversial in part because it seems to bracket in advance the possibility of the human in its rights discourse.

But acting under the silhouette of personhood also permits corporations to influence policy as equally interested stakeholders. If the bundling of risk in securitization helps to render liability an abstraction, then the privatization of protection from, say, economic harm inexorably places social decision in the (small) hands of bottom-line priorities. There are already many cases in the water industry where the corporation assumes the right over water as a risk in return, effectively pricing the right to water beyond the poor and the vulnerable. Here one non-state actor, an NGO, must compensate for another non-state actor, a corporation, as the true purveyor of human interest, yet neither are necessarily the embodiment of a community of rights, those perhaps who might collectively vote their priorities according to public power. This is not a tussle between minimal and maximal risk but a matter of how social responsibility is priced, secured. Similarly, while the language of subcontracting is now entrenched it is accompanied by a tranching of social action in which the corporation in its responsible personhood can justly claim decisive participation (or not, depending on its own version of risk assessment). It is not that any diminution of state power is to be questioned but that mediating functions are being overwritten by contentious claims to risk and security that the market itself is supposed to arbitrate. In this light, personhood is not symptomatic of the right to sanction but, rather, it precisely signals the displacement of rights in general.

For those who doubt sometimes whether the current leader of the "free world" is human at all, the story of corporate personhood has been a long-standing material correlative. Again, the notions of corporate man as either holistic or atomized are not new in themselves: it is the basis of their corroboration, or what we might call "liability," that is recalibrating what is extant of the human in human rights in its constitutive consistency. According to this logic, the liquification of homo economicus with state leadership is the apotheosis of the effulgence of "persons of (accrued) interest" where humans as humans might have been. Thus, as we have noted, the 14th Amendment on due process (originally to protect freed slaves) has long been cynically viewed as capitalist doublespeak: constitutional protections commensurate with personhood are combined with abjuring the same legal processes when prosecution might be at hand. At those moments the best mechanism for avoiding due process (and taxes) is a geographic adherence to minimal rights—basically statelessness. Indeed, a transnational corporation like Nike goes one better—why pretend to have an office in Bermuda when one can have "Nike Innovate CV," a utopian space that exists only in the minds of their tax accountants—how can we pay taxes, they argue, in a place that does not exist? Alternatively, in the United States, where money and politics traditionally and passionately embrace, few would have predicted their enthusiastic coupling would be guaranteed by the First Amendment, where the right to free expression becomes the right to freely express corporate protections. Personhood is basically state protections for supra-state transactions: it is the calculation not of what is rightfully human, but of what is selectively human according to the laws of capital circulation and value realization. Like security, personhood is not an absolute: it offers, ironically, all the fungibility of strategic essentialism or, for corporate theorists, what might be called "reverse hybridity mismatch," personhood as essentially a statistical foible.

The principles of personhood have been used to negotiate corporate malfeasance rather than prosecute it to such an extent it has been introjected as a state paradigm—it has become a cost of rights in general and a cost of the right to reproduce this economic substantiality in particular. Again, this does not ratify a subject but guarantees the right to personhood as proxy. A third dimension generalizes this condition in the antinomy of core rights and core commodities. It is the sign of political economy that cannot be undone simply by shifting the logic of capital circulation onto the limits of a sovereign state form. The stateless, the refugee, the migrant, those seeking political asylum, might collectively be characterized as failed state subjects (even if this is far from being a shared condition as such) but even when the social and political paroxysms are legible in producing their movement, the role of transborder economic logic often goes unremarked precisely because it follows such movement. Yet transnational capital of this kind is not a flight from failed sovereignty so much as an expression of sovereignty in flight. Neoliberalism remains Janus-faced about the fate of the state, because its partiality for individual entrepreneurialism and free markets is not necessarily averse to state contracts or institutional securitization (both through guaranteeing money and in the provision of military might). While the specter of state solidarity of the Global South had represented a major and potentially fatal challenge to the imperial preconditions of the Peace of Westphalia, the general collapse of state infrastructure is a greater fear because it renders the accumulation of property itself insecure. The fundamental rights to food, water, and shelter are not necessarily diminished by rescaling self-determination, yet undoing market prerogatives in core commodities in particular underlines the difficulties in maintaining the rights of non-state actors (distinct, of course, from terrorists and corporate stands ins). Some say Article 28 of the UDHR is impossible to achieve in the current world system ("Everyone is entitled to a social and international order in which the rights and freedoms set forth in this Declaration can be fully realized"), where profits are to be made, geopolitical and otherwise, in rewarding dictatorships and authoritarianism, or where fiscal responsibility can be off-shored or rendered conveniently abstract. The phrase "fully realized" in Article 28 is deeply prescient, because whatever is sought in the right cannot be made commensurable with "full realization" in capitalism's value form. Both are horizons rather than goals, yet the horizon of one often recedes in direct proportion to the realization of the other.

The passage from core commodities to core rights can be rendered as legally negotiable, but as Marx once noted with regard to the demands of capital and labor over the working day, "there is here, therefore, an antinomy, right against right, both equally bearing the seal of the law of exchanges. Between equal rights, force decides" (*Capital*, Volume One). One could think of this in terms of the Cochabamba "water wars," for instance, in which the forces of water privatization (companies like Bechtel, etc.) were dealt a significant rebuke by a broad popular movement. Given the struggles over water access and management since, Cochabamba now marks something of a skirmish, with the war over water operating at the scale of globalization itself. Thus, the lessons of Cochabamba may usefully be connected to recent water crises in Detroit and Puerto Rico, but particularly the Dakota Access Pipeline protests at Standing Rock that began in 2016. The moment of solidarity around the latter was important on so many levels, not just in the forceful connections made within and among Sioux tribes, but in the substantial claims of indigenous rights and resources in general (including access to clean water). The message was clear: the privatization of core commodities is central to the antinomy of rights and security, between human rights and contemporary neoliberal capitalism.

So how do these three elements inform a political economy of rights, beyond the depressing insistence that tiny hands can manage global risk by executive order? Because most human rights discourses have arisen within conditions of capitalism as a posited norm they tend to be reactive and reformist, but not absolutely so. The security of securitization, the personhood of corporatism, and the commodification of basic conditions of life, reveal the limits of rights discourse whenever globalization's baseline in political economy is left in place. The trans and supranationalism of such discourses have intensified under neoliberalism in part because the latter is also interested in the strategic disarticulation of state sovereignty. Populism putatively stands against both forms of globalism, yet it is an ideology supple and differentiated enough to sacrifice the claims of one in the service of maintaining the other. Populism's version of political reform, therefore, would seem to challenge market machination yet pushes far harder against human rights that might supersede the protections actually girding protectionism. An overarching hesitation within globalization concerns the relationship between the above elements and neoliberalism's overall push for privatization. In a world of limited liability, privatization legalizes the retreat from moral and/or economic obligations and effectively minimizes the terms of any social contract (debt can be socialized; property, not so much). Of course, there are more obvious moments when rights are suspended—the occasional shock doctrine and the imminence of terror divide and diminish in similar ways, while there are rarely clauses in the language and practice of offshoring and subcontracting that purport to be an enhancement of human rights. The political economy of rights historically points to a much more flexible regard to universality which means less that rights are simply subject to, for instance, capitalist imperatives, but that rights are the sum of material conditions which include both economic and social forces. The latter are greater even than the small hands that otherwise embrace them, and that is both a resource of hope and inevitably one of danger. Once one has justifiably peeled away the shibboleths and pieties that attend normative rights discourses, the political challenges reposition the scales of opposition. There are certainly rights to be fought and won, but if their basis does not shake the central axes of capital logic, including the commandment that is private property, then securitization will continue to overdetermine the social security of rights itself and the hands that can actually hold them.

David Harvey has suggested that neoliberalism means the financialization of everything (33). Here we might think of small hands not just in terms of greedy financiers, or their powerful gatekeepers in high governmental office, but also as that which intimates a scalar saturation of the everyday, so that securitization becomes an extension or confirmation of the cost of living. This can be discerned, for instance, in the otherwise mundane provisions of retirement infrastructures, both public and private, that use financialization to secure well-being beyond the sale of labor. Rather than think of this as simply inexorable complicity, attention to the financialization of the individual offers a way into new forms of counter-hegemonic delinking in which the relay of human rights becomes disruptive. How? First, the differentiation of human rights into positive and negative represents a material grammar of disjunction. What is proper to property is a rights discourse for the individual but it is not immanently secure across its relations. This means distinguishing rights that are preventative from those that are obligatory. The conservative reading of such difference often makes state obligations over entitlements an equivalent of coercion vis-à-vis individual liberty. Given the characteristics of globalization outlined above and the porosity of borders for financialization, it is easy to see how corporate personhood might exploit the space of this disjunction. Neoliberalism, from this perspective, is the transubstantiation of rights through which genuine demands of the subject qua the state are displaced by, for instance, a signifying logic linking the privacy of the individual to the private, privatization, and privation. Thus, a positive right as resistance is not simply the defense of the individual, but the deconstruction of personhood as a function of property. Such a counter-displacement is also counter-intuitive because it necessitates the promulgation of a certain insecurity, albeit around the notion of securitization itself.

Second, and following from this, neoliberalism's commodification of primary means of sustainability paradoxically makes risk management a condition for the production of populations at risk. The lesson of water privatization in this regard underlines both the prescience of local organization in challenging the nostrums of accumulation by dispossession, and the necessity of a trans-local networked solidarity, one that would permit the articulation of a right to water back along its commodity chain to the source, as it were, of risky pricing. The global reconstitution of rights thus also entails a collocation and co-location of contemporary neoliberal logic, specifically in the synergy of financialization with corporate transnationalism. For some, this would mean principally using the state as a rights lever, one that would call to account pricing and privatization as a matter of law. This is not an unproblematic strategy since states within globalization always factor in questions of comparative advantage, that can include protecting those businesses that produce it (as well as sustaining a more traditional comprador desire to engage for personal advantage). Yet this is where rights discourses have to interrogate the structural components of risk and link rights to risks at a global scale. The defamiliarization of security, personhood, and commodification does not in itself place rights in the hands best able to shape their inalienability across populations and states, citizen subjects or not. If the limits of international financial institutions are by now well known, this has done little to allay the fears that transnational NGOs have a tendency to reproduce them (and not just because they often work in tandem with such institutions). The intercession of rights is initially a reading practice of how globalization currently proceeds, and thus it attends to capital logic. By contesting the grounds of capitalism's concepts of security, the reader of rights can better articulate a global security more worthy of the term, and fathom a global populace that can legitimately hold it.

Works Cited

Baxi, Upendra. 2007. *The Future of Human Rights.* 3rd ed. Oxford: Oxford University Press.

Chomsky, Noam. 2007. *Failed States: The Abuse of Power and the Assault on Democracy.* New York: Holt.

De Feyter, Koen. 2005. *Human Rights: Social Justice in the Age of the Market.* London: Zed Books.

Dienst, Richard. 2011. *The Bonds of Debt: Borrowing Against the Common Good.* New York: Verso.

Harvey, David. 2007. *A Brief History of Neoliberalism.* Oxford: Oxford University Press.

LiPuma, Edward. 2017. *The Social Life of Financial Derivatives.* Durham: Duke University Press.

Marx, Karl. 1992. *Capital.* Vol. 1. Translated by Ben Fowkes. London: Penguin.

———. 1993. *Capital.* Vol. 3. Translated by David Fernbach. London: Penguin.

Nash, Kate. 2013. "Global Capitalism and Human Rights." *Journal of Globalization Studies* 4 (1, May): 63–77.

Rancière, Jacques. 2004. "Who Is the Subject of the Rights of Man?" *South Atlantic Quarterly* 103 (2/3, Spring/Summer): 297–310.

PART II

Securitization, Toxicity, and the Future of Rights

CHAPTER 8

The Littoral Combat Ship, or the Designs of Liquid Sovereignty

Diren Valayden

In a discussion paper for the US Agency for International Development, James G. Stavridis and Reuben E. Brigety (2012) argue that the challenges of national security in a post-Cold War world can only be met through the joint efforts of the military, diplomatic, humanitarian, and development sectors. They call this new approach "strategic humanitarianism," one that combines "combat and compassion" within the framework of a rights-based approach to development. On paper, "strategic humanitarianism" evokes traditional counter-insurgency programs designed to pacify populations through development aid alongside military intervention (cf. Wall et al. 2017). As Stavridis and Brigety acknowledge, their proposal could be perceived as a militarization of humanitarian aid, or as others have argued, the instrumentalization of human rights principles for military ends (Perugini and Gordon 2015; Douzinas 2007). "Strategic humanitarianism," however, goes beyond the

D. Valayden (✉)
Binghamton University, Binghamton, NY, USA
e-mail: valayden@binghamton.edu

A. S. Moore and S. Pinto (eds.), *Writing Beyond the State*, Palgrave Studies in Literature, Culture and Human Rights,
https://doi.org/10.1007/978-3-030-34456-6_8

incorporation of humanitarian and human rights law into military training. It provides an epistemological basis for a range of dominant actors to view crises as "complex" and ongoing, and the international justification (under the pretext of "conflict prevention" and "conflict resolution") to restructure whole societies by reforming their security apparatuses (cf. Civic and Miklaucic 2011; Commission on Human Security 2003).

The governance of "complex" crises implies, since the turn of the century, the novel yoking of development and security, whereby, as Mark Duffield (2014, 2) argues, "underdevelopment" is treated as "dangerous" and aid policy has shifted from technical assistance—US President Truman's 1949 "Point Four speech" was emblematic of this technicist approach—to "conflict resolution and societal transformation." As Duffield points out, "complex" crises require responses that go "beyond the capabilities or legitimacy of individual Northern governments" and thus draw in "governments, NGOs, military establishments and private companies" in new "strategic networks and complexes" (2). This new development-security nexus signals a shift in North–South relations, "from hierarchical and territorial relations of governments to polyarchical, non-territorial and networked relations of governance" (2). In this context, I want to suggest that the basis for warfare is being rethought. In other words, the development-security nexus and the shift in the nature of global relations it signals have epistemological implications for the understanding, justification, and waging of war. Consequently, we need to rethink the critique of war in terms of the vested interests of a military-industrial complex (i.e. parasitic defense corporations influencing public policy for profits). Rather, warfare has become part of a global system of governance that simultaneously includes securitization and the forestalling of imminent catastrophes (Ophir 2010).

Stavridis and Brigety (2012, 50), while painting the United States as the standard-bearer of a new global moral order, acknowledge the operational challenges that are all but nudging us in a post-Westphalian order of sovereign states. In their view, the NATO operation in Libya displayed all the dimensions of a complex crisis: while warplanes were bombing military targets, humanitarian emergencies were developing all over the country and beyond. First, there was the need to repatriate expat workers from countries unable to carry out airlift operations for their nationals (e.g. Nigeria and Bangladesh). Second, the hastily constructed migrant camps in Tunisia and Egypt were quickly overwhelmed, meaning that the emergency increased the risk of region-wide social and political destabilization. In response, several UN agencies together with the involved NATO militaries were forced to carry out, in their words, "one of the largest humanitarian airlifts in history." The characterization of the mission as a "humanitarian airlift," of course, obscures the fact that the bombing campaign itself contributed to the humanitarian emergency: the military campaign had initiated and subsequently managed an imminent catastrophe. In this situation, as the first missiles are fired, a "complex" operation is simultaneously set in motion—one that involves private interests, different countries that provide logistical support, and NGOs and UN agencies that contribute to risk mitigation. The involvement of "strategic networks and complexes" in managing emergencies means that, as Adi Ophir (2010) has argued, "no sovereign can claim today a monopoly over the [declaration of a state of] exception" because determining the threshold of catastrophe itself becomes contested and ambiguous.[1]

The loss of state monopoly over "the exception," the means of violence, and "territoriality" (Sassen 2000) has not led to a general "uncertainty" or "incalculability" (in terms of governance), as some theorists of risk societies emphasize (Beck 2009). Instead, I want to stress here that all kinds of techniques and technologies, drawing their methodologies and epistemologies from architecture, design, or urban planning, have been put in place to mitigate risks and to plan for future disasters (Collier and Lakoff 2015). Rather than the end of sovereignty, we are witnessing the metamorphosis of its categories beyond the "Westphalian fiction of the timeless territorial integrity of nation-states" (Bystrom and Slaughter 2018, 7), a work of translation that is being undertaken by various military and security analysts and practitioners who seek to ground armed intervention spatially, normatively, and ontologically. Though the noisy debates about a "clash of civilizations" have tended to obscure this more insidious reinvention of sovereignty post-9/11, what we are witnessing is the attempt (already underway) to embed warfare as the general horizon and orientation of social life. Worked upon in various sectors and by myriad professionals, practitioners, and entities, we are and have been planning as Hiba Bou Akar (2018) argues in her analysis of Beirut, "for the war yet to come."

In this essay, I analyze the US Navy's new warship, the Littoral Combat Ship (hereafter, LCS), as exemplary of the new work of grounding war and armed intervention spatially, normatively, and ontologically. Indeed, the LCS can be read as a concrete attempt to define a new urban spatiality, the littoral, that can be made legible to future war planning. The "urban littoral" emerged in two US Navy white papers, as a new spatial category into which warfare can be projected in an age where wars between states are disappearing. It defined the littoral as the area on land reachable by sea-based weapons, and the sea equivalent that can be affected by land-based attacks.[2] In the urban littoral, it is projected that humanitarian emergencies and military action will become part of the fabric of life itself. In other words, the urban littoral emerges from the US Navy's white papers as an "imaginative geography" (Said 1979) wherein the reinvention of post-Westphalian sovereignty might be beheld and analyzed. My analysis shows how design thinking has become key to this reinvention. Owing to its modular design, the LCS seeks to naturalize the interchangeability of humanitarian and military missions. Designed to operate at the threshold of combat and compassion, the LCS thus embeds "strategic humanitarianism" by virtue of its very existence. I will conclude with a reflection on the implications of the naturalization of combat and compassion for the liberal rights regime: rights discourse cannot be imagined as an outside from which a critique of military violence can be mounted.

The Urban Spatiality of the Littoral

In September 1992, the US Navy published a white paper (*...From the Sea*) that announced a "new strategic direction" and declared "a fundamental shift away from open-ocean warfighting *on the sea* toward joint operations conducted *from the sea*" (emphasis mine). The declaration of a fundamental shift was no overstatement in this context, for the document indeed tore up the foundational concept, "open-ocean warfighting," that had guided maritime strategy from the nineteenth century to the end of the Cold War. The Navy announced "a shift in focus to littoral operations" (operations in coastal zones, as opposed to on the high seas) as global threats recede in comparison to regional challenges, but warned: "Mastery of the littoral should not be presumed. It does not derive directly from command of the high seas. It is an objective which requires our focused skills and resources." In a second paper, published two years later, *Forward...From the Sea*, the new emphasis was further confirmed, noting that the "vital interests"—economic, political, and military interests "for which the United States is willing to fight"—lie at the "endpoint of 'highways of the seas' [...] that stretch from the United States to the farthest point on the globe."

In the thinking of Alfred T. Mahan and Sir Julian Corbett, the two strategists who shaped naval warfare for much of the twentieth century, navies fought on the open seas and armies focused on land operations. The littoral was reduced to an issue of *tactical* maneuvers but not of *strategic* thinking. It is indeed the spectral presence of Mahan and Corbett that is being exorcized by the two position papers of the US Navy. Mahan, along with fellow Navy-enthusiast Theodore Roosevelt, played a key role in defining the US Navy's strategic thinking as President of the US Naval War College (Karsten 1971). Both men saw the importance of building a modern imperial fleet that could confer command of the seas to the United States. But it was Mahan (1890) who *conceptually* framed the fate of nations and empires in terms of their "sea power." It is to him that the Navy owes the formulation of the seas as a "great highway" (25) and of "warfighting on the sea" as the quintessence of "control of the seas." In Mahan's view, since sea commerce is of vital importance to the wealth of nations, the protection of economic interests has often led to violent confrontations; yet, wars over political interests that were unrelated to sea commerce have also been influenced "in their conduct and issue" by "control of the sea." "Therefore," he argues, "the history of sea power, while embracing in its broad sweep all that tends to make a people great upon the sea or by the sea, is largely a military history" (1).

If in Mahan we might locate the ideological and political component of the US Navy's strategic thinking throughout the twentieth century, in Corbett we may find the more sober, philosophical one. Corbett (1911) translated Clausewitz's thinking, which he deemed too continental, into maritime strategy, in order to postulate a theory of naval warfare and to anchor the notion of "command of the sea" in scientific principles. Command of the sea, according to Corbett, "means nothing but the control of maritime communications, whether for commercial or military purposes. The object of naval warfare is the control of communications (on which the life of a nation depends), and not, as in land warfare, the conquest of territory" (90). "The object of naval warfare must always be directly or indirectly either to secure the command of the sea or to prevent the enemy from securing it" (87). Despite Corbett's scientific aspirations, it is a very biblical imagery that underpins his theory of command of the sea, for the high seas are viewed as a "barrier" that the Royal Navy both opens up for Britain to influence events in distant lands and shuts down to prevent enemy attacks. Command of the sea can never be absolute. It remains in a "state of dispute," and naval strategy is concerned with securing it, because unlike territory it can never be possessed (87–90).

"Sea power" and "command of the sea" held for much of the twentieth century as the two strategic concepts of sovereign claims upon the world and its oceans. By the end of the Cold War, however, US naval strategy would be turned upside down—and with it, the *place* of sovereignty *in the world*. In a paper published in 1995 in the *Naval War College Review*, titled "The Littoral Arena," Rear Admiral Yedidia Ya'ari (1995) of the Israeli Navy first sketched out the dramatic shifts in naval thinking that would have to accompany a change of focus from command of the sea to littoral warfare, not least, "the implications it [the littoral arena] has for prevailing concepts of ship design." The journal republished the article in 2018, describing it as "an analytical performance worthy of any Old Testament prophet" (Hughes 2018, 97). The prophecy was not simply a question of strategy and conceptual innovation, for it went further and defined a whole new space for military intervention, and hence a new way of seeing and relating to the world.

In the littoral, Ya'ari contends, threats are not only defined by their "intensity" but by their "density." Warships patrolling the littoral are not only forced "to maintain a constant, all-dimensional state of alert" because of the threat of attack at any moment from modern radar-guided surface-to-sea missiles, but also have to deal with a "clutter" situation, in the form of "civilian tankers, freighters, fishing boats, and aircraft going about their daily business" (83). The crew is thus placed under severe stress because the ship is a "constant target in the littoral," and the survivability of the ship and its crew "requires as a normal operating mode the highest level of *everything, all the time*" (87, emphasis in original). The problem for the US Navy is that its ships were designed to operate and fight on the open ocean. The survivability of a fleet could be created through synergy, that is, "by combining several types of ships, with the capabilities of one compensating for the deficiencies of others" (84). Such "defense in depth" is not possible in the littoral, not only because of clutter, but also because smart missiles, which can be launched in salvos, make the warships constant targets. The ships built for the open ocean are thus unsuited for the littoral where maneuverability is vital: "One can certainly carry a big stick with today's surface ships; it is hard to walk softly, harder still to walk safely" (89).

Ya'ari concludes that even as the US Navy's two position papers announced a shift in strategic thinking, in terms of ship design, "the paradigm is still the historic battles of the forties in the Atlantic and Pacific." Writing in 1995, Ya'ari contends that "we are entering the next century, and also a dramatic transition from the open ocean to the shallow seas, with a severe lack of relevant experience" (93). To regain maneuverability in a cluttered geographical space, the US Navy sought to commission a specific warship at the turn of the millennium: LCS. But the littoral is also an urban concept in the Navy's imaginary: "clutter," or such "civilian tankers, freighters, fishing boats, and aircraft going about their daily business," evokes a particular spatial imaginary. Clutter exists close to ports, in busy channels connecting seas and oceans, and in waterways that link maritime trade. The urban is here extended to include the territorial waters claimed by a state, together with the air, underwater, and cyberspaces that it controls. The whole "volume" of a given spatial configuration is taken into account, and not simply the area to be targeted (Elden 2013). The littoral is thus all that extends and emerges from the social fabric of urban existence itself.

It should not be surprising, therefore, that the LCS program originated from a ship-design concept known as the "streetfighter." The new streetfighter ships, proposed in a 1999 paper by Vice Admiral Arthur Cebrowski and Captain Wayne P. Hughes, Jr. (1999), embodied the new strategic direction of the Navy by equipping warships to fight in the littoral regions of the world. As the authors argue, the streetfighter's "core task" is to "compete for control of the enemy's 'streets' – his home waters [and] back alleys" consisting of small islands and shallow waters where "blue-water Navy" cannot operate. "His unsafe streets are cluttered with coastal traders, fishing boats, oil rigs, and boat people of all types who may be innocent or hostile," and it will fall to the streetfighter to "clear out the clutter and sort friend from foe." At a time when urban warfare was beginning to weigh heavily on military minds occupied with the recent Balkan wars and, for the US military, the nightmare of Mogadishu, the littoral was being imagined as a new category of urban space.

The urbanization of naval warfare and strategy has become even more apparent today, as Western militaries readily speak of the "urban littoral" as combat combining the "worst of both worlds" i.e. the intensity and density of the city and the coastal spaces (McCarthy 2018). In the "urban littoral" war means engagement in spaces that are densely populated with civilians, that contain the licit and illicit circuitries of population movements and commercial life, and that house the critical infrastructures that sustain urbanization. That is, an interface must be found between violence and the rhythm of city life itself (cf. Graham 2011). In such a situation, a humanitarian crisis is always imminent, giving a seabound dimension to the concept of "the three block war." Modern military operations might involve traditional warfighting, peacekeeping, and humanitarian missions within three contiguous city blocks. The infamous mission creep—the gradual increase of the number of objectives to be accomplished beyond the original scope of the military intervention—seems to be inevitable. As such, while the urban littoral provided the Navy with a new challenge, it was also an opportunity to update its fleet. The LCS was born as a new program for projecting power in an urbanizing world where combat and compassion could be launched from the same platform.

The Norm and Form of the LCS Program

The military's appetite for new weapons cannot be simply explained nor fully described by the notion of a military-industrial complex, i.e. in terms of the ways through which defense corporations influence public policy. At stake is a new relationship between "war-making" and "state-making" (Tilly 1985), or between violence and sovereignty. Many have already argued that the so-called war on terror has upset the spatial and temporal distinctions between war and peace: Derek Gregory (2011) speaks of an "everywhere war" whereby the modalities of war are extended across societies beyond conventional battlefields, while others have noted how the "war on terror" eschews the conventional distinctions between wartime and peacetime (Dudziak 2012). Since the turn of the century, wars have not only made and remade states in the Global South but the impact of the war on terror has itself changed the character of life on the so-called homefront. At an astonishing pace, these changes have been felt across the spheres of law enforcement and its militarization, border management, the liberal rights regime, and the management of crises and emergencies. This diffused character of war means there is no normative "outside" or principle of limitation on sovereign violence. The absolute authority to kill and maim is claimed in the name of humanity, human rights, freedom, and security.

The diffusion of endless warfare everywhere does not imply that war is delocalized. As I argued above, cities are increasingly seen as the sites of war—a state of affairs evolving in the context of "urbanization without development," or urban growth without the investment in infrastructure and public services that normatively accompanies urbanization (Davis 2006). For many security and military analysts, the link between under-development and violence seem to be inevitable. The 2002 *National Security Strategy of the United States* (2002, 1) spelled it out clearly:

"America is now threatened less by conquering states than we are by failing ones." Military and security analysts speak of nothing short of a "new development and security paradigm" ushered in by 9/11, one that treats "complex emergencies and fragile states" as security problems (Natsios 2005). The key challenge is the integration of apparently disparate and conflicting elements such as humanitarianism, development, the liberal rights regime, and warfare within a single framework. The term "complexity" has increasingly served the ideological purposes of systematizing rights-based development, humanitarian actions, and war within a system of governance that has eventually surpassed the international system of nation-states.[3]

Into the world of so-called complex systems, enter the LCS, a weapon whose design reveals much about this brave new world of warfighting on the urban littoral. The idea for the LCS program was born in the Department of Defense Office for Force Transformation (OFT), which was set up by then Secretary of Defense Donald Rumsfeld in October 2001. The tasks given to OFT were to transform US military capabilities and to generate new concepts for war-making in the twenty-first century. When first conceived, the LCS program would have equipped the US Navy with 52 new ships, or close to 15% of the fleet. The first ship was launched in 2005, and up to 2015, a total of 23 had been funded. By then, the program had faltered. Initially budgeted at $250m per ship, it had also more than doubled in cost. The first ships suffered mechanical, structural, and maintenance failures, and combat-readiness was significantly off schedule due to design problems (Axe 2011). The littoral concept was itself proving to be a hard sell, with the new administration's Secretary of the Navy, Ray Mabus, declaring the need for a name change: "Well, if it's like a frigate, let's call it a frigate [...] It will be the same ship, the same program of record, just with an appropriate and traditional name" (quoted in LaGrone 2015). And so, the ship was renamed a frigate and up-gunned. While the ship's name might have changed, the core principles that guided the LCS program remained intact.

Of those core principles, the LCS program's focus on modularity is what concerns me most here. The LCS has been described as "a program to pursue a modular small combatant" (Wills 2016). Two models, built by General Dynamics and Lockheed Martin, have to date been commissioned. Rather than focusing on each model, I will summarize, for brevity and clarity, their characteristics and consider them as one ship design, the LCS. The emphasis on size means that maneuverability is greatly enhanced; the USS Freedom (the first LCS commissioned by the US Navy in 2008) has a speed of 47 knots compared to the roughly 30 knots of most destroyers and frigates in operation. It has a flight deck for helicopter launch, as well as capabilities to transport and deploy unmanned autonomous vehicles. The core innovation lies in its modular design: the sensor and weapons suites are separated from the hull, meaning that a variety of mission modules can be swapped in according to strategic and operational needs. This "plug and play" function signals the LCS's attraction as the vessel that embodies the new strategic direction of the US Navy, wherein the breadth and variety of naval missions are foundational to naval power. When first envisaged, at least 90 mission modules were proposed to be used for deterrence, crisis response and management, and humanitarian assistance, as well as conventional naval fighting capabilities such as mine, anti-submarine, and anti-surface warfare. The modules are designed to be able to fit into standard-sized containers that can be carried on the ship or airlifted when needed.

The LCS is a low signature warship—that is, it was designed with a reduced radar profile with the littoral arena clearly in mind. Since detection is unavoidable in littoral regions, because of radar saturation and surveillance technologies (in addition to the presence of old-fashioned civilian vessels that can report back the sighting of warships), the goal is to delay it as much as possible. Once detected, then, the ship must use its maneuverability to avoid enemy attacks. In addition to its reduced radar profile and its maneuverability, and given the fact that it can operate in shallow waters, the LCS is designed to have more port access than the traditional vessels that have operated as part of a blue water navy. This is crucial to the US Maritime Strategy, as laid out in the 2015 document *A Cooperative Strategy for 21st Century Seapower*. If the first foundational principle of US Maritime Strategy is "forward naval presence" (i.e. military presence across all corners of the globe), the second is the creation of a "global network of navies" through joint operations with allies and partners across the planet (Dunford et al. 2015, 2).

Like all modern warships, the LCS was designed with the latest cyber technologies available, following a trend in securitization that seeks to tilt the human–machine interface in favor of the latter (Gros 2012). Automating various aspects of the ship means it requires a reduced crew size compared to traditional warships, thus providing another cost-cutting incentive for the US Navy. A reduced crew operating a networked architecture forces personnel to multitask on board the vessel, leading to a rigorous training program. This has led the US Navy to embrace a simulation program (the San Diego-based "LCS University") similar to its Air Force counterpart, whereby the crew is trained on land before active duty (Prine 2017). For the LCS, the Navy has abandoned rotating crews on- and off-board, and instead uses two teams that rotate on the same ship, thus increasing "ownership" and ensuring that maintenance is carried out (Cordle 2017; Navy 2016). The crew flies home instead of rotating to another ship that takes them back, and the LCS remains deployed. Thus, the small crew size of the LCS along with automation has allowed innovation at the level of organizational behavior.

Crewing a vessel might seem a simple case of economics, but it fits within the US Navy's new concept of "dispersed lethality" that emerged from a 2014 LCS wargame intended to shift the LCS program to a frigate variant. Dispersed lethality relies on dispersing rather than concentrating force, thus enabling strikes at enemies anytime and anyplace. Hence, surface combatants need crews that are trained and battle-ready at all times. Ownership over a vessel, in this scenario, increases its preparedness because it is adequately maintained. If surface combatants have been generally used to defending more valuable units, such as submarines and aircraft carriers, dispersed lethality puts emphasis on upgrading every ship's offensive power so that they might also be called in for offensive strategies. Those warships could now take on an enemy fleet that might try to deny sea access to the US Navy (anti-access and sea denial being two of the major preoccupations of post-Cold War strategy). Finally, dispersed lethality seeks to make use of the possibilities offered by cyber technologies to connect the individual units of the fleet to each other. Each warship thus acts as the communication node in a vast network deployed over the globe.

A crucial component of the LCS was that its platform architecture would include its ability to operate at the threshold of complexity. Within current military discourse, complexity represents an obscure object of desire: it is the image of the world on which strategy is modeled, and it is at the same time, something that is malleable to willpower and suitable weapons systems. At the same time, according to military understandings of complexity, achieving total knowledge of complex systems is impossible. Hence, strategy and operations will always have to work with imperfect knowledge. The LCS was designed to turn this kind of epistemological uncertainty into an advantage, using its modular design to make adversaries guess whether it was on a humanitarian or military mission. I argue that in fact, modularity allows the LCS to naturalize the relationship between violence and normative principles of humanitarianism. That is, military humanitarianism does not simply involve an ideological or instrumental relationship, but a naturalization of the interchangeability of the principles of humanity and those of violence. This involves, moreover, implementing a relationship of deception through weapon design and military strategy. As I go on to argue in the next section, the condition of possibility for the naturalization of the relationship between violence and humanitarianism was the prospect of drawing on technological advantages through "network centric warfare" and the non-normative (and even anti-normative), process-oriented approach of design thinking. Those two forms of thinking allowed the LCS to be integrated into a novel way to rethink post-sovereign violence.

Hiding in Plain Sight

The idea of "network centric warfare" (NCW) emerged in the late 1990s as a way to rethink war for two putative reasons: (1) the economic, social, and technological ecosystems in which human beings operate have changed, so the military must follow suit, and (2) the enemies facing the United States are no longer predictable state actors. In their 1998 paper, Cebrowski and Garstka (1998) argue that "fundamental changes are affecting the very character of war. Who can make war is changing as a result of weapons proliferation and the fact that the tools of war increasingly are marketplace commodities[.] [These are changes that] affect the where, the when, and the how of war." Previous modes of warfare were "platform-centric," that is, they relied on deploying platforms such as planes, ships, or tanks in tactical formations. In contrast, war now needs to be network-centric. This means that war-makers need to leverage the capabilities offered by information technologies and direct war through the network itself. By linking all the elements of the military through the network, the "speed of command" increases and generates a competitive advantage in the battlefield. The nodes in the network also organize themselves from the bottom-up; commanders and regular troops (or "end-users," in a military language that increasingly borrows from management jargon) assemble to swarm the enemy and disassemble once the action is completed (cf. Bousquet 2008).

Rapid assembly and disassembly, emerging through decentralized command would ostensibly lead to the "self-synchronization" of fleets in battle. This kind of self-organization is designed to overcome a key factuality of warfare, namely that situational awareness deteriorates in the battlefield, or the fact, stated another way, that "no plan survives initial contact with the enemy" (Cebrowski and Garstka 1998). Thus, the infinite tactical innovations that self-synchronized fleets can generate aims to reduce and obliterate what Carl Von Clausewitz ([1832] 1989, 119–121) called friction, or the "evil" that prevents a real war from approximating the ideal ("war on paper"). Friction, in Clausewitz's term is the "infinity of petty circumstances" that happen by chance, and which are impossible to calculate. Reducing fiction is thus a key goal of militaries in general. NCW manages friction in two different innovative ways. On the one hand, it follows many technologically determinist approaches that project the elimination of age-old obstacles through technological innovation. In Cebrowski and Grastka's plan, for instance, it is assumed that the shift from platform-centric to network-centric warfare will solve the problem of friction by leveraging the possibilities offered by new technologies.

On the other hand, however, NCW also inverts Clausewitz's theory. Whereas the old Prussian strategist was concerned about friction within his own troops, his contemporaries focus on how to increase its impact in enemy ranks. If Clausewitz ([1832] 1989, 120) declared that friction was "a force that theory can never quite define," today's theorists turn to complexity theory and design thinking as epistemological and methodological principles to weaponize friction. As Cebrowski once declared, success will lie in "manipulating complexity" and in the "ability to shift the terrible burden of warfare complexity and the risks it carrie[s] away from you onto your opponent" (quoted in Blaker 2006, 132).[4] A revamped naval fleet should be equipped to manipulate complexity through its tactics: swarming the enemy with large numbers of combat entities, and creating information overload by multiplying the variety of platforms leading the attack, united through their "dispersed lethality." With the LCS, something else was also proposed. By virtue of its very design (i.e. the platform architecture), the ship was to create "uncertainty as to mission and capabilities of a given platform" (Johnson and Cebrowski 2005, iii). In other words, the LCS embedded uncertainty in its very design. Along with tactics, design thinking (the likes of which produced the LCS as a weapon par excellence of NCW doctrine) emerges as key to the manipulations of complexity and risk.

As a general rule, design encapsulates both the end result and the process. In the case of the LCS and the modularity built into its design, the end result is the ability to have "plug-and-play" modules that allow a ship to shift between mission packages without being taken out of commission. Embedded within this type of platform is a thinking process that becomes compulsory for those who command the vessel: namely their "situation awareness" and their ability to maintain it must remain open ended and flexible, with effects for how and what solutions may be reached in combat. Given that the LCS is capable of switching between humanitarian and combat missions while at sea, it becomes less obvious to its adversaries what kind of ship they are facing. Military design thinking is geared toward fostering this problem-solving capability in its end users. Complexity theory or design thinking, in the hands of security and military analysts, has served key ideological roles in naturalizing the link between combat and compassion, and in making the two appear interchangeable. In complex and adaptive systems (as current wars are imagined), humanitarian emergencies and violent interventions are inevitable so the argument goes. Militaries and humanitarians are thus both engaged in neutralizing threats to humanity; the military fights insurgent or criminal groups that pose a threat to the global system, while humanitarians must prevent those displaced by warfighting from creating destabilizing ripple effects through the system.

The appeal of design—as methodology, field of practice, and style of thinking—to the new military thinkers of "complex systems" is obvious. As a methodology, design defines the range of practical skills that military personnel requires to master the relations between planning and execution, and thus also defines the skills and proficiencies needed to master the emergence of complexity (Banach and Ryan 2009). But design thinking is more than simply practical mastery; it always suggests what is possible and what the world might be. This inherent speculative quality opens the door for endless innovation in an organization that is anchored by hierarchy, ritual, sacrifice, and routine (Zweibelson et al. 2017). Through design thinking, innovation can function in much the same way as it does in the new economy: as catalyst and product. Design, as Bruno Latour (2008) argues, "is made to be interpreted in the language of signs," and collapses the distinction between the material and symbolic dimensions of things. As such, when we speak of the design of the LCS, we are speaking of the ship as a manipulator of signs—the platform capabilities (in terms of its lethality); its networked dimension (is it on its own or part of a dispersed fleet?); and its capability to shift mission packages. The goal of the military is to have a weapon that can *hide in plain sight* by blending with the "clutter" in the littoral and navigating at speed like its imagined enemies.

Even though the LCS is equipped with stealth capabilities, the emphasis is less on avoiding detection than on transforming the data that the enemy can generate about it into white noise by creating information overload in terms of its location, intent, and lethal capabilities. By creating complexity for the enemy, it stretches its own legibility in the information ecology of potential adversaries and embeds an "epistemology of deception" (Goldberg 2012). At gunpoint, the enemy is forced to be transparent about its intent, capabilities, and location, while the LCS is involved in "manipulating complexity." Complexity, design, and networking point toward this new modality of sovereign violence emerging not so much in law, but rather, in the vulgar discourses of the military. The LCS is the weapon system that has been created for societies that are constantly preparing for war: its 90 mission modules that can be swapped according to evolving complex crises provide flexibility to the warship. As importantly, modularity offers a degree of manipulating the appearance of the LCS, integrating its lethality among civilian traffic in the urban littoral. With its ability to blur the distinction between armed and humanitarian interventions—combat and compassion—it also aims to disable potential adversaries by hindering their decision-making processes. The danger with this system of disruption and deception is that it will also disable all normative principles, such as the system of rights and intervention in the name of humanity, by absorbing them within the new modalities of violence.

Conclusion

In the introduction, I alluded to the fact that warfare is now becoming part of the system of governance, and inevitably, is becoming gradually embedded in social life. Societies and especially cities are increasingly designed and planned according to the principles of "the war yet to come" (Bou Akar 2018). The justification for such planning is often based, we are told, on the unpredictability of attacks, the increasing and deliberate targeting of civilians, and vulnerability to system disruption. This new social disposition to fight wars necessitates a particular conceptualization of social life—life is increasingly viewed as complex. According to this new social ontology, warfighting will necessarily create or deepen humanitarian crises and human rights violations, and the military must be equally equipped to deal with those emergencies. The LCS is in some way a perfectly designed weapon, at least in theory, to fight such wars.

Its modular design allows it to switch between humanitarian and military missions as needed; its hull and speed allow it to navigate the shallow waters of coastal megacities where future urban warfare is projected to occur; its cyber capacities allow it to leverage a networked fleet in combat, etc. More importantly, according to its military proponents, it can leverage complexity to its own advantage in a world that is supposedly more complex.

Complexity, as one of its leading theorists, Edgar Morin (2005, 10), once argued is a "problem word and not a solution word." Complexity was supposed to eliminate reductionist accounts of the world, and in the process reveal relations, nonlinearity, and hetero-temporalities as modalities of social interaction. In Morin's account, "complex thought" would be a way to problematize scientific and humanistic inquiry into the contemporary human condition. While military thinkers have accepted the latter aspect of complexity as a problematic, they have also found in complexity a solution to rethink and project warfare in a post-Westphalian international system. Security and military analysts are concerned about how to fight a war in and around the coastal megacities of the Global South against irregular forces or against criminal elements who may harbor terrorist cells. Yet, such warfare in the urban littorals cannot be allowed to create major disruptions to the economic and political system, for repercussions will also be felt in the Global North given the high degree of global connectivity. Furthermore, population density in megacities means that violence will inevitably lead to humanitarian emergencies.

This knot of problems (humanitarian, developmental, armed intervention) has been approached in military discourse through the concept of complexity. Yet, labeling problems "complex" has also served as a solution for militaries to justify violence. This is because complexity is the solution word that allows the relationship between military intervention and humanitarianism to be naturalized. It makes the link between the lack of central governance (state authority) and violence appear as self-evident—a lack that can only be approached through combat and compassion. As I argued above, the process that links militarization and humanitarianism is embedded in the design of weapons systems while accompanying styles of thought—design thinking, complexity and systems theory, etc.—seek to modify the practices and behaviors of those involved in the security-development-humanitarian nexus. As it touches everyone, warfare extends beyond the confines of a military-industrial complex and permeates within a system of governance itself. The LCS might be a slice of the problem, but in its design we can glimpse a broader sketching of the designs of a post-sovereign global moral order.

Notes

1. Adi Ophir (2010, 79) has argued that creating and keeping a population "at the verge of a humanitarian catastrophe" has become a key component of post-sovereign governmentality. Since, this process of catastrophization draws in multiple agents (NGOs, International agencies, medical practitioners, militaries, monitoring agencies, states, etc.), determining the "threshold of catastrophe" is always contested, thus preventing sovereigns from declaring absolute authority over "the exception."
2. In international law, the strip of coastal sea over which states exercise territorial control was initially defined by the cannon-shot rule: sovereignty ended with the range of artillery fire. Initially 3 miles, now states claim 6–12 miles of territorial sovereignty over coastal waters. The 1982 United Nations Convention on the Law of the Sea further extended an Exclusive Economic Zone of two hundred nautical miles from the coast of any state.
3. David Chandler (2014) has labeled this development, security, humanitarian nexus as the "governance of complexity" pointing to the fact that practitioners in those fields increasingly draw upon nonlinear and non-territorial understandings of intervention, while they eschew the paradigms bequeathed by the state-system.
4. The first theorist of war to be credited as the innovator of this approach to complexity is the maverick US Air Force pilot John Boyd, whose ideas have been influential on the conceptualization of network-centric warfare, but whose influence went all the way to the White House during the first Gulf War (Osinga 2007; on Clausewitz see Jullien 1996, 22).

Works Cited

Axe, David. 2011. "How the Navy's Warship of the Future Ran Aground." *Wired*. Accessed August 3, 2018. https://www.wired.com/2011/08/future-warship-ran-aground/.

Banach, Stefan J., and Alex Ryan. 2009. "The Art of Design: A Design Methodology." *Military Review* 89 (2): 105–115.

Beck, Ulrich. 2009. *World at Risk*. Translated by Ciaran Cronin. Cambridge, UK and Malden, MA: Polity Press.

Blaker, James. 2006. "Arthur K. Cebrowski: A Retrospective." *Naval War College Review* 59 (2): 129–145.

Bou Akar, Hiba. 2018. *For the War Yet to Come: Planning Beirut's Frontiers.* Stanford: Stanford University Press.

Bousquet, Antoine. 2008. "Chaoplexic Warfare or the Future of Military Organization." *International Affairs* 84 (5): 915–929.

Bystrom, Kerry, and Joseph R. Slaughter. 2018. "The Sea of International Politics: Fluidity, Solvency, and Drift in the Global South Atlantic." In *Global South Atlantic*, edited by Kerry Bystrom and Joseph R. Slaughter, 1–30. New York: Fordham University Press.

Cebrowski, Arthur, and John J. Garstka. 1998. "Network-Centric Warfare: Its Origins and Future: Arising from Fundamental Challenges in American Society and Business, Military Operations Will Capitalize on the Advances and Advantages of Information Technology." *U.S. Naval Institute Proceedings* 124: 28–35.

Chandler, David. 2014. "Beyond Neoliberalism: Resilience, the New Art of Governing Complexity." *Resilience* 2 (1): 47–63.

Civic, Melanne A., and Michael Miklaucic. 2011. *Monopoly of Force: The Nexus of DDR and SSR*. Washington, DC: National Defense University Press.

Von Clausevitz, Carl. [1832] 1989. *On War*. Translated by Michael Howard and Peter Paret. Princeton: Princeton University Press.

Collier, Stephen, and Andrew Lakoff. 2015. "Vital Systems Security: Reflexive Biopolitics and the Government of Emergency." *Theory, Culture & Society* 32 (2): 19–51.

Commission on Human Security. 2003. *Human Security Now*. New York: United Nations.

Corbett, Julian Stafford. 1911. *Some Principles of Maritime Strategy*. London and New York: Longmans, Green.

Cordle, John. 2017. "Good Riddance to Rotational Crews." *U.S. Naval Institute Proceedings*. Accessed July 19, 2018. https://www.usni.org/magazines/proceedings/2017-06/good-riddance-rotational-crews.

Davis, Mike. 2006. *Planet of Slums*. London and New York: Verso.

Douzinas, Costas. 2007. "The Many Faces of Humanitarianism." *Parrhesia* 2: 1–28.

Dudziak, Mary. 2012. *War Time: An Idea, Its History, Its Consequences*. Oxford: Oxford University Press.

Duffield, Mark R. 2014. *Global Governance and the New Wars: The Merging of Development and Security*. London and New York: Zed Books.

Dunford, Joseph F., Jr., Jonathan W. Greenert, and Paul F. Zukunft. 2015. *A Cooperative Strategy for 21st Century Seapower*. Accessed August 1, 2018. http://www.navy.mil/local/maritime/150227-CS21R-Final.pdf.

Elden, Stuart. 2013. "Secure the Volume: Vertical Geopolitics and the Depth of Power." *Political Geography* 34: 35–51.

Goldberg, David Theo. 2012. "Epistemologies of Deception: Topologies of the Extra/Ordinary." *The Salon* 5. Accessed August 12, 2018. http://jwtc.org.za/salon_volume_5/david_theo_goldberg.htm.

Graham, Stephen. 2011. "When Life Itself Is War: On the Urbanization of Military and Security Doctrine." *International Journal of Urban and Regional Research* 36 (1): 136–155.

Gregory, Derek. 2011. "The Everywhere War." *Geographical Journal* 177 (3): 238–250.

Gros, Frédéric. 2012. *Le Principe Sécurité*. Paris: Gallimard.

Hughes, Wayne P. 2018. "A Prophet for Our Times." *Naval War College Review* 67 (3, Summer): 96–97.

Hughes, Wayne P., and Arthur Cebrowski. 1999. "Rebalancing the Fleet." *U.S. Naval Institute Proceedings* 125 (11, November): 31–34.

Johnson, Stuart E., and Arthur K. Cebrowski. 2005. *Alternative Fleet Architecture Design*. Washington, DC: National Defense University Press. Accessed August 3, 2018. http://ndupress.ndu.edu/Portals/68/Documents/DefenseTechnologyPapers/DTP-019.pdf?ver=2017-06-22-143006-157.

Jullien, François. 1996. *Traité de l'efficacité*. Paris: Bernard Grasset.

Karsten, Peter. 1971. "The Nature of 'Influence': Roosevelt, Mahan and the Concept of Sea Power." *American Quarterly* 23 (4): 585–600.

LaGrone, Sam. 2015. "SNA: Modified Littoral Combat Ships to Be Designated Frigates." *USNI News*. Accessed August 13, 2018. https://news.usni.org/2015/01/15/sna-modified-littoral-combat-ship-class-changed-fast-frigate.

Latour, Bruno. 2008. *A Cautious Prometheus? A Few Steps Toward a Philosophy of Design (with Special Attention to Peter Sloterdijk)*. Keynote Lecture for the Networks of Design Meeting of the Design History Society, Falmouth, Cornwall.

Mahan, Alfred Thayer. 1890. *The Influence of Sea Power Upon History*. Boston: Little, Brown and Co.

McCarthy, Dayton. 2018. "The Worst of Both Worlds: An Analysis of Urban Littoral Combat." Accessed December 10, 2018. https://www.army.gov.au/our-future/australian-army-research-centre/australian-army-research-centre-publications/army-25.

Morin, Edgar. 2005. *Introduction à la pensée complexe*. Paris: Seuil.

Natsios, Andrew S. 2005. "The Nine Principles of Reconstruction and Development." *Parameters* 35 (3): 4–20.

Navy. 2016. Accessed July 19, 2018. http://www.navy.mil/submit/display.asp?story_id=96574.

Ophir, Adi. 2010. "The Politics of Catastrophization: Emergency and Exception." In *Contemporary States of Emergency: The Politics of Military and Humanitarian Interventions*, edited by Didier Fassin and Mariella Pandolfi, 59–88. New York: Zone Books.

Osinga, Frans P. B. 2007. *Science, Strategy and War: The Strategic Theory of John Boyd*. Oxford and New York: Routledge.

Perugini, Nicola, and Neve Gordon. 2015. *The Human Right to Dominate*. New York: Oxford University Press.

Prine, Carl. 2017. "Once Maligned, LCS Program Now a Model in Navy Training." *The San Diego Union-Tribune*. Accessed July 19, 2018. http://www.sandiegouniontribune.com/military/sd-me-littoral-ship-20170901-story.html#.

Said, Edward W. 1979. *Orientalism*. New York: Vintage Books.

Sassen, Saskia. 2000. "Territory and Territoriality in the Global Economy." *International Sociology* 15 (2): 372–393.

Stavridis, James G., and Reuben E. Brigety. 2012. "Combat and Compassion." In *Frontiers in Development*, edited by Rajiv Shah and Steven Radelet. Accessed October 30, 2018. https://www.usaid.gov/sites/default/files/documents/1868/USAID_eBook.pdf.

Tilly, Charles. 1985. "War Making and State Making as Organized Crime." In *Bringing the State Back In*, edited by Peter B. Evans, Dietrich Rueschemeyer, and Theda Skocpol. Cambridge and New York: Cambridge University Press.

United States. 2002. *The National Security Strategy of the United States of America*. Washington: President of the U.S.

Wall, Tyler, Parastou Saberi, and Will Jackson. 2017. *Destroy, Build, Secure: Readings on Pacification*. Ottawa: Red Quill Books.

Wills, Steven. 2016. "Why Choose the Littoral Combat Ship? Because It Is the Best Option." *War on the Rocks*. Accessed on July 17, 2018. https://warontherocks.com/2016/01/why-choose-the-littoral-combat-ship-because-it-is-the-best-option/.

Ya'ari, Yedidia. 1995. "The Littoral Arena: A Word of Caution." *Naval War College Review* 48 (2, Spring): 7–21.

Zweibelson, Ben, Lars Hedstöm, Magnus Lindström, and Ulrica Pettersson. 2017. "The Art of Military Design: Swedish Armed Forces and the Contemporary Security Environment." *Kungl Krigsvetenskapsakademiens Handlingar Och Tidskrift* 3: 83–97.

CHAPTER 9

Psychology, Torture, Networks: Or, Structure as the Subject of Human Rights

Stephanie Athey

This essay argues that attention to networks and networked phenomena may move human rights activism beyond a preoccupation with violations as these are embodied in the particular state, nation, regime, or in the sovereign subject. Since the late 1990s and across the twenty-first century, network analysis has taken a variety of forms and drawn a range of adherents in the sciences, communications, arts, and the social sciences. Network study is finding that *how* people (and organizations) are linked to others, meaning the quality, history, pattern, and frequency of those relationships and interactions, weighs significantly on practices as diverse as the spread of epidemics or the spread of ideas. Connections and their specific characteristics strongly influence patterns of behavior be it sexual, political, or consumer behavior (Papachristos 2011).

Network analysis provokes a reorientation in human rights toward structure—the networked forms and patterns of connection among persons, policies, organizational incentives, professional codes, constituencies, and infrastructures that together drive, enable, sustain, and

S. Athey (✉)
Lasell University, Newton, MA, USA
e-mail: sathey@lasell.edu

A. S. Moore and S. Pinto (eds.), *Writing Beyond the State*,
Palgrave Studies in Literature, Culture and Human Rights,
https://doi.org/10.1007/978-3-030-34456-6_9

deny, say, chronic hunger, massacre, or environmental racism. Networks can deliver consequences in ways that are predictable if not always precise, but they distribute their work, and therefore culpability, across relationships in ways we rarely question. To take structure as the subject of human rights is to ask how those relationships are forged and where they might be weakened, severed, or reconfigured; it is to stretch our present understanding of human rights, perpetrators, and violation. Accounting for networks demands we forge instruments of accountability, legal and otherwise, that take aim at forms of influence, connection, and complicity that range from the nefarious conspiracy to the more subtle moral deference inculcated and embraced as "professionalism." If we posit agency in relationships not persons, if we pose structure as a question, rife with alternatives, it suggests that work for human rights becomes deeply restructural, demanding new configurations of society and continual efforts to jerry-rig, improvise, and reroute available networks, relationships, and tools in the effort. Public action must on the one hand, make it possible to detect, dismantle, and prosecute networks, and on the other, retrieve justice as a daily, collaborative, interactive, and affirmative practice broader than the law.

I come to this position through work on US torture and complicity, work that has led me to contend specifically with the forms of public and professional complicity legible in ethics codes, journalism, activist spectacle, political theater, commerce regulations, contractual agreements, and funding routines. In *Torture's Echo and the National Security Imagination*, I argue that ending torture requires torture be seen as a networked phenomenon. More specifically, responsibility and participation in the torture conducted by the United States over the first decades of the twenty-first century require an altered analysis of state torture as a collaborative practice perpetrated by a network. Fine scholarship on torture has documented its bureaucratized features. But the public understanding has yet to make a large conceptual switch: we need to unseat a common perception of state torture as an incident or an act perpetrated by a torturer, and to refigure it instead as a collaborative, compartmentalized, networked process that assembles and divides communities and distributes and stratifies resources across them.

In other words, as I argue elsewhere, whether state torture occurs in a raid, in a local prison, during a street corner confrontation or in a secret offshore installation, and whether that practice incorporates the waterboard, electric cables, sensory assault, isolation, rape, forced standing, the enemas the United States termed "rectal feeding," or none of these, a collaborative process is at work. A network of human actors identifies and targets a marginal population, apprehends representative subjects, coordinates their environment and their pain, and justifies their misery, communicating terror broadly and translating that terror and justification into a particular distribution of economic, political, and social resources. The work of torture would be impossible to sustain or deny without a variety of transnational, technical networks for transportation and supply, or without the practical, professional, interagency networks and the host of interpersonal ties and obligations they represent, including the teams of lawyers, medical "experts," spectators, and apologists necessary to generate and sustain state torture.

Without further restating the case laid out in the book, this essay posits then that extended professional networks are necessary to state torture. For a prime example of torture, complicity, and impunity, and therefore the culpability of networks, the essay points to a seemingly unlikely culprit, the Association of American Psychologists (APA), the largest and most influential association governing the accreditation and licensure of mental health professionals worldwide. That professional association has forged and maintained numerous longstanding ties that bind its work, initiatives, leadership, and even its ethics directorate to the US Department of Defense, the US Central Intelligence Agency and a number of intelligence agencies and security firms abroad. This essay uses this case, although not to condemn psychology or to separate it neatly from other academic disciplines. All disciplines would benefit from a searching human rights audit that reviews our institutions, professional routines, codes of practice, and entanglements with unsavory benefactors. Instead, this essay uses psychology, the APA, its compromised ethics directorate and top management to make an argument about networked violence that, in turn, holds promise and challenge for human rights thinking and organizing generally.

An important case in late 2017 will briefly illustrate the culpability of networks and their place in the struggle for justice. In *Salim v. Mitchell* the American Civil Liberties Union (ACLU) successfully brought two psychologists to trial for US torture inflicted at secret overseas installations. Psychologists James E. Mitchell and Bruce Jessen had been commissioned by the CIA to design and in many cases personally undertake a program of torture against war on terror captives. The defendants were the first the government did not shield from prosecution with a claim to "state secrets," a powerful argument that a case should be dismissed without a hearing. Instead, *Salim v. Mitchell* became the first criminal case to receive a hearing in US court and there prosecute US actors for the torture of captives taken in the post-9/11 raids and wars. An undisclosed settlement was reached with the two plaintiffs who survived Mitchell and Jessen's brand of CIA torture and with the family of the third, Gul Rahman, who was tortured to death (Ladin 2017).

While singling out individual plaintiffs and perpetrators enables litigation like this and its success, too often it also enables professional structures and the tradecraft passed along such structures to escape critical analysis as well as moral and legal culpability. This case involving psychology, torture, and the CIA points up decades-old professional and financial entanglements among universities, private think tanks, the Pentagon, and specific networks of scholars and schools of psychology has left a clear trail of mutual benefit and social harm. *Salim v. Mitchell* is a victory, though several details should disquiet us and direct our attention away from individuals and toward supporting networks: the Senate Select Committee on Intelligence that studied the CIA's detention and interrogation program found that years prior to the settlement the CIA had signed a multimillion dollar, multiyear indemnification contract with Mitchell, Jessen and Mitchell-Jessen Associates, meaning US taxpayers would foot their legal bills and fund any settlements through 2021. This hefty assurance came on top of the $180 million the CIA paid to their company and the $81 million Mitchell and Jessen gained personally from designing a program that put the stamp of "innovation" and "science" to torture techniques that were well-known and studied by psychologists, the CIA, and the Pentagon since the 1950s (SSCI 2014, 16–17; Emmons 2017).

Like the CIA, it turns out the APA had also prepared a defense for psychologists engaged in torture and other degradations. In 2002, the APA issued a Code of Ethics derided by the World Medical Association as the "Nuremberg" defense (WMA 2003; Pope 2018a). Article 1.02 of that code, in particular, directs psychologists to inform their collaborators when their duties violate professional ethics; however, "*if the conflict is unresolvable* via *such means, psychologists may adhere to the requirements of the law, regulations, or other governing legal authority*" (emphasis added, Burton and Kagan 2007; APA 2020).[1] In other words, the military psychologists who, for instance, designed Behavioral Science Consulting Teams for Guantánamo, shared detainee medical data with interrogators, and themselves participated in the torture of captives like Mohamed al-Qahtani (Fink 2016; Woodward 2009), or the independent psychologists involved in torture like Mitchell and Jessen, could and did claim to be just following orders.

The Nuremberg defense lurking in the ethics code is more than a subtlety; at trial, Mitchell and Jessen drew a direct line from the code to torture in one of their motions to dismiss. The psychologists pointed to their contractual relationship and argued they "simply did business with the CIA pursuant to their contracts" (Ladin 2017). They compared themselves to a gassing technician who provided Zyklon B to the Nazis, citing his acquittal by a British military tribunal. The Nuremberg trials, of course, established the opposite rule. "Just following orders" was an insufficient defense; "even though only the Nazis had final say on which prisoners would be gassed." Private contractors including the owner of the Zyklon B chemical company were found guilty for supplying illegal means to the Nazis at a profit (Ladin 2017).

As public outcry grew about psychologists at Guantánamo, quiet complaints about James Mitchell also arose from *within* the CIA's Office of Medical Services, a group that had assured the White House that waterboarding left no lasting damage (Cole 2009, 191–195). APA leadership responded with a Task Force on Psychological Ethics in National Security, which together with the CIA's Professional Standards Advisory Committee and a head CIA director of operations and psychologist, Kirk Hubbard, prepared the 2005 version of the Code of Ethics. An independent inquiry into the APA's complicity in torture issued by Hoffman et al. in 2015 found the task force a sham and that all these groups coordinated carefully with the military and White House to ensure the Code's precise alignment with the language of still-secret "torture memos" issued by the White House Office of Legal Counsel. The Hoffman report found the intent here, as in 2002, was to "loosen" any ethical restrictions that could damage professional livelihoods and to ensure that the longstanding pipeline of support and employment from the security state to the psychology profession remained intact (Hoffman et al. 2015, 91, 274–276, 304–305).

Just as damning, the APA facilitators of these new codes received contracts, grants, or appointments supplied by the Pentagon or Mitchell and Jessen's company. Recipients of such funds and positions included former APA president Joseph Matarazzo—who had opined in an ethics consultation that sleep deprivation did not constitute torture—and APA member and CIA advisor and contractor, Mel Gravitz—who dismissed a complaint against Mitchell saying the Hippocratic "do no harm" oath obligated psychologists to protect groups like the nation (Hoffman et al. 2015, 157–159). Along with Matarazzo and Gravitz, Ethics Director Steven Behnke and Hubbard were identified as funding recipients (Hoffman et al. 2015, 178).[2]

This nutshell history of the *Salim v. Mitchell* perpetrators only grazes the surface of the professional structures, payments, meetings, and ties exposed in an independent review by David Hoffman and the separate shadow report by dissident APA members that preceded it, entitled *All the President's Psychologists* (Hoffman et al. 2015; Soldz et al. 2015). In fact, news of several psychologists' involvement in torture activity appeared earlier in mainstream publications and widely circulated human rights reports (Lewis 2004a, b; PHR 2005, 43–47; Shane 2008; Kaye 2010). The ties Soldz and Hoffman found linking White House lawyers and torture memos, the Department of Defense, the CIA, RAND corporation and the APA produced figures like John Leso, the Behavioral Science Unit pioneer at Guantánamo, or Mitchell and Jessen who tested out the psychological theory of "learned helplessness" to condition human beings in a CIA facility in Thailand. But isolating the work of Mitchell and Jessen from other academic professionals and accomplices, and from the profession of psychology itself, only follows a dangerous and limiting precedent in work toward justice and human rights. These men seem identifiable as perpetrators because they were in the room where torture occurred, but they would not be there if it were not for others who comprised the "six degrees of separation" linking one organization to another. An altered understanding of violence practice needs to alter our conception of perpetrators and networked culpability. The actions of those not in the room are integral to the damage done.

To pursue such a networked conception of culpability and justice work, this essay reaches back to the longer history of collaboration between national security and behavioral science. That collaboration not only generated network science but also greatly inflected the decolonizing, "cold war" contexts affecting the development of human rights discourse. Owing to the origins of human rights instruments in Western legal frameworks that focused on the freedoms and obligations that connect the individual to the state and vice versa, human rights discourse has undertaken an excruciatingly difficult task: the pursuit of justice and human flourishing through a painstaking and narrow focus on seeming sovereigns—the particular state, nation, regime, or the individual perpetrator. These supposedly sovereign agents become the targets of prosecution or blame.

Interestingly, the early twentieth-century collaboration between psychology and security gave rise to networks for command, communication, and control in ways that seemed to threaten those sovereign human subjects. Indeed twentieth-century US torture took shape at that nexus. Yet as network thinking has evolved since, many see in networks the possibility of more emancipatory projects. Networks, as we will see, produce patterns of interdependence and interactivity that embody forms of "distributed sovereignty" or non-sovereignty (Jagoda 2016, 14). This essay considers the value of network thinking for human rights organizing and explores its potential for prosecuting violence networks and reinventing justice work as an undertaking well beyond law.

The Rise of Networks and Behavioral Psychology

Networks join more than humans of course, and the rise of contemporary network thinking is rooted in the emergence of programmable machines in the early part of the twentieth century. Key patterns in the working relationships and infrastructure joining intelligence, the military, and psychology were laid at that time. Still, many accounts of that rise condense a longer history to focus on the United States from the 1940s through the 1990s when "the network" achieved sufficient explanatory power to represent phenomena as disparate as "the human brain, the global economy and geopolitics" (Jagoda 2016). An unmistakable move from "machine" metaphors for connection and control to "network" metaphors has accompanied this cultural shift (Selisker 2016).

Jagoda points to three material transformations across the period that intersected to assist this rise of networks, first, the systemization of innovations in science and engineering that, allied with a nascent military-industrial complex, leveraged general systems theory during and after World War II to advance work in computation, cryptography, and cybernetics. Cybernetics was a 1948 coinage meaning the study of "command and control in the machine and the animal." The work both captured and precipitated a general reorientation in many disciplines as they began to rethink their objects of study in terms of systems of information and communication (Selisker 2016, 99, 103). From 1946 to 1953, the Josiah Macy, Jr. Foundation, at one point a funding arm of the CIA (Marks

1979), hosted interdisciplinary conferences devoted to cybernetic possibilities. These supported dialogue across fields of psychology, neuroscience, circuit theory, anthropology, evolutionary biology, and mathematical logic models (Tudico 2012, 35).

This ferment stirred a second material transformation, expanding engineering interest in interconnected technologies for communication, command, and control, especially electronics and media. This development, again with assistance from military and governmental structures, gradually assembled the Internet. By the mid-nineties, this emergent communication technology came to "impact everyday experiences of most first-world subjects, initially in the US," and by the twenty-first century, to generate an infrastructure and "material reality for billions of people around the world" (Jagoda 2016, 12).

Third and finally, the spread of the network concept can be linked to the material proliferation of free market and neoliberal institutions, ideology, and the instruments of finance capital. Resistance to those "globalizing" changes, from the anti-colonial, civil rights, and anti-war countercultures of the 1960s to the human rights organizing of the 1970s and 80s, also found networks to be critical organizational models and points for intervention (Jagoda 2016, 13). However, as Selisker stresses, "the notion of programming humans developed before and alongside, not after, the notion of programming machines" (Selisker 2016, 99). Behaviorist psychology had an early start demonstrating the possibilities of systematized command, communication, and control. In 1914, after Pavlov and before Skinner, James B. Watson argued that behaviorism entailed an experimental approach to conditioning animals through external stimulus that, at last, distinguished psychology from philosophy as a scientific discipline. Watson was a key figure promoting the relevance of this science to industry, politics, and the military and was instrumental in the creation of the US Division of Psychological Warfare in World War II (Selisker 2016, 10–11).

Throughout those years, the Pentagon and CIA engaged psychologists, psychiatrists, and neurologists at major research institutions to pursue studies of command and control, boosting these men to prominence by funding human experimentation aimed at "modifying individual behavior by covert means." Harold Wolff, neurologist at Cornell University, aimed to tell the Agency "how a man can be made to think, 'feel,' and behave according to the wishes of other men, and, conversely how a man can avoid being influenced in this manner" (Marks 1979, 157–158).

Experiments followed military and CIA interests as well as the psychologists' own, and they studied a range of hallucinogens and other chemicals, electricity, sensory deprivation and overload, lobotomy, hypnosis, and a variety of other inventive, even whimsical, means. An overlooked aspect of this psychology–security partnership was the proliferation of assessment instruments created to predict one's susceptibility to coercion or one's resilience in the face of violence (Marks 1979). Profit-generating assessment packages have become fully integrated into military recruitment and training practice since.

No reliable means to control behavior emerged from this work, but it did have tangible and lasting results. One result is the widespread and enduring fascination with CIA "science," its experiments, and its capabilities, an atmospheric investment one finds everywhere in popular culture. However, the most enduring outcomes of this experimentation have been the routines and structures developed over this time that sustain funding relationships, university influence, professional ties, and organizations. In 2006, APA Division 19 (Military Psychologists) announced the US Department of Defense was the largest employer of psychologists worldwide, a claim repeated in a 2012 publication that noted:

> the psy sciences play a key role in manning contemporary wars: They work to fashion recruitment and training programs, to render (or declare) soldiers fit for re-deployment and to manage disability claims, among numerous other tasks. We also need to consider the deployment of psychiatry, psychology, and neurology either to enhance a military's own troops or, increasingly, to debilitate enemies through the weaponization of such technologies. Developments in military neurology are key here, and as a recent report by the Royal Society on neuroscience, conflict and security points out, international law lags far behind these developments. (Howell 2012, 3)

Constant interactivity across these decades aligned national security and the interest of psychology in behavioral science. It is notable that in 1967, two psychologists published major studies, each signaling a critical future path for behavioral science experimentation: social networks and coercion. One author was Stanley Milgram, the psychologist best known for his "obedience to authority" research years earlier. The obedience experiments determined that when asked to do so by an authority figure, people were willing to administer shocks to others despite their audible suffering. Milgram's 1967 experiment, however, approached influence from the direction of acquaintance networks. He quantified the "small world" principle, the belief that any two people are likely to be connected through a short sequence of intermediate acquaintances. He found that a random subject could direct a postcard by US mail to any specified stranger in the United States, simply by passing that postcard through five or six intermediaries, beginning with someone the subject knew and instructing that recipient to pass it on to someone she knew (Kleinberg 1999).

The second study in 1967 was Martin Seligman's work on "learned helplessness." He demonstrated dogs forced to endure electrical shocks soon became completely compliant, losing even the will to escape those shocks. At his home decades later, in December of 2001, Seligman hosted a meeting that introduced a new generation of the CIA to "learned helplessness" and to two of its proponents eager to work with the CIA, James Elmer Mitchell and his colleague John "Bruce" Jessen. What followed were frequent meetings and conversations among top officials from Defense, the CIA, the RAND corporation, Mitchell, Jessen, the head of the APA Ethics Office, and four past and present APA presidents, two of whom served on a CIA advisory group at this time. Seligman's "learned helplessness" became the twenty-first century "scientific" support for CIA and Defense "enhanced interrogation techniques."

As solid partners in the emergence of networks for command, several branches of social psychology and behavioral economics remain integral to our contemporary networked lives, fields that are still working as did Milgram and Seligman, right at the crossroads between persuasion and coercion. Insight from these fields is now "employed to determine the news we read, the products we buy, the cultural and intellectual spheres we inhabit, and the human networks, online and in real life, of which we are a part" (Shaw 2017).

Liberalism, Non-sovereignty, and the Potential of Networks

As they were envisioned by military science and a fearful public in the mid-twentieth century, network models smacked of totalitarian futures and threatened to undermine nebulous boundaries between the programmable human and machine. Those are the fears, as both Melley and Selisker point out, that underlie the flowering of a US cultural investment in imagining what is distinctly human and "American," i.e. the "liberal human" with "individualism," "agency," "autonomy," "bodily integrity," and the like (Selisker 2016, 8). That same conceptual groundwork (riddled with racial, gendered, religious exclusions, and the like) now seems to hamper a variety of emancipatory projects including work in human rights.

For many, however, network thinking portends the opposite, promising to lead well away from liberal humanist tools and the command and control models first sought through militarized science. Instead, those who engage in network analysis often note how networks confound this liberal humanist sense of "agency" and sovereignty. Sociologist Andrew Papachristos used a form of network analysis to determine that gang homicides in Chicago were in fact "murder by social structure." Using arrest records and affiliations to map interactions, he found that among these gangs, the organization, number, and kinds of connections among members patterned an organizational memory. In groups predicated on the interdependence of their members, dominance contests and alliances with rival gangs created patterns that persist in that memory and guided daily interactions. That is, a structured pattern and memory dictated the range of individual action that might come as a result of any act of aggression. New members inherit this networked memory and method and use it as a schematic for their actions; the result is a challenge to older notions of agency: "While an individual member pulls the trigger, it is the structure that determines who kills whom" (Papachristos 2009, 84). In other words, while individual participants in a violence network tend to be the focus of investigation or blame, it is the organizational memory, intragroup codes, structure, and quality of relationships that inform, direct, and limit individual action. The organizational memory and structure endure, even as individuals are replaced. Networks, as Jagoda would say, "distribute sovereignty" or non-sovereignty (Jagoda 2016, 14).

For those who study them, networks introduce new questions and pose tough challenges. How does one chart the quality, frequency, quantity, and pattern of interactions within a network? Scholars note the number and distribution of ties among entities can produce different actions, affects, and outcomes. It matters, for instance, whether most are linked by and through their relationship with one centralized person/node (a star-like structure expanding outward from a single point, less dense), or whether everyone in a structure knows and interacts with most everyone else as in a friendship clique, small working group, or a street gang (cohesive or "closed" structures). Papachristos notes that when it comes to network analysis criminology is behind the curve, not yet using social network analysis to challenge old models of action or motive. When phenomena are studied as networks, unexpected dynamics appear, e.g. third or fourth parties whose small and indirect interactions may turn out to drive behavior or may illuminate factors that are now mostly rendered in abstractions. Network analysis, he writes, can "unpack the black box often associated with ideas such as 'peer influence,' 'group processes,' or 'facilitation effects'" (Papachristos 2011, 114). "Peer influence" and "facilitation effects" saturate the examples drawn from the APA, the Office of Legal Counsel, or the military, precisely the elements of torture networks that evade legal accountability.

Networks also pose questions of strategy and boundaries. They are said to represent and embody "more complex forms of ideology" that can reconfigure analysis, objectives, and tactics in political work. As importantly, network thinking promises to "reformulate the parameters of human identity and interrelation" (Jagoda 2016, 14). The result gives the nonhuman a bigger role in events. Decentering the human may take the form of a post-human or transhuman "new materialism," a project that jettisons conceptual dualism of all kinds to argue instead that mind, body, and all matter are resolutely material, interconnected, and interactive (Barad 2015). Network or relational thinking that collapses the human and nonhuman this way "changes the types of questions asked…as well as the settings and objects scrutinized" (Jacobs 2012, 417). Genetically modified organisms, floods, viruses, shipping routes, particles, decaying equipment, all contribute to change (instigating maintenance, disruption, and breakdowns) in ways "irreducible to what humans do to them" (Passoth et al. 2012, 3–4). Because of the critical role played by contact between human and nonhuman, some scholars reach beyond the network metaphors for connectivity to point to *ecologies* or "heterogenous ecologies of entities acting" (Jacobs 2012, 417).

So too, in network relations, action itself becomes unsettled, and scholars speak of agency without actors. Agency is not a precondition of action nor is it a property of persons or things, instead "it is a relational, ever-changing outcome" of connections between (Passoth et al. 2012, 4; Barad 2015). In outlining principles of his Actor–Network Theory, Bruno Latour uses the figure of "translation" and mutation to conceive of the agency or action sparked by relational ties. Latour has described nodes in a network as mediators or "translators" to signal that new energy is produced at points of connection. Mediators translate or transform stimulus they receive, not simply react to it or pass it on intact. What is more, mediators are being acted on by multiple forces, any mediator is situated in multiple networks at one time, as he says, "many people and things are at work in any individual" (Latour 2005, 54).

The radical and complex relationality of matter that binds human and nonhuman is both science and politics, and it has been greatly advanced by feminist physics, by work on quantum phenomena, as well as indigenous feminisms. In particular, indigenous feminisms have continued to remind transhumanists that interconnectivity and interaction among entities do not make for equivalence among those entities. It is critical to continue making a claim to the "human" and "rights," but those claims must be firmly situated in a wholly revised theoretical framework committed to identifying inequities and interdependence among the broadest range of entities, animate and inanimate beings (Hua and Ray 2016). In their warning about false equivalence, Hua and Ray point to the steep challenges posed by network thinking and ecologies. There is a tendency to visualize complex network structures through a web-like graph of nodes and the ties between them. This can appear to flatten the relationships they chart, making nodes (entities, mediators) all appear equal in influence. The result can be a flattening of the real power differentials that inflect all connections and interactions. Such representations can mask the reality that many networks, like violence networks, exist largely to assign and enact racial, sexual, gendered, linguistic, and religious subordination.

Similarly, our methods of representing or theorizing structures of connection and interactivity can obscure the impact of past configurations on the present. Writing about contemporary indigenous communities in North America and their struggles to reconnect with sacred objects or exert control over natural resources, Hua and Ray note that "structural dispossessions" precipitated the current structure of interaction among those communities, local and federal governments, landscapes, artifacts, and private interests. Any relational analysis needs to map structural dispossessions that still inflect the active shape of things, e.g. racism, gender violence, privation, and trauma (Hua and Ray). Accounts of networked phenomena must register what Karen Barad calls histories of loss (Barad 2015). Networks distribute culpability or sovereignty and they carry forward the past.

Rethinking Interactivity and Justice

Seeing torture as a networked phenomenon helps us anticipate and contend with torture impunity. It is important to note, however, that every organization and player in the APA story remained keenly attuned to the perils of those legal mechanisms to target individuals, embarrass institutions, and curtail funding. Professional networks continue to invest considerable resources in insulating themselves from legal accountability. Nevertheless, in the case of torture lawyers, intelligence agencies, and psychologists—military, CIA, and civilian—we have seen that the resilience, pliability, and fluid nature of the professionalized, transnational forms of torture collaboration long ago outstripped our legal mechanisms for accountability, invested as those mechanisms are, in individual or state sovereignty.

Human rights organizing has proceeded as an array of networks in continuous tension with the liberal foundations of rights discourse. As anthropologist Sally Engle Merry and many critics have argued, rights are part of the expansion of the modernist vision of the North promoting democracy, rule of law, capitalism and the free market, "Eurocentric in origin and inspiration with its investment in the person, the state, the community...autonomy, choice, bodily integrity and equality are ideas embedded in the legal documents that constitute human rights law" (Merry 2006, 48). Human rights networks, therefore, must grapple with the sovereign frameworks for human rights prosecutions even as we build networked or quantum understandings of entanglement and relationality as means to rethink justice itself. I look first, briefly, at possibilities for prosecuting networked culpability within the system of law we have and then turn to some collective efforts beyond the law that are busily creating their own work-arounds and reconfigurations.

In an excellent piece on twenty-first-century frameworks for accountability, legal scholar Karen Hoffman details the status, as of 2017, of cases being pressed against US actors for torture, nationally and internationally. She argues that certain hard-won innovations that challenge a nation's sovereign jurisdiction are too fragile to be exercised in cases of US torture. The principle of Universal Jurisdiction for torture, invoked to pursue Pinochet for atrocities in Chile, for instance, has secured important interpretations that demonstrate heinous action anywhere can be pursued by any national courts irrespective of their connection to the crimes. Pinochet rulings also underscored that head-of-state or "high official" immunity cannot protect torturers (Hoffman 2017, 117). Yet states invoking Universal Jurisdiction to investigate and prosecute torture have found themselves under enormous pressure from the United States to end investigations. In the case of Spain and Belgium, national legislatures responded to US pressure with new law that undermined universal jurisdiction and limited a prosecutor's reach. In other words, nations leverage the networked realities of global power to shore up sovereignty when it suits them. Hoffman concludes that torture prosecutions have and will fare somewhat better using traditional forms of jurisdiction within states.

US jurisprudence has developed a challenge to the premise of sovereign perpetrators. Racketeering law allows prosecutions of leaders and members of organizations who order or profit from the criminal activity of their associates, an approach to networks and violence that promotes a distributed configuration of injury, guilt, knowledge of outcome, and intention. Known as RICO prosecutions, they target commerce involving "criminal enterprise and activity" not limited to one state. Geoffrey Law writes that RICO, though initially designed to fight the mob, has now been applied "in cases involving organizations that few people would mistake for the Mafia, including Major League Baseball, the Key West Police Department and the Catholic Church" (Law). RICO moves toward a recognition of distributed agency and therefore distributed culpability.

Altogether different models refined by transitional justice efforts internationally also begin to unsettle the notion of individual perpetrators and agency. In the wake of gross societal violation, transitional justice models locate justice in a basic set of five intersecting requisites. One such requirement of justice is memorialization, the comprehensive inscription in public memory of the violence and its multilevel toll. This measure is complemented by truth seeking, criminal justice, reparations, and, most intriguing in this instance, "guarantees of non-repetition" (ICTJ). A guarantee that gross violation will not be repeated cannot be met with verbal commitments, or the revision of Ethics codes, or with new leaders and ethics directors, though all are essential and all of these we have seen in the case of the APA. Instead the guarantee to non-repetition requires institutional fumigation and reconfiguration so organizations, professional practices, and networks facilitating the violations, often within the judicial and security sectors, either no longer operate or are rethought and reassembled in a manner that guarantees non-repetition of the violence. This provision of transitional justice targets organizations that may have "connived in the violation" or "aided and abetted in repression" (UNSC 2004, 20).

Where RICO prosecutions acknowledge the complicity of networked actors, transitional justice frameworks identify structural complicity and demand the dis-assembly and restructuring of such networks on the level of funding, professional training and routines, incentives, and the like. Transitional justice therefore recognizes that the work of justice must achieve a restorative threshold higher than that reached by law. In doing so, transitional justice efforts acknowledge, if problematically, the need for collectively driven transformations that originate outside of or alongside international legal standards.

For instance, the first comprehensive UN Security Council document on transitional justice points toward "integration" (UNSC 2004, 4): "Strategies must be holistic, incorporating integrated attention" (UNSC 2004, 9) and "due regard...to indigenous and informal traditions for administering justice or settling disputes, to help them to continue their often vital role and to do so in conformity with both international standards and local tradition" (UNSC 2004, 12). Of course, the work of "conforming" international standards to local tradition, and vice versa, is a paradox and central crux. The UN Security Council's chosen term, integration, edges toward but does not quite imagine the "international" and "indigenous" as systems of meaning that emerged together, each already embedded in the reality of the other. In the UN prescription, the international and indigenous seem to be frameworks on paper, parallel, opposing, apart. We might instead conceive of them as always already entangled: interconnecting, interpenetrating systems, mutually unsettling, and impacting. The latter imagines an inescapable, interdependent networked reality, marked by inequity and structural dispossession but also intersections and relays ripe for rerouting.

Such rerouting, of course, is already underway. While various efforts within institutionalized systems of law grapple slowly with how to prosecute networked culpability and promote justice as a higher threshold of non-repetition and restoration, collective efforts have been busy creating their own work-arounds and reconfigurations. Human rights praxis has long conceived of oppression as structural and understood justice as a group creation, interactive and participatory. Such organizing, however, has not necessarily conceived of its modes of resistance or the violations themselves as networked phenomena. Rethinking human rights efforts as networked challenges to networked violence can spur the political imagination, driving us to identify and acknowledge multiple new points of complicity that then suggest new locations and resources for disrupting the network. That deeper understanding of networked culpability must come from within a more refined and ready understanding of our own entanglements. That is, network thinking demands we expose sites of our own unacknowledged complicity in the structures large and small that drive violations of human rights. The "six degrees of separation" by which we ourselves are joined to the problem, participate and share culpability, these become junctures ripe for resistance and powerful restructuring.

The work of psychologists can again provide a good example. Indigenous communities confronting trauma have worked to decipher and reckon with harmful entanglements, and in doing so, such communities have pushed psychologists, understandably, and other social and development workers to deeper understandings of the complicity of their own professions and personal networks in violence and harmful routines. The combination has led to wholesale cross-disciplinary and communally based innovations. El Salvador's civilian communities who had suffered the brunt of mass violations during the civil war of the 1980s illustrate this. People convening there in the midst of violence pushed Jesuit scholar and Spanish social psychologist Ignacio Martín-Baró to new formulations of theory and practice. Before he was killed by the military in 1989, he determined healing required a thorough, lived critique of individualism. Martín-Baró came to demand psychologists align with the oppressed not the state and that they overturn the models of health promoted by the Western medicine and by European-American psychology.

In a scathing critique of the APA's complicity in torture in 2007, psychologists Mark Burton and Carolyn Kagan turned precisely here, to the legacy of El Salvadorans and Martín-Baró: "the security apparatus in North American psychology is the hegemonic force in world psychology, one that touches us all." Moreover, "the imperialist state has for years harnessed psychology for social control through anti-democratic, pro-system propaganda in core countries of the West or those who resist the West" (Burton and Kagan 2007, 486). To counter this, "radical psychology should study the paradigm of social control exerted by the state and its construction of psychological life" (Burton and Kagan 2007, 486).

Allied with liberation theology and popular pedagogy, Martín-Baró's liberation psychology argued trauma or suffering were shared social things, not a personal injury or "secret distress" (Burton 2004, 585). Mental health was not "the matter of individuals' satisfactory functioning in society." It entailed just the opposite, a transformation of society. Problems in mental health signaled the "crystallization within individuals of aberrant and dehumanizing social relations" (Lykes and Sibly 2014, 212). Because psychosocial problems evolve at the collective and social level, they "must also be solved collectively" (Lykes and Sibly 2014,

211). Health required participatory creation of new notions of "rights" and "treatment" (Burton 2004, 586). Martín-Baró foregrounded the people's "right to understand" the structural processes that cause social-psychic disruptions including militarization. A refugee project built on the Martín-Baró model and focused on Burma's persecuted Shan ethnic community also articulated rights to structural analysis: communities "had the right to understand their political and economic situation as well as why that situation existed" (Lykes and Sibly 2014, 221). Similarly, people had the right to undertake the restructural, to fashion their own solutions and work for systemic change, not simply personal transformation. In other words, structure is the subject of human rights.

The restructural work of human rights certainly means, in part, creating new communities, new networks. For example, using Martín-Baró's PSL (*Psicología Social de la Liberación*) as a foundation, the US-based Icarus Project extends the model of mental health as an intersectional social justice issue. Convening communities across the States, the effort names itself a "support network and education project by and for people who experience the world in ways that are often diagnosed as mental illness. We advance social justice by fostering mutual aid practices that reconnect healing and collective liberation. We transform ourselves through transforming the world around us" (Icarus 2018). Paul Farmer has learned from a similar commitment to the poor in Haiti that communities must lead their own healing, "to rethread social relations toward well-being" (Lykes and Sibly 2014, 212). The act of "rethreading social relations" is evocative of the structural and restructural subject of human rights that requires unwinding and winding new connections.

To take the actor–network or quantum models seriously for human rights work would mean to reject the abstraction that is "the communal" or "the community." Communities are not a priori, nor are they a prelude to action, but they are always emerging, morphing, or dissipating in a constant flux. What factors and conditions galvanize everyday entanglements to generate social movement is as important a question as what legal mechanisms or disruptions can hold a violence network to account. At any given time, what are the varieties of persons, entities, conditions, and complex social practices (contagion, shipping, professional promotion) that in colliding, induce or stymie the forward motion of "organizing" or social movements? Cultivating an ecology for connectivity and motion demands more specific attention to the "hows of becoming active" (Passoth et al. 2012, 5).

As PSL or liberation psychology suggests, then, sustaining a non-sovereign alternative for justice requires robust communal and professional forums that exercise justice as an ongoing right to understand structural entanglements, a practice of critique, self-critique, and new circuit-building. Such justice also requires the constant work of gathering contingent communities and rerouting our ties to structures of violence. ACLU legal director David Cole (2017) writes that major changes at the level of the Supreme Court began with street-level interactions. A new style of "long form persuasion," encouraged canvassers to inquire in depth, not about beliefs, but about opponents' own social networks (their prior entanglements)—e.g. what family members or friends had experienced a particular problem or struggle. And then to listen at length to their anxieties and fears.[3] The work is in cultivating an entire ecology, human and nonhuman, for connectivity. It is perhaps the neighborhood, the open door, and the resident at home that translate personal meanings and experience, transform the activist, and thereby alter the activism. These ad hoc, communal encounters built new circuits that in turn rerouted the law.

Conclusion

I have used the knotted history and present of the CIA, Department of Defense, and APA to argue that making violence networks salient is important collaborative work in a world where too often jurisprudence and activism both focus on the individual perpetrator and where "professionalism" too easily disguises complicit action. Indeed, one pitfall inherent in this work is our tendency to conceive of transnational, corporate, state, even disciplinary networks themselves as the new sovereigns, all-controlling, impenetrable, inevitable. Given the mystique and power cultivated by the intelligence organizations and military-industrial bureaucracies, or the great cost and influence of the North American university system of credentialing and advancement, it is not uncommon for participants as well as the public to overestimate the power, reach, and efficiency of the bureaucratic machine.

However, as Jagoda reminds us, the lived experience of networks is completely different, even avowedly non-sovereign. Our everyday experience of interconnectivity is not one of control but more often of breakdowns, delays, frustration, distraction, and isolation even in connection. We seem to wait endlessly on upgrades and seek out patches, plug-ins, and work-arounds. Networked relations of all kinds require constant maintenance, even when they are not being hacked or coping with a security breach. By nature, networks are multiple, amorphous, and porous; participation levels are dynamic and participants fluid (Jagoda). All of these features make violence networks alive with possibilities for reconfiguration and intervention. Human rights networks, interactive chains of entities in constant translation, are consistently embedded in violence although engaged in rerouting and restructuring its impact. Violence networks are not static but emergent, with restructural potential, and networks for justice must continually critique their own entanglements with them.

The sovereign culprit must cede way, or stand beside, models of networked culpability. The case of the APA participation in networked violence shines a light on the need for the academic and public sectors to inspect our own industries, disciplines, and justice work with the courage modeled by dissident psychologists. All fields need to take seriously the force of professional codes and deference in our own networks, tracing the power to which we are party, the structural dispossessions that made that so, and the intersectional power relations in which we are situated. The distributed models of professionalism, justice work, and "networking" discussed here call on us to think relationally, hone listening, cultivate new communities, and sharpen our role in rejecting or restructuring our own professional routines and national security relationships alike.

Notes

1. The author thanks historian Lean Sweeney for perceptive contributions to this essay. Not until 2010 and again 2017, under persistent membership pressure, was the Nuremberg line in the APA ethics code successfully removed.
2. After the 2015 Hoffman review of APA, the Ethics Office determined to outsource complaints entirely, suggesting potential violations be adjudicated by "appropriate" bodies, such as the military and government agencies (Pope 2018b).
3. For a fine reading of examples of a networked approach to law in the United States, see David Cole's *Engines of Liberty.* He traces three effective, rights-based campaigns that began with small public support and ended with US Supreme Court victories that reinterpreted law. He considers the National Rifle Association's success reinterpreting the second amendment

to refer to personal gun rights not just militias, second, the victory of marriage equality activists in *Obergefell*, and finally the (limited) rights gained on the books for (some) detainees in the war on terror.

Works Cited

American Psychological Association. 2020. "Ethical Principles of Psychologists and Code of Conduct." See 2010 Amendment 1.02. Accessed January 26, 2020. http://www.apa.org/ethics/code.

Athey, Stephanie. (Under review). *Torture's Echo and the National Security Imagination.*

Barad, Karen. 2015. "Interview: Matter Feels, Converses, Suffers, Desires, Yearns and Remembers." *New Materialism: Interviews and Cartographies*, October 1. https://quod.lib.umich.edu/o/ohp/11515701.0001.001/1:4.3/--new-materialism-interviews-cartographies?rgn=div2;view=fulltext.

Burton, Mark. 2004. "Viva Nacho: Liberating Psychology in Latin America." *The Psychologist* 17 (10): 585–587.

Burton, Mark, and Carolyn Kagan. 2007. "Psychologists and Torture: More Than a Question of Interrogations." *The Psychologist* 20 (8, August): 484–487.

Cole, David, ed. 2009. *The Torture Memos: Rationalizing the Unthinkable*. New York: The New Press.

Cole, David. 2017. *Engines of Liberty: How Citizen Movements Succeed*. New York: Basic Books.

Emmons, Alex. 2017. "Historic Settlement Reached on Behalf of CIA Torture Victims." *The Intercept*, August 17. https://theintercept.com/2017/08/17/cia-torture-settlement-aclu-mitchell-jessen/.

Fink, Sherri. 2016. "Where Even Nightmares Are Classified: Psychiatric Care at Guantanamo." *New York Times*, November 12. http://nyti.ms/2erngaa.

Hoffman, Karen. 2017. "Redress for 'Some Folks': Pursuing Justice for Victims of Torture Through Traditional Grounds of Jurisdiction." *Georgia Journal of International and Comparative Law* 46: 97–128.

Hoffman, David H., et. al. 2015. *Report to the Special Committee of the Board of Directors of the American Psychological Association. Independent Review Relating to APA Ethics Guidelines, National Security Interrogations, and Torture.* http://www.apa.org/independent-review/APA-FINAL-Report-7.2.15.pdf.

Howell, Alison. 2012. "The International Political Sociology of Psychology and Mental Health." *International Political Sociology* 6 (3, September): 331–333. https://doi.org/10.1111/j.1749-5687.2012.00166_7.x.

Hua, Julietta, and Kasturi Ray. 2016. "The Lives of Things: Native Objects, Human Rights and NDN-Indian Relationality." *Prose Studies*, Special Issue, *Revaluing the Human: The Moral Economy of Human Rights* 28 (1): 12–33.

Icarus Project. 2018, September 1. https://theicarusproject.net/what-we-do/.
International Center for Transitional Justice. *Institutional Reform*. https://www.ictj.org/our-work/transitional-justice-issues/institutional-reform.
Jacobs, Jane M. 2012. "Urban Geographies I: Still Thinking Cities Relationally." *Progress in Human Geography* 36 (3, June): 412–422. https://doi.org/10.1177/0309132511421715.
Jagoda, Patrick. 2016. *Network Aesthetics*. Chicago: University of Chicago Press.
Kaye, Jeffrey. 2010. "APA Scrubs Pages Linking It to CIA Torture Workshops." *ShadowProof*, May 16, 2010. https://shadowproof.com/2010/05/16/apa-scrubs-pages-linking-it-to-cia-torture-workshops/.
Kleinberg, Jon. 1999. The Small-World Phenomenon: An Algorithmic Perspective. *Cornell Computer Science Technical Report* 99–1776 (October). https://www.cs.cornell.edu/home/kleinber/swn.d/swn.html.
Ladin, Dror. 2017. "CIA Torture Psychologists Compare Themselves to Nazi Poison Gas Manufacturer as a Defense." *ACLU Speak Freely Blog*, July 25. https://www.aclu.org/blog/national-security/torture/cia-torture-psychologists-compare-themselves-nazi-poison-gas?redirect=blog/speak-freely.
Latour, Bruno. 2005. *Reassembling the Social: An Introduction to Actor-Network-Theory*. New York: Oxford University Press.
Law, Geoffrey Nathan. n.d. "Understanding RICO Conspiracy Laws." https://www.federalcharges.com/Understanding-RICO-Conspiracy-Laws/.
Lewis, Neil A. 2004a. "Broad Use of Harsh Tactics Is Described at Cuba Base." *New York Times*, October 17. https://www.nytimes.com/2004/10/17/politics/broad-use-of-harsh-tactics-is-described-at-cuba-base.html.
———. 2004b. "Red Cross Finds Detainee Abuse in Guantánamo." *New York Times*, November 30. https://www.nytimes.com/2004/11/30/politics/red-cross-finds-detainee-abuse-in-guantanamo.html.
Lykes, M. Brinton, and Erin Sibly. 2014. "Liberation Psychology and Pragmatic Solidarity: North-South Collaborations Through the Ignacío Martín-Baro Fund." *Peace and Conflict: Journal of Peace Psychology* 20 (3): 209–223.
Marks, John. 1979. *The Search for the Manchurian Candidate: The CIA and Mind Control*. New York: Times Books.
Merry, Sally Engle. 2006. "Transnational Human Rights and Local Activism: Mapping the Middle." *American Anthropologist* 108 (1): 38–51.
Papachristos, Andrew V. 2009. "Murder by Structure: Dominance Relations and the Social Structure of Gang Homicide." *American Journal of Sociology* 115 (1): 74–128.
———. 2011. "The Coming of a Networked Criminology?" In *Measuring Crime and Criminality: Advances in Criminological Theory 17*, edited by John MacDonald, 101–140. No location: Transaction Publishers.

Passoth, Jan Hendrick, Birgit Peuker, and Michael Schilmeier. 2012. "Introduction." In *Agency Without Actors? New Approaches to Collective Action*. New York: Routledge.

Physicians for Human Rights (PHR). 2005. *Break Them Down: Systematic Use of Torture by US Forces*. https://s3.amazonaws.com/PHR_Reports/break-them-down.pdf.

Pope, Kenneth S. 2018a. "A Human Rights and Ethics Crisis Facing the World's Largest Organization of Psychologists: Accepting Responsibility, Understanding Causes, Implementing Solutions." August 27. https://kspope.com/apa/crisis.php.

———. 2018b. "The American Psychological Association Outsources Adjudication of Ethics Complaints: 5 Far-Reaching Consequences." July 22. https://kspope.com/ethicsoutsourcing.php.

Selisker, Scott. 2016. *Human Programming: Brainwashing, Automatons and American Unfreedom*. Minneapolis: University of Minnesota.

Senate Select Committee on Intelligence (SSCI). 2014. *Senate Intelligence Committee Report on Torture, Committee Study of the Central Intelligence Agency's Detention and Interrogation Program*. Declassified Version, April 3, 2014. New York: Melville House Publishing.

Shane, Scott. 2008. "Chinese Inspired Interrogations at Guantanamo." *New York Times*, July 8. https://www.nytimes.com/2008/07/02/us/02detain.html.

Shaw, Tamsin. 2017. "Invisible Manipulators of Your Mind." *New York Review of Books*, April 20. http://www.nybooks.com/articles/2017/04/20/kahneman-tversky-invisible-mind-manipulators.

Soldz, Stephen, Nathaniel Raymond, and Steven Reiser. 2015. *All the President's Psychologists: The American Psychology Association's Secret Complicity with the White House and US Intelligence Community in Support of the CIA's "Enhanced" Interrogation Program*. Full text at *New York Times*, April 30, 2015. https://www.nytimes.com/interactive/2015/05/01/us/document-report.html?fbclid=IwAR1ntyY0wHnu4A_ioeKOAuWLdQaudxkD2m4xctOOzdthwTeoiklKAAZUc6k.

Tudico, Christopher. 2012. "The History of the Josiah Macy Jr. Foundation." New York: Josiah Macy Jr. Foundation.

United Nations Security Council. 2004. *The Rule of Law and Transitional Justice in Conflict and Post-Conflict Societies*. S/2004/616. *International Center for Transitional Justice*. https://www.ictj.org/gallery-items/principles; PDF at http://archive.ipu.org/splz-e/unga07/law.pdf.

Woodward, Bob. 2009. "Guantanamo Detainee Was Tortured, Says Official Overseeing Military Trials." *Washington Post*, January 14, 2009. http://www.washingtonpost.com/wp-dyn/content/article/2009/01/13/AR2009011303372.html?noredirect=on.

World Medical Association. 2003. "Physicians Under Threat, Warns WMA President, Press Release." *World Medical Association*, June 23, 2003. http://web.archive.org/web/20030715220823/http://www.wma.net/e/press/2003_9.htm.

CHAPTER 10

Mediterranean Returns: Migration and the Poetics of Lamentation

Angela Naimou

The Mediterranean Sea is only one of 20 active "Refugee Situations" currently spotlighted by the UNHCR, and it involves a small fraction of the more than 68 million people living in displaced, refugee, or "refugee-like" "situations" globally (UNHCR 2018a, b). But as the only "situation" that borders multiple EU states and the North African and Middle Eastern states with which they are so heavily involved, it is a highly visible site for the conflict between the freedom to move from war or insecurity and the sanctions against it. The Mediterranean situation highlights the many ways that state and humanitarian actors work to transform persons on the move into legal identities to be managed: the migrant to detain, imprison, offer temporary protection, or put in camps; the "infiltrator," to use Israel's legal term for irregular border crossers, to punish; the victim of trafficking or smuggling to rescue, forcibly repatriate, or remove to a third country; the refuge seeker to care for, manage, or grant asylum to; or, the dead to inspect or to let go. These are some of the futures

A. Naimou (✉)
Clemson University, Clemson, SC, USA
e-mail: anaimou@clemson.edu

A. S. Moore and S. Pinto (eds.), *Writing Beyond the State*, Palgrave Studies in Literature, Culture and Human Rights, https://doi.org/10.1007/978-3-030-34456-6_10

designed for the crossers to find. Meanwhile, people's experiences, movements, and desires exceed the legal categories that seek to contain them. Tensions between the legal and extra-legal meanings of such terms as *refugee*, *asylee*, *migrant*, *alien*, *foreigner*, *exile*, *deportee*, or *infiltrator*, play out explicitly in this essay, confounded by the state-centered discourse that conceals the workings of a global migration regime.

The hostility that African migrants and refuge seekers encounter have led the Mediterranean to serve as a vital coordinate for theories of blackness that take the afterlife of slavery as a grounding condition, where blackness is always being "in the wake"—what Christina Sharpe theorizes as a position "in the modalities of Black life lived in, as, under, despite Black death: to think and be and act from there" (2016, 22). Sharpe names this thinking and being and acting as "wake work," and she outlines its generative possibilities as a site of artistic production and consciousness in the black diaspora. She draws from the blunt diagnosis that "today's scene in the Mediterranean reveals slavery's *afterlife*...black suffering and death in the Mediterranean sustains and resuscitates European democratic society" (Woods and Saucier 2015). In this view, nonracial humanitarian critiques of the crisis are both figure and ground of antiblackness. What Europe's border regimes enable—the Libyan torture camps and slave auctions, or the Israeli expulsions of Eritrean and Sudanese nationals through so-called Voluntary Departure policies—are just the more spectacular instances of a deep racial migration order, where migrants and refugees and local residents play out a stunningly incoherent but internationally coordinated and punitive border politics on sea and land.

The Mediterranean as a storied space of intercultural creativity, "the open, the cosmic, the infinite" (Diagne, foreword to Cassin 2016), lives not as an abstraction but as a "strategic crossroads for global energy, telecommunication, security, trade, and fishing interests," one where a disingenuous "war on human smuggling" has been unfolding as the proper response to the deaths of crossers (Albahari 2016, 277–278). Humanitarianism has been invoked as a challenge to the harshness of border regimes, even as humanitarian efforts may cause harm in their ostensible aim to improve border policies. As Miriam Ticktin has claimed, humanitarian border discourse may implicitly require that border crossers possess an impossible kind of "innocence," one free "from desire, will, or agency" (Ticktin 2016, 257); they may presume a context-free temporality of emergency and crisis that requires urgency (262); and they may prioritize "compassion" in the structure of humanitarian feeling, to be given conditionally but received gratefully (264). In short, the language of "humanitarian borders" can transform those who cross them into a new category that strengthens humanitarian-military border regimes: innocent victims created by a sudden emergency who need the world's compassion.

This essay considers how poems by Jehan Bseiso, Warsan Shire, and Aracelis Girmay confront the racial and imperial violence of the border regime by remaking a poetics of grief. In different ways, these poets pull from a broader poetic repertoire of elegy and lamentation to make poems that refuse conventional and state-sponsored responses to the dead. The now-conventional understanding of the English elegy as mimetic of the mourning process, moving from grief to consolation or completed mourning, remains central to English-language contemporary poetry of loss, but becomes plainly inadequate as a response to the recursive and future-oriented violence that is the border regime. Elegies for politically orchestrated, anticipated mass death inhabit a future tense: they are "proleptic elegies" for the victims that will come (Spargo 2004), and this elegiac mode has relied on nationalist and humanitarian frames that need to be reconsidered. Elegiac poetry may imagine the future to lament the present, just as powerfully as it returns us to moments of past grief.

The concept of return can help us think about how poetry responds to the politics of refuge in the Mediterranean and to the capacity for poetry to generate and perform a space and time of grief. Return signals ever-recurring, unending sorrow in poetry of lamentation in Arabic and English poetic traditions. The Arabic poetry of lamentation, *rithā'* (رثاء), can play on a lexical relation between *aoud*, "to return" (عودة), and *'id*, "holiday" (عيد), which gives the meaning of return or recurrence, as holidays or festivals are recurrences, but which also has another related meaning of "recurrent care, sorrow, or chronic disease."[1] The English elegiac tradition as a poetic mode of mourning can, like the Arabic tradition, be understood as a return to grief, and elegies to the Mediterranean refugee dead revisit these basic questions about the shape and time of mourning; the source of violence, justice, ethics; the past and future of diaspora; and the work of elegy to mourn at once too late and in advance. I focus on Shire and Girmay as each figure the Mediterranean Sea as a site of returns—returns failed, incomplete, forced, or impossible. The concept of returns organizes a broad poetics of the Mediterranean—what has been called the "world's deadliest border" (Albahari 2016). It highlights the patterns of refugee crossings and blockings at work in international and transnational migration regimes.

Return is a concept of displacement already multiply burdened: burdened by its promise to end indefinite exile and dispossession, as in the Palestinian demand for the "right of return" [حق العـودة] (*Ḥaq al-ʿawda*); burdened by the nonliteral return given the force of law, as in the Israeli "Law of Return"; and, burdened by the nicer names we give to deportation—as in repatriation (return to the patria), and as in state or UN managed "voluntary returns" or "voluntary departures," named "voluntary" despite or because they are often unwanted returns that people agree to from pressure, inhospitality, and despair. Burdened too by the presumption that the refugee would prefer not to burden host countries, that they'd prefer to return home as soon as it were possible. For philosopher Barbara Cassin, the concept of return is a fantasy of origins and a lesson that language is the true home we inhabit: in the term *nostalgia* (*nostos*, "return," and *algos*, "pain" or "suffering") she finds the mythos of return: Greek roots for a term invented by the Swiss and exemplified by Odysseus's perpetually desired and perpetually deferred return.[2]

Shire and Girmay experiment with modes of grief in poetry that move between mourning and lamentation; in doing so, their poems expand our available languages for responding to military-humanitarian borders. These poems put pressure on the conventions of elegy: their poetics of grief test the limits and contradictions of humanitarian response, where the dead have been made into spectacle and metonym for global crisis, and where the disingenuous mourners adopt the key of humanitarian grief in their public statements. They express grief but also map the networks of death making, from the conflict or insecurity in "home" countries to state reception and expulsion policies, illustrated in the humanitarian Mare Nostrum rescue operations (2013–2014) and the punitive Israeli policies of voluntary departure for Eritrean and Sudanese nationals. They also trace lines of imagined affiliation between poetic speakers, at times shifting between the imagined black diaspora generated by the history of the transatlantic slave trade and particular diasporas from African states prompted by events of the twentieth and twenty-first century.

Shire is a Nairobi-born and London-based poet, with Somali family ties. Girmay describes herself as Santa Ana, California-born, with routes from "Eritrea, Puerto Rico, and African America," living in New York City. Shire and Girmay contend with the question of how diasporic routes and flows might organize a response to an international and global order of forcible returns. They chart the effects of human rights policies and practices that often must collude with the state and international agreements that make such disastrous outcomes and outsized hostility to those seeking refuge without prior authorization. And they chart diasporic lines of interpretive affiliation and distance—as when ululation and English elegy converge in Girmay's cycle "Elelegy"—as well as through the actual routes people take, as with the Eritrean, Sudanese, Somali, Syrian, and Iraqi nationals who share vessels, departure points, and pathways by land.

The diasporic mode can reconceptualize "return" not to an originary homeland but as one of the many hazards and punishments of unauthorized migration, the diasporas to be lamented not only for the cause of displacement but also for the global attempts to stop the journey before survivors arrive, or to make their arrival a temporary and reversible condition.[3] Here, I want to think about the forms that refugee futurity takes when we think about the sea and the many returns it enables: the sending or bringing, the coming or going back of those who traverse it; but also, the returns it brings to states and organizations in the senses of political gain and economic profit; and the conceptual returns it brings to theory and poetry on the recurrence of forced migration itself and the grief it so often gives way to.

One response to this aesthetic problem is Jehan Bseiso's short poem "No Search, No Rescue." A Palestinian poet, activist, and aid worker based in Cairo, Bseiso originally posted the poem on The Electronic Intifada website in April 2015, a month with a record death toll in the Mediterranean. The poem opens with a dedication "to the families and lovers at the bottom of the sea, trying to reach Europe." Its speakers are smugglers and the survivors of shipwrecks who lament the dead and continue their migration. The poem's organizing refrain also reverses the presumed centrality of Europe: "Your Sea, Mare, Bahr. Our war, our Harb." The line transliterates the Arabic for sea, "bahr" (بحر) to anagrammatically reflect the word for war, "harb" (حرب). It refers to the Latin *Mare Nostrum*, "our sea," the ancient Roman imperial name for the Mediterranean, later revived as part of Italian colonial ambitions in Africa in the 1880s and then again by Mussolini and Italian nationalism. *Mare Nostrum* was also the name for the Italian government's short-lived military humanitarian anti-smuggling search and rescue air and naval operation along the Libyan and Italian coasts (2013–2014), launched after two major shipwrecks: on October 3, 2013, when more than 360 refugees, the majority from Eritrea, drowned off the coast of Lampedusa; and then on October

11, 2013, when a boat capsized and left at least 34 dead, the majority from Syria and Palestine.

While quickly superseded by Frontex's more minimal assistance and more punitive focus on border control, Operation Mare Nostrum's search and rescue component was seen by supporters as saving lives and holding the potential to make a radical claim of responsibility for refugees outside the current political imaginary of sovereignty, citizenship, and asylum.[4] The poem's title suggests that the 2015 rise in the number of deaths represented not only the loss of search and rescue operations but also the long-term harm built into Mediterranean military-humanitarian borders. "No Search, No Rescue" does not mourn the dead in the sense that it does not move from grief to consolation, and it gives no closure by commemorating one set of victims; instead, it gives the sense that people will continue to "overcome war and poverty only to drown in your sea" or become survivors with "maps on our backs. / Long way from home" (Bseiso 2015).

Two poems by Shire, titled "Home" and "Conversations about Home (At the Deportation Centre)," are not explicitly elegies. Moving between humanitarian appeals and bleak assessments of state power, "Home" was written and circulated widely online in writing and audio in the fall of 2015 as an intervention in public debates over whether refugees deserved to be welcomed by Europe. It opens with the sense of urgency that anyone, including you, would feel in conditions of terror:

> no one leaves home unless
> home is the mouth of a shark
> you only run for the border
> when you see the whole city running as well. (Shire 2015, n.p.)

The poem was read aloud in public places by famous people, made into Youtube videos, and went viral through social media. It was a call to renew public feeling and change policy.[5]

Its poetics of intervention are underscored when we read "Home" (2015) as a rewrite of Shire's earlier poem, "Conversations about Home (At the Deportation Centre)," written in 2009 and published in her 2011 book *teaching my mother how to give birth*. Shire wrote "Conversations" after visiting with a group of young undocumented refugees from Somalia, Eritrea, Congo, and Sudan living in the abandoned Somali embassy in Rome, a city whose outskirts house "The Identification and Expulsion Center," a massive detention complex. The title locates the poem at the "deportation centre"; the news account of its composition locates the poet at the "abandoned embassy." Inhabiting both place names are the unauthorized forms of black life that dread future deportation, abandoned by diplomatic channels to legality. "Conversations" does not have the relentless momentum of short enjambed lines: it's a prose poem of first-person voices, answering the question of how they fell into a time out of place:

> They ask me *how did you get here?* Can't you see it on my body? The Libyan desert red with immigrant bodies, the Gulf of Aden bloated, the city of Rome with no jacket. I hope the journey meant more than miles because all of my children are in the water. I thought the sea was safer than the land. […] I spent days and nights in the stomach of the truck, I did not come out the same. Sometimes it feels like someone else is wearing my body.

If there is an explanation here, it is presumed to be useless: this is titled a conversation, not an asylum interview; this is a deportation centre, not a welcome one. The 2015 poem's line—"no one puts their children in a boat / unless the water is safer than the land"—is in the conditional present tense, to undo the finality it carries for a thinking speaker-subject in the original poem—"I thought the sea was safer than the land." "Home" is designed to intervene before it is too late (again), but it is the reworking of poem in many ways about being, already, too late: "Conversations" gives voice to those who thought they *had* escaped, only to face imminent return to the mouth of the shark. Where the 2015 poem becomes an opportunity to recalibrate the time of deportability into one of hospitality, the 2011 poem ends by quietly reminding us that time will yield a different kind of return—the inevitable meeting again of listener and speaker in an afterlife, beyond the realm of land and water and legal channels of incorporation or expulsion:

> All I can say is, I was once like you, the apathy, the pity, the ungrateful placement and now my home is the mouth of a shark, now my home is the barrel of a gun. I'll see you on the other side. (Shire 2011, 27)

As a poem that signals the need to be timely, "Home" nonetheless highlights its own belatedness and the deliberate belatedness of those who would welcome refuge and asylum seekers. Shire rearranges the humanitarian failures in the 2011 poem into a kind of second chance for Europe in the 2015 poem: but what led Shire to write "Home" and propelled its wide circulation also haunts its present-tense temporality. The summer of 2015 had been the highest death toll in the Mediterranean Sea, to be surpassed the next year.

A poem voicing its urgency to intervene does so in response to the fact that its arrival is in some way already too late. Elegy may be most explicitly suited to this temporality of belatedness, as the genre of poetry where lateness is the explicit occasion for reflection. Aracelis Girmay's poem cycle "Elelegy" takes grief as its main temporality and route back to the Mediterranean. It is an attempt to rethink the capacity of contemporary poetry to arrange grief over ongoing deaths through the form of elegy and to address black diasporic futurity by addressing the dead. In doing so, Girmay's poetry moves between three competing modes for thinking about the racial and geopolitical forms of contemporary migration around the sea: the poetry of lamentation; theories of blackness in the afterlife of slavery; and, a critique of imperial, state, and international practices at borders and toward people trying to move against a global system largely hostile to refugee futures.[6] Diaspora, in this context, can structure transnational elegy both in the poet's claimed relation to the dead and in the poet's object of criticism: in this case, an uneven but global war and migration politics that trades in mass violence—what some states see as their attempts to minimize the "pull" factors of migration—while refusing to claim such politics as explicitly hostile to human life and the right to move.

Girmay's book contains two poem cycles: "Elelegy" and the title cycle, "the black maria." "Elelegy" marks the October 2013 drowning, mentioned above, of more than 300 people, nearly all Eritrean, off the coast of the Italian island of Lampedusa, a name that has become shorthand for shipwrecked people trying to reach the European side of the sea. Girmay notes that "*elelegy* means to place itself in both the English elegiac tradition and the ululatory traditions of grieving and joy in cultures of North and East Africa," merging the individual poet's writing and the collective's embodiment in sounds of intense affect, outside of language. Girmay does not identify the robust tradition of lament in Arabic poetry but she channels its mode. Like ululation, the *rithā'* (رثاء) is an expressive mode of "uninhibited grief": it was originally performed by women as part of funerary rites for male next of kin. As verses in rhymed prose, *rithā'* moved beyond women's funerary rites to become the prized mode for the collective lamentation and celebration of social and religious heroes who fell in battle: the war dead.[7]

As the poetry of mourning, the English elegy responds both to its own poetic tradition and to contemporary social forms for experiencing loss and grief. Elegy originally referred to an ancient Greek verse form used for miscellaneous subjects, though it carried a mood of sadness or lament: elegy thus was once more capacious and open to lamentation as a social expression of grief. Hurley and O'Neill chart the history of how the Reformation changed religious mourning rituals and praying for the souls of the dead and ushered in the modern English elegy as a secular mode. Criticism of the genre of English elegy has focused on the movement from grief to consolation; the lament and then the transcending of pain; elegy as a "work of mourning" (Freud) that leads to successful and complete working through of mourning. Modern elegies (Ramazani 1994) have diminished the distinction between elegy as a movement to consolation and mourning and the "elegiac" as a poetic representation of melancholia. Yet all elegy begins with the response and return to loss. As a "mimesis of mourning," elegy arranges grief as an imaginative return to the time and space of loss—it is a turn back, toward a grief remembered (Ramazani 1994, 29). Girmay's "elelegy" stages grief as a mode of return tied to an assemblage of poetic forms and themes of return: together, these returns invoke mourning and hold on to it as indefinite. Even when the poem cycle follows the general elegiac pattern of lament, praise, and solace, it retains a sense of un-completable grief—as Judith Butler describes it, "one is hit by waves…Something takes hold of you: where does it come from?" (Butler 2004, 21).

Incompleteness is sometimes conceptualized as itself a return: we keep returning to the same problem rather than moving decisively and fully beyond it. "Elelegy" emphasizes the role of lamentation within the diminished distinction between mourning and melancholia common to the modern elegy, what Jahan Ramazani describes as its mode of melancholic mourning. The second cycle, "The Black Maria," for black seas (from the Latin *mare*) constellates the "Elelegy" poems on Eritrean deaths with elegies, estrangements, and survival stories in the U.S.: most especially of black killings by police power. Here the poems activate the other meanings of "black maria"—as astronomers' misnomer for the moon's shadows, what they thought were dark waters on its surface—and as the term for vehicles for mass detention by police. Where the first cycle addresses the sea in its insensibility to the deaths of people in it, the second reflects on human insensibility to the pain of others. In this way *the black maria* pulls U.S. and Eritrean national contexts into a poetics of black diaspora figuring a collectivity of mourners and a mourning of the collective dead. It shows that incompleteness is not always a pathologized melancholic resistance to fully accepting someone's death but that incompleteness is the very structure of ongoing politically-constructed destruction of human dignity. Under these terms, the dying has gone on for so long and the killing has not stopped. How can mourning be successful when the collective violence could be stopped but isn't? Or when the dying is treated *as if* it were up to the victims themselves to stop it, thrown as they are into illegality?[8]

The return to loss shapes "Elelegy" in more ways: its imagined return to a collective mourning tradition in the extra "ele" generates its own tensions with the individual elegist's grief. Its lament is patterned as a historical repetition of mourning the collective dead—in slavery, then empire, then civil war, then postcolonial state violence, then border and migration policies—all in one poem, all addressed to "you / on that ship, stuttering across the sea," the Eritreans in the Mediterranean:

> It is October, 2013,
> off the coast of Lampedusa,
>
> the Italian fishermen whose
> grandfathers, nearly a hundred years ago, barred
>
> our grandfathers from
> our grandfathers' land
>
> … [these]
> grandfathers meet again through you
> & the fishermen who,
>
> some of them, pull you from the sea, who,
> some of them, watch you drown
>
> out of ruin, out of hate, out of fear. (Girmay 2016, 21–22)

A short rhyme later in the cycle returns us to this image to apostrophize the dead:

Luam, who says to the dead,
--sea near Lampedusa

I saw the hundred
fishes from a distance
& this is what I knew:

they were not fishes,
they were you. (Girmay 2016, 39)

Most poems in "Elelegy" are addressed to the dead or to the sea or both, as if they were one. In "Elelegy," the Mediterranean Sea is caught in the temporal hold of unfinished pasts and over-determined futures. More than once, Girmay names poems simply "to the sea (any)," joining the Mediterranean to the black maria and a litany of other bodies of water—the Red Sea, the Caribbean Sea, "the Afterworld Sea/Sea of Death," "any sea," the Atlantic Ocean, the Mississippi, the Tallahatchie (Girmay 2016, 13, 74).

The poem cycle does not confine itself to a tradition of individual mourning, centered on the individual psychology of the mourner. In seeking a collective formal expression of mourning, the poem cycle enacts a stealth critique of citizenship- and state-based concepts of mourning. In doing so, Girmay's poetics also lament the border regime's transformation of the dead into a dead that cannot be properly individuated—the undocumented dead whose identification by name may be lost, even as they get conscripted into public expressions of mourning by politicians. Refusing the comfort of pathetic fallacy, Girmay returns repeatedly to the *in*-sensibility of the sea to the human world, even as the speaker addresses it. One of the poems titled "to the sea (any)," ends this way:

Sea-
blackness, our Eurydice,
at the shoreline when we ask,

Where are our dead, have you carried them
Back to us? You repeat only,

Who, who? (Girmay 2016, 30)

The sea is insensible but speaks back. Its answer is itself a question that reveals the sea as one of forgetting, not merely insensible because it is water but insensible because it seems to once have had the capacity to remember and feel grief: as if it once knew the living world but has forgotten its names. In this moment, the sea confirms its otherworldliness, echoing the Eurydice of Rainer Maria Rilke's 1907 poem "Orpheus. Eurydice. Hermes." The poem takes the ancient Mediterranean story of Orpheus's desire to pull his dead beloved back with him into the world of the living. Eurydice's would-have-been miraculous return ultimately fails once Orpheus disobeys the condition that he does not look back at his beloved until their passage into the living world is complete. It registers the moment he looks back through Eurydice's transformation: "She was already loosened like long hair / poured out like fallen rain." By the time Hermes informs her that her beloved has looked back, "she could not understand, and softly answered / Who?" (Rilke 1995, 59).

In this failed crossing from death into life, Orpheus's look back as they ascended from the Underworld was an intervention too early. But Orpheus's failure to achieve the near-impossible underscores the grim truth that his intervention—the effort to keep Eurydice alive, to save her from death—had always already been too late. Rilke's poem reflects on the interior affective changes of death within Eurydice, making elegy or mourning no longer the appropriate aesthetic or affective register: "being dead / filled her beyond fulfillment. Like a fruit," Eurydice is "suffused" with her "own mystery and sweetness": "she was filled with her vast death, which was so new" (Rilke 1995, 57).

In Girmay's poem, Eurydice's transformation becomes that of the sea, a body having already become taken by its own fullness of death—what Girmay treats as a figure (a "who"), sometimes a "you," who is "talkless 'witness'" and "body of bodies" (2016, 11). Girmay accesses this relation of wonderment to death and obliviousness to life, attributing Eurydice's lines to the sea as the scene of death and a body incapable of mourning. In doing so the poem cycle raises questions about who and why and how we collectively choose (or decline) to mourn the unauthorized refugees that become the collective dead, as they continue to be made almost immediately by international agreements and practices that, despite refugee resettlement and asylum procedures, are hostile to the freedom to migrate.

In an essay on Randall Jarrell's 1940 poem "The Refugees" (revised in 1949), critic R. Clifton Spargo sees the poem's grief for the Jewish refugees who will be denied refuge as a proleptic elegy. He writes: "Split thus between the report of an impossible intervention (it is too late for these refugees) and the remaining possibility of a real political intervention in immigration policy (because it is not too late for others), the speaker's fatalism interrogates contemporary American anti-immigration policies that were actively yielding refugees to suffering and death all across occupied Europe." Spargo sees an ethical possibility in the useless mourning. He sees an elegy to "those who die by orchestrated violence" as having a special potential to "upset norms" in that it "comments on a political division that casts some lives as more worthy than others" (52–53). Elegy can become an "act of futile dissent."

One torture survivor from Eritrea's isolated coastal prison recounts a grim joke on the futility of dissent and human insensibility: "There is a saying in prison: If you scream, only the sea will hear you" (Human Rights Council 2016, Section 5.265, 66). It highlights Girmay's deliberate futility in apostrophizing what will not and cannot hear her words, a way, however indirect, of holding onto the power and meaning of a scream or a lament despite the likelihood that nobody will hear or feel or respond to it. In thinking about the Mediterranean and what he terms the "crimes of peace" that end in deaths of people trying to cross the sea, Albahari reminds us of this sea's insensibility: "the sea does nothing by itself. The sea does not militarily preclude passage through its straits. It does not dictate immigration policies. It does not sign bilateral agreements or make development aid conditional on migration containment. It does not reject people. It does not traffic in persons, nor does it rescue them" (Albahari 2016, 278–279).

Spargo's reading shows the limits nationalist and humanitarian frames can have on the proleptic elegy, when refugee suffering is recentered on subjects who can do the grieving and then taken as a given, that refugee deaths are as natural as antiblackness, or what Sharpe calls "the weather." To mourn is also to claim a relation to the lost where there may have been none before. When the elegists can choose themselves and their subjects, the refugee dead are put into the frame wrought by one who claims the power to mourn them. The displacement and mode of death make it difficult for the refugee dead to be returned to their communities, to have the stability of funereal rites, to be mourned by the family and friends who would have claimed the body in its former time and place.

When the capacity to perform grief serves as the main coordinates for both elegy and refugee futures, an unethical dimension to the social practice of mourning becomes possible, where a public acknowledgment of mourning the dead not only conceals but intensifies the precarity that ensures mass killings, as when state leaders pronounce the deaths as "tragedies" caused by smugglers or misguided migrants rather than by states, wars, or extreme economic insecurity (Albahari 2016, 278). To decenter the mourner and the grappling with political injustice in poetic form can be a challenge for elegies for the refugee dead.

As others note in their work on elegy, there is a difficulty even in naming a genre that performs grief: to mourn is a task, a process, an ethics, and a practice that presumes deep feeling, even an undoing of the self. But to mourn is also to assume a position, to fulfill a role, to take on an artistic form, all possible without feeling affectively the loss. What can be the poet's relationship to the lost but the beginning of a relationship that has to work up the feeling of intimacy and grief despite levels of abstraction—to grieve publicly for the death of those you did not know, who would not have been lawfully able to occupy the same space as you, who cannot prompt the feeling of "imagined community" as fellow compatriots? Critics of poetic and social forms for practicing grief have underscored in various ways the relationship between the genre of elegy and democracy (McGrath 2014), elegy and citizen-centered ethical responsibility (Spargo 2004, 2005), elegy and aggressive nationalism (Butler 2004), elegy and transnationalism (Ramazani 2010), elegy and the breakdown of cultural norms for mourning (Ramazani 1994), and allegory and postdictatorial mourning (Avelar 1999). "Incomplete mourning" (which Spargo sees as an ethical resistance to conditions of violence) here represents the temporality of ongoing refugee and migrant precarity, where the elegy is not to mourn those particular lives but the continuation of an international and global system that is necropolitical.

Girmay stages these problems with elegy as poetic and political ones. There are moments when the elegist and the dead and even the sea are not central figures of the poems, but instead a man with his son who feels the wind stirring the trees, and in this way knows that his brother has died in the Mediterranean, even as he tells his son that his uncle will return home soon: as the speaker announces "you are going now/into that other realm" unaccompanied by the rituals of home, "preyed over by the symbolic grief / of government, & no one allowed / who knows your name, to claim you," the speaker apostrophizes the dead and conjures the image of his brother, as if the poetic act of elegy might work against the Creon-like edict against claiming and burying one's own dead (Girmay 2016, 28).

"Elelegy" holds onto the tension between two cultural forms for sounding grief, sounded out at the same time. Anyone in the company of a professional mourner, or surrounded by wails or keening, can at once spontaneously feel grief and know that the body and mind are being manipulated to produce that response, independently from the feeling one might have had otherwise in that moment. "Elelegy" pushes against the elegiac tradition at some level, merging it with the ululatory tradition of collective grieving, where eloquent statements of the dead have no place, where instead the collective shares in grief that sounds like shouts broken and shaped only by moving the tongue against the roof of the mouth, insisting on hitting against the limits of the body to make sound.

Not only the refuge seekers but the refugee crises, too, can be emptied of their history and the returns they make for others—the going back, the coming to, the exchange made, or the profit gained. Here we can think again about the Eritrean and Sudanese refugees who ventured onto the Mediterranean Sea to die or survive the crossing. How do we think about "return" when we consider that, for some crossers, this was not the first search for asylum? A group of researchers released a report in January 2018 on Israel's Voluntary Departure Program. Based in Berlin and with experience working with refugee communities residing in Israel under several NGOs, the researchers interviewed Eritrean survivors of the Mediterranean passage who went on to gain asylum in Germany. The report explains Israel's shift to a policy of forcible deportations for the more than 37,000 people residing in Israel after irregularly crossing its southern border with Egypt. Legally defined as "infiltrators," 71% are Eritrean (21% Sudanese) nationals. Israeli courts have recognized the virtual impossibility for them to even apply for asylum in Israel, let alone receive it, and the state's policy has been "to make their lives miserable" until they leave, despite UNHCR statements that Eritrean and Sudanese nationals are recognized to deserve refugee and asylee status at high rates elsewhere in the world (Birger et al. 2018, 6)—highlighting the fundamentally flawed and easily short-circuited formal processes for recognizing refugees according to specific definitions and specific political or NGO bodies. Unable to repatriate the "infiltrators" to Eritrea or Sudan directly, Israel has improvised its own back to Africa plan: sending these would-be asylum seekers to an unnamed third country (according to the survivors interviewed, they are sent either to Rwanda or to Uganda) with promises of dignity, asylum, a work permit, a good future, and $3500 cash. Survivors testify that in practice, they were promptly taken from airports upon arrival, stripped of their travel documents, kept against their will, robbed, beaten, incarcerated, and then thrown into the dangerous smugglers' route. So their new displacement begins: from Israel to Rwanda or Uganda, through Uganda to South Sudan, to Sudan, through the Sahara Desert to Libya, and then across the Mediterranean Sea to Europe, where over 90% of those who survive receive asylum. Some were forcibly deported to Eritrea by one of these third countries.

Follow the route and survivor testimony (Fig. 10.1), and it becomes clear that Israel's practice amounts to a state policy of expulsion and harm or death. The survivors interviewed by these researchers lamented those who didn't survive, some having been like them "voluntarily departed" from Israel:

> [In the Sahara] people died and we buried them... This life... I don't want to remember this. It's hard to think about this... At night, it returns to our head. It returns. (Kiflom, quoted in Birger et al. 2018, 26)

Their testimony enters the dead into the record of this report as people the survivors remember, people the survivors literally were among who could have been survivors. It echoes the interviews Shire turned into "Conversations about Home (at the Deportation Centre)" in that both aim to bear witness and intervene before it's too late, again—the poem ending with the speaker anticipating death ("I'll see you on the other side") (Shire 2011, 27). How is the problem of lived memory and the voicing of grief shared and *not* shared between these refugee survivors and an elegist from the diaspora? How do both positions return us back to the problem of the elegy and its nationalism, the elegy in the midst of another refugee crisis?[9]

The Eritreans interviewed in the report left Israel 2014–2015 to make the same sea crossing as those on the vessel of October 2013 near Lampedusa, and the same crossings of many others. Among the most publicized crossings is called by the Forensic Architecture research agency the "Left-to-Die Boat" case of 2011, investigated under their Forensic Oceanography project in order to bring evidence to a series of pending legal cases filed by NGOs concerned over the "nonassistance to people in distress at sea" (Forensic Architecture). In the 2011 case, sixty-three people in

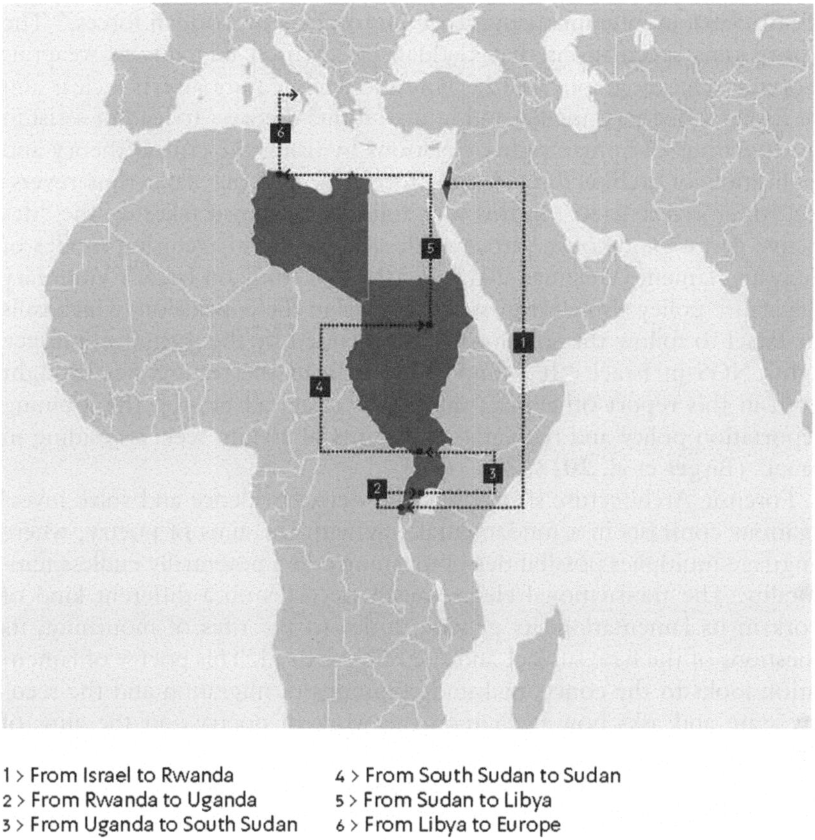

Fig. 10.1 Map of voluntary departure survivors' routes (Birger et al. 2018, 15). Reprinted by permission

distress died despite drifting slowly in the "most highly surveilled section of sea in the entire world" (Forensic Architecture). Forensic Oceanography's report maps the slow temporality of drift: it shows the vessel leaving the Libyan coast, becoming distressed, and then drifting back to Libya, where the few survivors were imprisoned. Survivors described Gaddafi forces encouraging or even forcing them onto vessels and launching them toward Europe—"Migrants making these crossings had at times to rely on paying smugglers and Gaddafi forces. There were also widespread reports of Sub-Saharan migrants being forced into boats by Gaddafi forces." The report joins speculations that Gaddafi forces used migrants as weapons (Forensic Oceanography 2012). Forensic Architecture asserts a clear aim for its work in court, media, and human rights theory—to lead or assist in investigations of human rights violations by using the critical theory and application of architecture, design, forensics, and big data, thus reversing "the forensic gaze"; in this way, founder Weizman takes up the "detective genre" and court battles while very insistently refusing modes of elegy and lament (Weizman 2017, 9–10). The study on Israel's Voluntary Departure policy also clearly asserts its aims in the conclusion, which calls for Israel to follow the solutions recommended by the forum on refugee rights NGS in Israel: "It is impossible to read the testimonies brought forth in this report otherwise; they are a clear call to stop the looming deportation policy and regularize the status of asylum seekers residing in Israel" (Birger et al. 2018, 37).

Forensic Architecture's imperative to detect evidence and solve investigations contrasts in a fundamental way with the aims of poetry, where language multiplies possibilities of meaning and a potentially endless temporality. The transnational elegiac aesthetic takes up a different kind of work in its lamentation, its generic duties to the rites of mourning, its questions of the lyric subject and the refugee dead. This poetry of lamentation looks to the conceptual underpinnings of migration and the security state and asks how it changes the work of poetry and the aims of elegy.

In a poem centered on Romare Bearden's collage painting "The Siren's Song," from the artist's Odysseus Series (1977), Girmay pleads with Bearden to help her resist the singularity of antiblackness. Bearden's Odysseus series is, like Homer's, about a return: ever so slowly and circuitously home, where home remains a site of danger or imminent departure. It's a moment in *the black maria* when the Mediterranean—as a site of return and revision by artists and intellectuals—promises to splice the ancient into the contemporary and the lament into the hopeful utterance. Bearden's black Odyssey returns to the fullness of ancient Greece and the Mediterranean, where Poseidon favors the Africans south of ancient Libya and always "wants to be with his friends there" (Bearden, quoted in O'Meally 2007, 13). For critic Robert G. O'Meally, who led the 2014–2015 exhibition of the Odyssey series at Columbia University, Bearden's Poseidon enters into a relationship of "antagonistic cooperation" with Odysseus, like an adversary in jazz improvisation whose obstacles thrown

Odysseus's way only serve to sharpen and heighten the polytropic figure's ingenuity (O'Meally 2007, 14). The series cuts and layers its figures into scenes of beauty held in that tension between the imperative to move homeward and its ever-receding horizon: it is to this black Mediterranean survival story that Girmay looks as her poetry expresses the desire not to be only the poetry of mourning.

Bearden depicts the "The Siren's Song" scene this way: at the center of a deep blue sky, in front of a gray-white sail, Bearden's black Odysseus is tied to the mast of his own ship. The yellow ropes crisscross tightly; his body is secured high on the mast but looks as if it is falling, suspended only by those ropes. O'Meally observes that Bearden has Odysseus hanging "on a cross," and another observes that Odysseus "seems to have been lynched on this high pole" (O'Meally 2007, 64). The image is layered by tension: the body looks limp from the pain of being bound. And it looks surrendered to a pose of ecstasy, listening to the Sirens' music that we can't hear. And it is a black body on a ship across a sea: the analogy to enslavement at once explicitly raised and resisted by Girmay in her wordplay on "the black maria" to mean blackness at sea and how both blackness and the sea are perpetually mis-seen, and what mourning comes from that.

Odysseus has chosen this moment of captivity to save his life without giving up the chance to hear beauty: he takes this temporary captivity to avoid the capture by the Sirens on his way home. In this way, it is a stunning image of blackness at sea incorporated into a poetics of Mediterranean returns. As the speaker of the poem, Girmay asks a question that is the poet's challenge in making a poetry of mourning: "How not to assign all blackness near the sea a captivity?" Overwhelmed by the returns on loss that the sea and states have delivered for so long, moved by Bearden's art as a return to the Ancient Mediterranean now filled with despair, she pleads with Bearden in short two-lined stanzas to "help [her] see" not only the captivity but also the un-captured that lies beyond, or hides itself deeper within, fugitively, the captive frame.

The poems discussed in this essay insist on writing beyond the state; they look past the oft-invoked claims of sovereignty and border protection to see their transnational necropolitical work. Bearden's Odysseus participates in the broader poetics I have sought to describe in this essay—one that involves a rethinking of ways to conceptualize the circuitous paths of leavings and returns generated by a world of border regimes. The Mediterranean returns considered here may extend lamentation as a diasporic poetics that at once grieves the fact of black suffering in the Mediterranean and yet pushes against its figuration as absolute singularity, what Sharpe describes as the "singularity" of physics—the collapse of all matter into a single point before falling into a black hole. I follow Vasuki Nesiah's point that "in this neoliberal age of 'democracy otherwise,' the question of what is due the dead is, as much as ever, intimately tied to what is due the living" (2015, 557). Such a poetics between elegy and lamentation invokes the limitations of humanitarianism while holding on to the need in our moment for a politics of grief as a politics of and for the living.

Acknowledgments Gratitude to all those who heard or read earlier versions of this essay. Special thanks to Walt Hunter and Brian McGrath for their early guidance and feedback and to Alexandra Moore and Samantha Pinto for ever incisive and generous comments.

Notes

1. I rely here on Suzanne Pinkney Stetkyvich's reading of this relationship between return and sorrow in Arabic poetry. See Stetkyvich (2002, 228–230). See also Meisami and Starkey (1998, 663). A fuller discussion of the artistic and political possibilities of lamentation and its relationship to maternalized and feminized politics is beyond the scope of this essay. For relevant readings, see essays by David Llloyd on keening and Mark Sanders on Antigone and customary law in *Loss: The Politics of Mourning*, edited by David L. Eng and David Kazanjian. For lamentation politics and theories of sovereignty, see Athena Athanasiou (2017).
2. Cassin writes *Nostalgia* in Corsica, a French island in the Mediterranean less affected than Lampedusa by unauthorized refugees than the Italian coast.
3. Actual dynamics between diasporic populations living abroad and national populations can be more complicated than diaspora as concept, of course. For a discussion of Eritrean diaspora and the state's implicit dependence on remittances, as well as the paradox that Eritreans living abroad enjoy more political recognition and economic rights than Eritrean nationals who live within the country, see Riggan (2013).
4. "No Search, No Rescue" was initially posted online. It was then published in Bhakti Shringarpure et al. (2018). For a fuller discussion of Operation Mare Nostrum, see Albahari (2015, 2016).
5. See Bausells and Shearlaw (2015), Kuo (2017), and Elgot (2015).
6. See Pinto (2013) for conceptualizing diaspora as "a set of aesthetic and interpretive strategies" of transnational black feminist poetry. Moving

between these registers asks that we think the multiple and varied "new diasporas" not reducible or rigidly analogous to the African diaspora of the transatlantic legal slave system (Goyal 2017).

7. Meisami and Starkey (1998, 663).
8. For a related discussion on racial melancholia, see Eng and Han (2000). See also Eng and Kazanjian (2013).
9. Recently, the UN announced a deal with Israel to halt these forced removals. Only hours later: "Israel's prime minister, Benjamin Netanyahu, suspended a deal he'd signed with the United Nations refugee agency [...] The agreement would have seen thousands of asylum seekers resettled in [Western] countries and others allowed to remain in Israel. As the government's earlier plans for mass deportations collapsed and the UN's alternative disintegrated under political pressure, about 39,000 Eritrean and Sudanese migrants are back in limbo. Some have been released from detention after the government's years-old secret deals to move refugees to Uganda and Rwanda also ran into difficulties." But even this agreement would have taken five years to implement (Lubell 2018).

Works Cited

Albahari, Maurizio. 2015. *Crimes of Peace: Mediterranean Migrations at the World's Deadliest Border*. Philadelphia: University of Pennsylvania Press.

———. 2016. "After the Shipwreck: Mourning and Citizenship in the Mediterranean, Our Sea." *Social Research: An International Quarterly* 83 (2 Summer): 275–294.

Athanasiou, Athena. 2017. *Agonistic Mourning: Political Dissidence and the Women in Black*. Edinburgh: Edinburgh University Press.

Avelar, Idelber. 1999. *The Untimely Present: Postdictatorial Latin American Fiction and the Task of Mourning*. Durham: Duke University Press.

Bausells, Marta, and Maeve Shearlaw. 2015. "Poets Speak Out for Refugees: 'No One Leaves Home, Unless Home Is the Mouth of a Shark.'" *The Guardian*, September 16. Last accessed August 15, 2018. https://www.theguardian.com/books/2015/sep/16/poets-speak-out-for-refugees-.

Birger, Lior, Shahar Shoham, and Liat Bolzman. 2018. "Better a Prison in Israel Than Dying Along the Way: Testimonies of Refugees Who 'Voluntarily' Departed Israel to Rwanda and Uganda and Gained Protection in Europe." Translation by Elizabeth Tsurkov. The Hotline for Refugees and Migrants. Last accessed August 15, 2018. Link to full report available online. https://hotline.org.il/en/publication/better-a-prison-in-israel-than-dying-on-the-way/.

Bseiso, Jehan. 2015. "No Search, No Rescue." *The Electronic Intifada Cairo*, 24 April 2015. Online. https://electronicintifada.net/content/poem-no-search-norescue/14461.

Butler, Judith. 2004. *Precarious Life: The Powers of Mourning and Violence*. London: Verso.

Cassin, Barbara. 2016. *Nostalgia: When Are We Ever at Home?* Translated by Pascale-Anne Brault. Foreword by Souleymane Bachir Diagne. New York: Fordham University Press.

Elgot, Jessica. 2015. "Benedict Cumberbatch Stuns Theatregoers with Anti-government Speech." *The Guardian*, October 30. Last accessed August 15, 2018. https://www.theguardian.com/uk-news/2015/oct/30/benedict-cumberbatch-stuns-theatregoers-anti-government-speech-refugees.

Eng, David L., and David Kazanjian, eds. 2013. *Loss: The Politics of Mourning*. Berkeley: University of California Press.

Eng, David L., and Shinhee Han. 2000. A Dialogue on Racial Melancholia. *Psychanalytic Dialogues* 10 (4): 667–700.

Forensic Oceanography. 2012. (*Charles Heller, Lorenzo Pezzani and Situ Studio*). "Report on the '*Left-To-Die Boat*.' Part of the European Research Council Project 'Forensic Architecture.'" Centre for Research Architecture, Goldsmiths, University of London, UK. Last accessed August 15, 2018. http://www.forensic-architecture.org/wp-content/uploads/2014/05/FO-report.pdf.

Girmay, Aracelis. 2016. *The Black Maria*. Rochester, NY: BOA Editions Ltd.

Goyal, Yogita. 2017. "We Need New Diasporas." *American Literary History* 29 (4): 640–663.

Human Rights Council. 2016. "Human Rights Situations That Require the Council's Attention Detailed Findings of the Commission of Inquiry on Human Rights in Eritrea." Thirty-Second Session Agenda Item 4. June 8. Last accessed August 15, 2018. https://www.ohchr.org/Documents/HRBodies/HRCouncil/CoIEritrea/A_HRC_32_CRP.1_read-only.pdf.

Kuo, Lily. 2017. "This Poem Is Now the Rallying Call for Refugees: 'No One Leaves Home Unless Home Is the Mouth of a Shark.'" *Quartz*, January 30. Last accessed August 15, 2018. https://qz.com/africa/897871/warsan-shires-poem-captures-the-reality-of-life-for-refugees-no-one-leaves-home-unless-home-is-the-mouth-of-a-shark/.

Lubell, Maayan. 2018. "Israel Suspends New Relocation Deal for African Migrants." *Reuters*, April 2. Accessed April 6, 2018.

McGrath, Brian. 2014. "Dead Men Running." *Diacritics* 42 (4): 80–96.

Meisami, Julie Scott, and Paul Starkey. 1998. "*rithā*'" Entry. *Encyclopedia of Arabic Literature*. 2 vols. London: Routledge.

Nesiah, Vasuki. 2015. "Counter-Sovereignty, Lamentation and Transgressive Publics." In Book Discussion: Bonnie Honig, Antigone, Interrupted. *Philosophy Today* 59 (3): 557–559.

O'Meally, Robert G. 2007. *Romare Bearden: A Black Odyssey*. New York: DC Moore Gallery.

Pinto, Samantha. 2013. *Difficult Diasporas: The Transnational Feminist Aesthetic of the Black Atlantic*. New York: New York University Press.

Ramazani, Jahan. 1994. *Poetry of Mourning: The Modern Elegy from Hardy to Heaney*. Chicago: University of Chicago Press.

Ramazani, Jahan. 2010. "Nationalism, Transnationalism, and the Poetry of Mourning." *Oxford Handbok of the Elegy*, edited by Karen Weisman. Oxford and New York: Oxford University Press.

Riggan, Jennifer. 2013. "Imagining Emigration: Debating National Duty in Eritrean Classrooms." *Africa Today* 60 (2): 84–106. Last accessed October 9, 2018.

Rilke, Rainer Maria. 1995. "Orpheus. Eurydice. Hermes." *Ahead of All Parting: The Selected Poetry and Prose of Rainer Maria Rilke* (English & German Edition), 55–60. Edited and Translated by Stephen Mitchell. New York: Random House.

Sharpe, Christina. 2016. *In the Wake: On Blackness and Being*. Durham: Duke University Press.

Shire, Warsan. 2011. "Conversations About Home (at the Deportation Centre)." *Teaching My Mother How to Give Birth*. London: Flipped Eye Publishing.

———. 2015. "Home." Genius.com. Last accessed August 15, 2018. https://genius.com/Warsan-shire-home-annotated.

Shringarpure, Bhakti, and Michael Bronner, Veruska Cantelli, Michael Busch, Jessica Rohan, and Melissa Smyth, et al. 2018. *Mediterranean*. New York: UpSet Press.

The Sirens' Song. 1977. Collage of Various Papers with Paint and Graphite on Fiberboard, 32 x 44 Inches. Collection of Dr. Alan and Pat Davidson. In Robert G. O'Meally, *Romare Bearden: A Black Odyssey*. DC Moore Gallery, 2007.

Spargo, R. Clifton. 2004. *The Ethics of Mourning*. Baltimore: Johns Hopkins University Press.

———. 2005. "The Ethical Uselessness of Grief: Randall Jarrell's 'The Refugees.'" *PMLA* 120 (1): 49–65.

Stetkyvich, Suzanna Pinckney. 2002. *The Poetics of Islamic Legitimacy: Myth, Gender, and Ceremony in the Classical Arabic Ode*. Bloomington: Indiana University Press.

Ticktin, Miriam. 2016. "Thinking Beyond Humanitarian Borders." *Social Research: An International Quarterly* 83 (2): 255–271. https://www.muse.jhu.edu/article/631162.

UN General Assembly, *194 (III). Palestine—Progress Report of the United Nations Mediator*, December 11, 1948, A/RES/194. Last accessed August 15, 2018. http://www.refworld.org/docid/4fe2e5672.html.

UNHCR. 2018a. "Refugees Operational Data Portal: Mediterranean Situation." Last accessed August 15, 2018. https://data2.unhcr.org/en/situations/mediterranean.

UNHCR. 2018b. "Global Trends: Forced Displacement in 2017." Last accessed August 15, 2018. http://www.unhcr.org/globaltrends2017/.

Weizman, Eyal. 2017. *Forensic Architecture: Violence at the Threshold of Detectability*. New York: Zone Books.

Woods, Tryon P., and P. Khalil Saucier. 2015. "Slavery's Afterlife in the Euro-Mediterranean Basin." *OpenDemocracy*. Last accessed August 16, 2018.

CHAPTER 11

Seeking Asylum: Mapping the Hidden Worlds of Migrant Detention Centers in Recent Literary Representations

Terri Tomsky

This chapter investigates the representational imaginary of today's most visually spectacular human rights challenge, specifically that of migrants crossing into Europe and North America within the context of increasing securitization. To study this issue, my chapter shifts focus away from the representation of the sovereign subject of the migrant or refugee, a figure often humanized in narratives for the purpose of empathy, in order to examine two separate but related issues: first, the representational challenge posed by the sheer numbers of non-status migrants; and, second, the effects these numbers are having upon the built environment and security infrastructure. To examine these issues in literature demands a change in perspective, from the local and individual, to the regional and global. The UNHCR estimates that there are some sixty million displaced

T. Tomsky (✉)
Department of English and Film Studies, University of Alberta,
Edmonton, AB, Canada
e-mail: tomsky@ualberta.ca

A. S. Moore and S. Pinto (eds.), *Writing Beyond the State*,
Palgrave Studies in Literature, Culture and Human Rights,
https://doi.org/10.1007/978-3-030-34456-6_11

people in the world, so this is a significant political concern (Fiske 2016, 6). But it also has a major cultural component and a complicated history. To begin with a simple observation: representations matter in the political context of migration. Many migrants, especially those claiming asylum, arrive at a border lacking the material possessions or legal documents to establish the legitimacy of their claims. Few, indeed, carry more than their stories. By their nature, such stories are designed to evoke sympathy, compassion, and fellow-feeling from their audience. However, to a state which is hostile toward or simply seeking to control migration, these stories are a risk that needs management. A counter-narrative must be developed, and thus we see representations of migration in media outlets that describe migrancy as an issue with a massive scale, in metaphors of "tides," "waves," or "floods." Such oceanic metaphors counter, because they drown out the sympathetic claims of individual voices.

In turn, groups opposing the anti-immigration rhetoric have sought to rehumanize the migrant through a body of literature that works to make legible the experience of irregular migrants—that is, those migrants without legal papers or full immigration status—and, particularly, their human rights violations within the broader setting of states' inhospitality. Already, there is a large and growing archive of cultural work—literary, nonfiction, visual, and digital—aimed at adults as well as children about and by asylum seekers and migrants, which have challenged dominant and pejorative misapprehensions of them as dangerous threats or invaders, as criminals or freeloaders, as well as other negative views about these subjects in relation to human rights and political community (e.g., Boie 2016; Greder 2007; Herd and Pincus 2016; Sanna 2016; Sacco 2010; Sayer 2015). Such texts relay the traumatic experience of displacement, and convey the scale of deaths, violence, the hostility of locals in the place they arrive, as well as other dangers of their journeys to readers. These works have a public-facing orientation, disarticulating a mainstream understanding of migrants as an unwanted intrusion or incursion on national sovereignty. Key to them is the foregrounding of an imaginative proximity between the narrator and the reader, an encounter, which establishes empathy and recognition of that subject as a sovereign subject and claimant of rights. In other words, such narratives seek to advance the migrant's human rights, often by making clear the violation of those rights. But, precisely because of their generic choice to focus on an individual or, at best, several individuals, their attempts to represent migration are bound by synecdoche. With a small part standing in for the whole, such texts resist the dehumanizing flattening of anti-immigration rhetoric by producing a different kind of flattening. Often, this is a flattening that rehearses the political impasse of romantic conventions, where a single individual's worth and value becomes articulated. At a point in history when the problem of migration is, in fact, massive, the efficacy of these gestures—of listening to every individual's story—can produce a kind of fatigue among its audience.

The positive interventions such texts have made cannot be denied, but this chapter addresses another body of texts, that *engage* rather than refuse the problem of scale. Specifically, I am interested in texts that dispense with humanizing narrative arcs, romantic appeals to empathy, the communicability of the migrant experience, the dramatic story of his or her journey, as well as the individualization of the refugee. I approach these texts cautiously since they appear to be antithetical to the human rights principle of "names, not numbers," to cite Carmine Menna, an optician from Lampedusa, Italy, who describes his experience rescuing forty-seven African migrants from a sinking ship in the Mediterranean (Kirby 2016). Indeed, Menna's act highlights the stakes of dispensing with humanization: what happens when non-status migrants, refugees and asylum seekers become numbers? For Menna, it is precisely his fleshly interaction with the migrants—pulling them physically out of the water by their hands, feeling how their "fingers...cemented into [his]...in a bond stronger and more intimate than an umbilical cord"—that affirmed to him that these were *people* rather than *abstractions* (Kirby 2017, 12). The texts I explore below confront the problem differently, imagining what possibilities emerge if we remain at the level of abstraction. I turn first to Canadian poet Dionne Brand's long-form poem *Inventory* (2006) and then to Canadian architect Tings Chak's graphic narrative *Undocumented: The Architecture of Migrant Detention* (2014) to consider how cultural texts can turn away from the individual accounts of human experience in order to call attention to a vast detention regime.

In this tactic, I want to suggest, these authors seek to foreground the *evidentiary*: the numbers of people, the systems, the infrastructures, and architectures through which migrant bodies are shuttled, distributed, and incarcerated. Such texts reflect what has been called the forensic turn in architecture, a movement that seeks to expose the way a built environment is also a "source of knowledge about historical events," opening up critical and juridical investigations into how the purposeful building of certain infrastructures creates the conditions and enables the practices that violate the human rights of their inhabitants (Weizman et al. 2010, 59). By foregrounding matter, material objects, and material environments, such texts show how infrastructures provide a witness to a particular set of politics perpetrated through their very formations. When these texts reveal the same or similar responses to irregular migration, the same buildings and processing centers being developed and deployed in different countries, it becomes clear that these are not solutions that have been designed with a single nation's interest. Instead, a larger pattern is evident that indicates the issue cannot be seen purely through the lens of the individual nation-state. Likewise, this suggests that a human rights response to the violation of migrants' rights should also be addressed globally. Indeed, these authors deflect attention from the individual refugee or migrant story in order to ask readers to reimagine their relationship far more broadly with the dispossessed and displaced; that is, to ask readers to consider the larger conditions and structures that create dispossession and that manage the dispossessed, and, by extension, think about those who have designed and designated these material environments.

Though the contexts are many, including the US-Mexican border and the so-called "jungle" at the French port of Calais, before it was demolished, the coast of the Mediterranean Sea is perhaps the dominant setting for representations of migration over the last decade. In many of these representations, the Mediterranean is framed as a space of "migration crisis," a view that tends to obfuscate the political decisions at work to deny safe and legal passage to those fleeing war and poverty (Jeandesboza and Pallister-Wilkins 2016). In the Mediterranean, the prosaic materials of mass migration, like the boats, migrant clothing, and shoes discovered on land have played a different, albeit also significant role in demonstrating the scale of migration. In Pozzallo, a port in Sicily, large numbers of "barely seaworthy" boats used to traffic migrants have been impounded and stacked to create what locals see as a makeshift memorial to their passengers (Dearden 2015). Other, more official, memorials have appeared in places that, because of their proximity to Africa, are key destinations for migrants. At some level, the memorials offer a tangible marker of mass migration, in place of the bodies of the so-called "lost migrants," to use the euphemism used to describe the drownings of desperate people. In Lampedusa, local authorities commissioned Mimmo Paladino to build a monument in 2008 on the southernmost end of the island, the closest European point to Tunisia. Paladino's "La Porta d'Europa" is in the form of an open doorway within a much larger yellow doorframe, adorned with bowls, shoes, and numbers, which figuratively represent the asylum seekers, who drowned in their efforts to reach Europe. Elsewhere, in the Canary Islands, lies a more unorthodox monument. As discussed in the epilogue to this volume and below, off the coast of Lanzarote, "Museo Atlantico," set up in 2016 by British artist Jason deCaires Taylor, commemorates those migrants who lost their lives crossing the Mediterranean less abstractly, providing instead a materialization of the people who lost their lives. His concrete sculptures, set out in twelve installations underwater, depict scores of humans on the ocean floor, in rafts and in lifeboats, and walking towards fortifications. An archive of the catastrophe in the Mediterranean, deCaires Taylor's monument is vivid in its realism and humanity: his human sculptures are clothed, often upright, contemplative, or gazing forward or upwards in a gesture that evokes futurity. Museo Atlantico calls to mind the global discourse of human rights protections, especially the UN's 1948 Universal Declaration with its focus on the inherent "dignity and worth of the human person [...] the equal rights of men and women" as well as their right to safety and protection, a concern raised by the Office of the High Commissioner for Human Rights over large movements of people in 2016 (OHCHR 2016). The last installation of deCaires Taylor's exhibits is a "human gyre," a spectacle of suffering represented by a circle made up of two hundred naked, prostrated bodies of men, women, and children. DeCaires Taylor's monument is an extraordinary feat which addresses the rights of those he represents as humans, as well as the complacency of Europe, displayed in his statues of self-absorbed spectators taking selfies directly in front of the migrants. Notably, his monument is situated in a UNESCO biosphere and designed to encourage the growth of coral (which is being depleted worldwide because of ocean acidification), and so it provokes his audience to think on climate change, a reality that is already causing major population disruption, though those displaced are often not designated refugees (Berchin et al. 2017). Even as a monument inaccessible to many because of its underwater location, deCaires Taylor's work conveys an awareness of the politics of visibility that renders many migrants unseen, unmourned, and insignificant.

Both these monuments then evoke the importance of commemorating the mass deaths of migrants materially, albeit in different ways. DeCaires Taylor's monument more forcefully highlights the necropolitics that guides contemporary modes of perception of the anonymous, sinking, and drowned asylum seekers. While his artwork certainly humanizes these subjects, his installations raise the question whether such refuge-seeking subjects are only humanized once they are dead. In other words, both "Museo Atlantico" and "La Porta d'Europa" crystalize a number of issues about the perilous state of irregular migration and what scholars have called "the deficit of human rights" (Balch, 38), that is the gap between the *promise* of human rights for all and the reality of closed borders, border camps, and the dangerous sea-crossings, often facilitated by the black market, which migrants undertake with the attendant risks of hypothermia, suffocation, fuel burns, substandard boats, fake lifejackets, etc. Recently, there has been an increasing violation of international humanitarian law when ships have refused their duty to rescue people in distress or stranded at sea, as per Article 98 of the 1982 United Nations Convention on the Law of the Sea (see also Angela Naimou's essay in this volume). Indeed, NGOs have estimated that there have been over 30,000 deaths since 2000 for those crossing the Mediterranean.[1] The fact that these fatalities have a conspicuous visibility is disturbing. The deaths of irregular migrants, particularly in the Mediterranean, tend to be hypervisible in ways that erase the living, the actual lives of asylum seekers and migrants. Certainly, the monuments, to differing degrees, mobilize a sense of pathos for the lives that were cut short. Yet, there is also a need to critically assess the discrepancy between our sympathy for the dead and the existence of what has been called the "global detention regime": the securitized containment of asylum seekers that denies them rights. It is important to ask questions about the militarization of borders as well as the lack of a safe and legal passage afforded to people fleeing war, what scholars have called "the 'letting die' of people at sea," and other humanitarian crises (Bigo 2015, 64). State hostility to migrants, in other words, is deeply implicated in the ongoing deaths of refugees and migrants, where the mass death of humans is more acceptable than granting them refuge.

In her 100-page poem, *Inventory*, Dionne Brand offers a bird's eye view of this calamity at a global level and suggests its causal relationship to the necropolitics of mass displacement. Her poetic-narrator is mesmerized by the international news that brings these realities inside her quiet home. She watches and listens "each hour, each night" (2006, 29) to a litany of news about killings around the world—"by mortars," "by suicide bomb" and "car bomb," "in collision," "in attack," "in fighting," "in firefight" (2006, 23), and the arrests, the deportations, the "drowning," and the "disappearances" of desperate migrants (2006, 38–39). While *Inventory* notes the effects of hostilities and conflict zones in places like Iraq, Sudan, the occupied territories in Palestine, and the racialized violence occurring daily in North America, as well as the many preventable deaths "by malaria, by haemorrhagic fevers, by hungers" (2006, 39), the poem also engages with the irregularization of migrants, the way policing, deportation, and imprisonment of non-status migrants pushes individuals to risk violence and death through unsafe journeys or border crossings. The narrator counts the deaths of migrants alongside a larger global tally of sufferings and killings, linked to colonial legacies and neo-imperial violence. The poetic narrator thus reflects on the precarity of lives of those caught "by fingerprint, by dogs and vigilantes" (2006, 39) and in "arrests near the tunnel,/ in arrest in La Migra in Brewster County" (2006, 39).

In her overview of "asylum/ in Traikirchen, at Brussels, at Helsinki" and the "deportations to Buenos Aires, Ricardo Barrientos," Brand reveals the global span of the securitization industrial complex that has been named the "ban-opticon" by political scientist, Didier Bigo to signal its objective: that is, to enforce borders and global security (2008, 32). Like Michel Foucualt's panopticon, the ban-opitcon represents "an escalating generalized surveillance" (2008, 31); however, unlike the panopticon, the ban-opitcon is not fixated with surveilling an entire population, and instead polices a specific minority found in "the transborder movement of individuals" (2008, 32). The ban-opticon is a global dispositif made up of heterogeneous practices, institutions, architectural structures, agencies, laws, and discourses (such as on security, threat, and criminalization), which seeks to regulate populations and exclude certain groups, typically a category of racialized "unwelcome" subject, while it "normalizes the non-excluded" (2008, 32). The ban-opticon, in other words, is a method of social sorting that reveals itself in punitive form and in its exceptional power; it constructs and so differentiates between desirable and undesirable subjects, legal and illegal subjects, and seeks to discipline—ban—those undesirables, to habituate them even, to their status as unwelcome.

Early in her poem, Brand's poetic narrator experiences the formidable power of the ban-opitcon wielding its securitization technologies as she waits at the airport, a border zone that orchestrates risk management, (in)security, and surveillance in biometric form and through the threatening presence of border guards. The effect—and affect—on bodies is palpable as "lines of visitors are fingerprinted/ eye-scanned, grow murderous" (2006, 16). People wait in "blenching queues [...] passive lines" at the "encampment of the airport" (2006, 17), while "guards blued and leathered, multiply" (2006, 16). Subjected to monitoring, human bodies are rendered at once anxious and uneasy, angry yet docile, and fearful of standing out. In contrast to this intensively policed space, which her narrator (as a citizen) is nevertheless able to navigate and traverse fairly smoothly, Brand thinks on the huge inequality that contemporary borders mean for different groups of people and gives an account of individuals who, for fear of deportation and detention, avoid these border crossings, many who end up "dreamless shipwrecked" (2006, 16). Her narrator enumerates those casualties: "thirteen drowned off the coast of Italy… twenty-one/ cockle-pickers by drowning at Morecambe Bay" (2006, 38). Her poem depicts an inventory of lives, anonymous and elusive, represented by numbers, rather than by names or as distinct individuals with complex feelings.

Sometimes, instead of figures, Brand represents these dispersed populations metonymically by the names of the detention facilities into which they are incarcerated by immigration authorities: "In childhood at Pagini, at Lampedusa and Regina /Pacis, at Safi army barracks" (2006, 39). Here the necropolitical gives way to the biopolitical administration of borders and bodies. The names of detention centers in Sicily, Southern Italy, and Malta may not be well known to readers of Brand's poem, though these facilities have proliferated in Europe over the last twenty years. The disenfranchised, racialized subject, who is seeking asylum, can be held in custody in such centers for years, and sometimes indefinitely. In designated detention centers, adults and children are set apart from society, warehoused, and locked up, while their identities and nationalities are ascertained.[2] Typically, such places enable the control and surveillance of unwanted migrants, where they are held with few rights and little to no political agency, while waiting for a decision about their status (there is no liberal presumption of innocence here).

The places named by Brand don't reveal much, but prompt the reader to search out their significance and histories. Pagani, for example, located on the island of Lesbos in Greece, refers to a children's refugee prison, whereas Regina Pacis, in Lecce, Southern Italy, is a holding facility for non-status migrants, run by Lecce's Catholic diocese and supported financially by the state. Both places have been mired in controversy, with Regina Pacis in particular linked to corruption as well as the physical and racial abuse of Muslim migrants (Albahari 2015, 52). Brand's reference to the drownings at Morecambe Bay relates to a beach in Lancashire, Northwest England, where twenty-one undocumented Chinese workers died in 2004. Unaware of the dangerous local conditions, exploited by criminal gangs, and unable to communicate in English, the migrants were working at night gathering cockles when they became trapped by the fast moving tides. Here, Brand calls attention to what became a national scandal in the UK as it exposed the under-regulation of labour, Britain's reliance on irregular migrants, often via human trafficking, the precarious or absent rights of migrants without legal documents, as well as their terrible working conditions, all of which prop up the normalcy of available cheap food in a neoliberal economy.

Brand's poem maps out a view of the global deportation system as well as the poverty and conflict that gives rise to displacement and migration in the first place, but her imaginative strategy for revealing this dilemma is conveyed in defamiliarizing terms, through the estranging logic of numbers and unknown place names. This tactic, which refuses a fuller, descriptive elaboration of those lives lost or those facilities that forcibly confine migrants, contrasts with other literary and visual representations, seen for instance in the graphic comics of Joe Sacco or in the non-fiction narratives of Michael Green and Andre Dao's 2017 volume, *They Cannot Take the Sky: Stories from Detention*. In Sacco's 2010 comic "The Unwanted," about asylum seekers arriving by boat from Africa to Malta, we can trace a process of re-humanization as Sacco foregrounds and visually amplifies the human faces and the words of the asylum seekers, creating points of empathic attachment for the reader. Lucy Fiske, a political scientist who has interviewed former detainees held in immigration detention centers has pointed out the need for what she calls a "re-humanizing" of asylum seekers and refugees, given the profoundly dehumanizing way they are treated by the detaining state. In her work with asylum seekers detained in Australia, Fiske writes that the refugees she spoke with often "appeal to a shared or universal humanity," a view that she sees as critical to "an implied belief that human status entails a guarantee of a minimum standard of treatment" (2016, 19). Here, the *voice* and *testimonial narrative* of the suffering victim is pivotal in establishing the humanity of the teller. In their anthology, Green and Dao reproduce this idea; by focalizing their stories on dramatic and humanizing testimony, their book casts their subjects, those incarcerated asylum seekers, as "resilient, suffering human beings"—the sovereign bearers of rights claims (2017, 317).

Brand's poem, in contrast, conveys a refusal to vocalize one individual (or group's) suffering over another. Her poem keeps at the forefront the sheer numbers, the vast scope and scale of the detained, the deported, the "vanished," the "faceless" and the "anonymously dead," who collectively reveal the structural violence that stymies free movement, as well as the barriers and detention mechanisms set up to deter and trap populations (2006, 78). Keeping count is significant because, as Fiske and others have noted in her analysis of non-citizen detentions and deaths, information is compiled unevenly; some states do not collect statistics and there is "no central database for recording the detention of non-citizens (including none for the European Union)" (Fiske 2016, 191).[3] While Brand's poem does not offer an accurate supplement to this lack of information, it nevertheless orients—and in fact, challenges—the reader towards a more critical, globalized view of the world and its widespread violations. Brand ends her poem on a bleak tone by telling her readers, "I have nothing soothing to tell you,/ that's not my job" (2006, 100). As she sees it, her poem must refute the lull of human(ized) stories, in order to "revise and revise this bristling list" of lives, a list that aims to galvanize outrage as it reminds readers of lives that would otherwise remain expendable or attract no attention (2006, 100). Her poem is no less a confrontation, which demands readers draw the connections, stay attuned, reflect, respond, and resist those structural inequalities produced by the configurations of today's exclusionary modes of belonging.

Canadian architect, Tings Chak similarly attends to the effects of the ban-opitcon on vulnerable populations through her engagement with the detention facilities themselves. Her graphic narrative, *Undocumented*, moves away from a view of border fatalities to explore what happens when undocumented migrants reach their destination; that is, she offers a close-up view of the detention centers to which non-status migrants are often banished. Chak's emphasis on detainment and the day-to-day operations within the detention facilities is unusual because as Eleni Coundouriotis has noted, many narratives about refugees and migrants repeatedly reiterate "the story of flight" where movement is the central topos, the dramatic motif which is key to "the imaginary of the refugee" fleeing persecution and war (2015, 78). Chak's focus thus reminds readers that, as Coundouriotis herself points out, "the story of *immobility*" is usually the accompanying, but downplayed reality of the refugee experience, a "consequence of flight" that shapes the lives of many refugees who must wait months, and sometimes years, in temporary camps (2015, 78, emphasis added). Indeed, mobility rather than stasis is emphasized (and perhaps venerated) in migrant stories because it signifies a "sense of agency and of movement toward a destiny" (2015, 78) and so functions to bolster the refugee's autonomy and hope "through the construction of her as a figure who can *walk* out from her circumstances and toward a restored normalcy (Coundouriotis 2015, 79, original emphasis). Chak's engagement with the architectures of migrant detention centers in Canada, by way of contrast, places emphasis on the production of immobility, the political governance that renders the stasis and rightlessness of the migrant as part of her critique of the disciplinary management of the immigrant other.

In her text, Chak exposes a different sort of Canada to the one typically enshrined through the official discourse of the state, which has long projected a positive image of itself as an inclusive "immigrant nation" that celebrates multiculturalism and promotes universal human rights in Canadian law, including the UN Convention Relating to the Status of Refugees, the Canadian Human Rights Commission, and the Truth and Reconciliation Commission. *Undocumented* offers a visual account of immigration detention facilities and points to the way these spaces function as legal grey zones, "sites of exclusion and seclusion," segregating undocumented individuals and subordinating them to an entirely different regime from that experienced by the rest of Canada (Chak 2014, 30). This discrepancy between Canada's inclusive rhetoric and its exclusionary treatment of non-status migrants is facilitated by the way such detention centers are designed. Immigration detention facilities are aptly known as "closed environments" which legal scholar Claudio Grossman defines as

> any place where persons are or may be deprived of their liberty by means of placement in a public or private setting in which a person is not permitted to leave at will by order of any judicial, administrative or other order, or by any other lawful authority. (2014, 125)

Like prisons or psychiatric units, immigration detention centers are also *closed* to the public in the sense that they are difficult to access—indeed, information about detention centers are often not made public—and so are subject to little oversight (Cornelisse 2010, 2). This has profound consequences for the guarantee of human rights claims of the individuals held there (and, for the most part, immigration detention centers appear to be inconsistent with international human rights obligations). The title of Chak's book, *Undocumented* suggests this lack of accountability. The word "undocumented" here refers to more than the precarious immigration status of the detainees; indeed, Chak's title illustrates the undocumented status of the detention buildings themselves: there is no public access to drawings, plans, or photographs of them. As highly securitized buildings, they are often off limits, and so, for a large part of her book,

Chak relies on an interview with the architect who designs detention centers to gather her information.

Undocumented highlights the hidden world of migrant detention centers—centers that are often unnoticed by locals—or, in Chak's phrase, that are "invisibilized" to local communities (University of Oxford Podcasts, 2014). The book offers a guide to readers to look anew within local spaces, to reconsider buildings, and imagine what life is like for those transferred to the detention regime. The book includes photographs, alongside line drawings, taken of the centers from the outside, which take up the first twenty-five pages of her book, to remind readers that these facilities are located across ordinary towns and small cities in Canada, such as in Napanee, Scarborough, Niagara, and Quebec City. In her book, Chak writes, "people without status are expelled to…buildings and landscapes so banal, that they can go by unnoticed" (2014, 10). In heightening attention to these sites of migrant incarceration, Chak reminds her reader that the invisibility of these facilities is a deliberate act: "We hide the things that we don't want to see or that we don't want seen" (2014, 18). Yet, the dramatization of migrant *lives* in the "holding centers" is mostly absent in her text (2014, 4). Rather than focusing on individual people, Chak instead analyzes the architecture of detention that shapes the inmates' experiences, which she annotates with short captions, taken from her interview with the architect or "stories borrowed from the lived experiences" of the detainees (2014, 1).

Her images capture the atmosphere of these centers, visually documenting the disciplinary confinement to which their inhabitants are subjected to as criminal other (though they have not been convicted of any crime) (Fig. 11.1). Her pictures track the ubiquitous surveillance, the locked doors, the caged windows, the small spaces that cause "white blindness," claustrophobia, and spatial disorientation, eroding the sense of one's own subjectivity (2014, 97). On one page, we can see twenty-five small panels of images displayed; of those, thirteen panels track different close-ups of CCTV cameras, mounted onto ceilings and walls, while the other twelve panels reveal a view from above, no doubt the angle captured by the surveillance camera (Fig. 11.2). The cumulative effect of knowing and seeing that constant policing is pervasive, leading to what Chak calls a "sense of spatial haunting – feeling the presence of someone else …who you can never catch a glimpse of" (2014, 96).

Chak's text makes apprehensible how irregularity is *felt* intensely, both physically and mentally. The experience of the detention facility reshapes

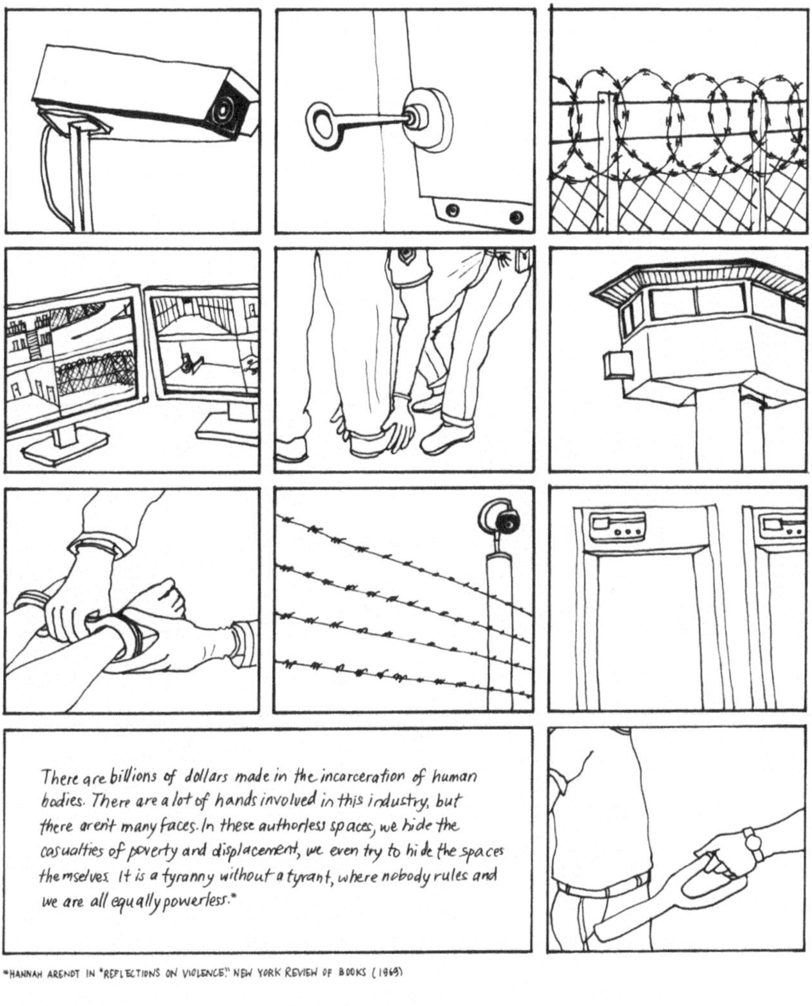

Fig. 11.1 Technologies of discipline and control in Tings Chak, *Undocumented* (2014). Reprinted by permission

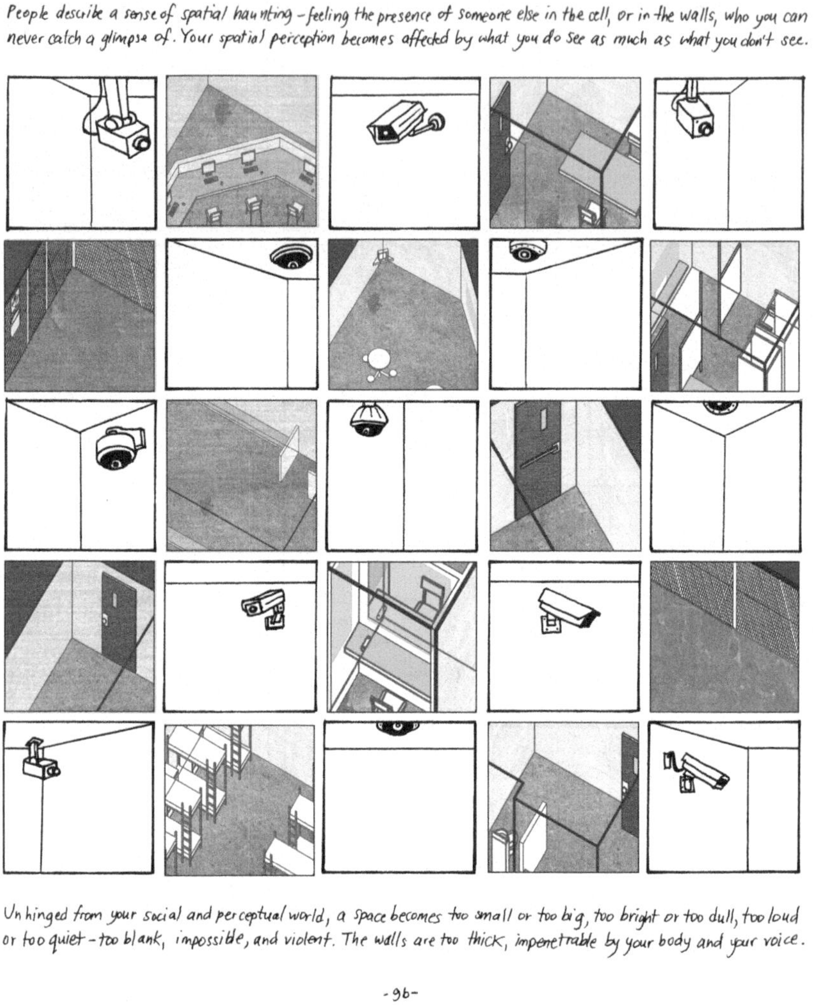

Fig. 11.2 Technologies of surveillance in Tings Chak, *Undocumented* (2014). Reprinted by permission

one's phenomenological relation to the world as detainees increasingly become "unhinged from [their] social and perceptual world" (2014, 96). Chak also draws the hoarded photos, secretly stashed food, and makeshift toilet-paper curtains to demonstrate the ways in which migrants seek to resist the conditions of the space, to sustain "a refuge, a home for the self" in a bid to reject their social and legal exclusion—that is, their social death—which is made explicit through the dehumanizing environment (2014, 106).

In line with Brand's defamiliarization technique, Chak checks the reader's voyeuristic gaze and desire to interpellate non-status people in various ways (for instance, labelling them as "illegals," "aliens," "shadow populations," etc.). Chak's illustrations turn the reader's curious gaze away from reading the human bodies held in detention centers, and guide it towards the scrutiny of those purposefully banal detention landscapes. Understanding dispossession through its built architecture, rather than through the humans who inhabit it, provokes and shifts readerly perception to the construction of a space of exclusion, a place without human rights and privileges, that exist within our home-towns and cities. In this way Chak induces the reader to a perception that resists a normative view of the ban-opticon, one that comes from a relatively safe position of privilege that casts the migrant prisoner as other or invisible. This perception is further consolidated by Chak's vocabulary, which dispenses with the often pejorative discourse associated with the ban-opticon; for instance, Chak makes a point of saying "mass displacement," rather than "mass migration" (2014, 1); and, she calls the inhabitants of the facility "detainees" rather than "migrant" to unsettle the euphemisms that sanitize what has been called the "conditions of structural subordination and exploitation" (Jansen 2015, 23–24). Moreover, even the terminology of "migrant" conceals the motivation of many refuge-seeking individuals and so minimizes, if not negates the state's political and legal obligations. Chak's emphasis on architectures concretizes the space for readers; and in doing so, insists that readers recognize the deliberative construction of these places and the processes involved in forcibly detaching subjects from the society in which they are residing.

In their assessment of securitization and the surveillance of asylum seekers within Canada and Europe, both Brand's and Chak's texts reveal the (in)visibility of the irregular migrant, a figure that is disproportionately noticed when dead, but whose lived experience of deportation and detention is obscured. While both texts provide new perceptual knowledge about the world, they also stress accountability, asking readers to take account (or to take a count, in Brand's case). Their shared political impulse challenges readers to consider what they are seeking as they read about mass displacement and mass incarceration. Both Brand's and Chak's representations refuse facile attachments and empty empathy, and so serve as a caution to readers to be more critical of easily felt sentiments towards individuals, since those feelings do not necessarily correspond to any political or social action toward justice. Their strategies of defamiliarization and detachment represent a stance of refusal or protest that implicates readers at a number of levels: from the empathic feelings that come out of reading refugee narratives in the "safe zone" of literary texts, in the comfort of our own homes in towns that might well harbour prison-like facilities for migrants (Keen 2007, 4)—to our participation in the ban-opticon, when as individuals, we fail to reflect on how the airport we pass through stratifies populations, the way borders are configured for the ease and mobility of some, and disabled for the unease and immobility of others. In their respective representations of a detention regime, Brand and Chak ask that readers become active participants in elaborating further meaning and connections across places, to reconsider spaces from the stories they tell about structural violence and racism. Texts that prioritize structures and numbers, which relay the challenge of comprehending scale over individual stories of migration, give rise to a critical perspective that illuminates politics at work. Such politics are revealing, helping readers see how migrant drownings, for example, caused by crossing the Mediterranean, are neither arbitrary nor accidents, but the violent effects of policies and infrastructures. But, just as importantly, they show that these policies and infrastructures are now no longer in the domain of the individual nation-state. The texts gesture towards the need for a collective, post-sovereign politics to what is inarguably a global human rights dilemma. The texts produced by Brand and Chak turn their gaze towards the securitization apparatus in order to refuse its opacity and its secrecy. As such, these representations offer critical interventions where readers can both apprehend and witness the violation of individual rights by the material realities of the global detention regime.

Notes

1. See *The Migrant Files*, an NGO funded agency for the estimates. UNHCR provides the highest figures for 2015, with over 3770 deaths; whereas 2016 saw over 3750 deaths in the Mediterranean crossing (UNHCR 2016).
2. Setting the detainees aside from mainstream society has led to particularly bad conditions at the detention facilities where they are incarcerated. Harmit Athwal notes the "misconduct...racism and degradation" that the migrants have been subjected to (2015, 52).
3. Jansen et al., note in their introduction that, while exact numbers are difficult to establish, there are several NGOs that have sought to map those numbers, such as *Migreurop* and *The Migrants Files*, that have been gathering data (2015, xii).

Works Cited

Albahari, Maurizio. 2015. *Crimes of Peace: Mediterranean Migrations at the World's Deadliest Border*. Philadelphia: University of Pennsylvania Press.

Athwal, Harmit. 2015. "'I Don't Have a Life to Live': Deaths and UK Detention." *Race & Class* 56 (3): 5–68.

Berchin, Issa Ibrahim, Isabela Blasi Valduga, Jéssica Garcia, and José Baltazar Salgueirinho Osório de Andrade Guerra. 2017. "Climate Change and Forced Migrations: An Effort Towards Recognizing Climate Refugees." *Geoforum* 84: 147–150.

Bigo, Didier. 2008. "Globalized (In)Security: The Field and the Ban-Opticon." In *Terror, Insecurity, and Liberty: Illiberal Practices of Liberal Regimes After 9/11*, edited by Didier Bigo and Anastassia Tsoukala, 10–48. London: Routledge.

———. 2015. "Death in the Mediterranean Sea: The Results of the Three Fields of Action of European Union Border Controls." In *The Irregularization of Migration in Contemporary Europe: Detention, Deportation, Drowning*, edited by Yolande Jansen et al., 55–37. London: Rowman & Littlefield International.

Boie, Kirsten. 2016. *Bestimmt Wird Alles Gut*. Stuttgart: Klett.

Brand, Dionne. 2006. *Inventory*. Toronto: McClelland & Stewart.

Chak, Tings. 2014. *Undocumented: The Architecture of Migrant Detention*. Montreal: The Architecture Observer.

Cornelisse, Galina. 2010. *Immigration Detention and Human Rights: Rethinking Territorial Sovereignty*. Leiden: Martinus Nijhoff.

Coundouriotis, Eleni. 2015. "In Flight: The Refugee Experience and Human Rights Narrative." In *The Routledge Companion to Literature and Human Rights*, edited by Sophia A. McClennen and Alexandra Schultheis Moore, 78–85. London: Routledge.

Dearden, Lizzie. 2015. "Mediterranean Migrant Crisis: Sicilian Port's Graveyard of Boats Provides Moving Memorial to the Dead." *The Independent*, August 6. https://www.independent.co.uk/news/world/europe/mediterranean-migrant-crisis-sicilian-ports-graveyard-of-boats-provides-moving-memorial-to-the-dead-10441878.html.

Fiske, Lucy. 2016. *Human Rights, Refugee Protest, and Immigration Detention*. London: Palgrave-Macmillan.

Greder, Armin. 2007. *The Island*, 2002. Crows Nest, NSW: Allen & Unwin.

Green, Michael, and Andre Dao, eds. 2017. *They Cannot Take the Sky: Stories from Detention*. Sydney, Australia: Allen & Unwin.

Grossman, Claudio. 2014. "Implementing Human Rights in Closed Environments Through the United Nations Convention Against Torture." *Law in Context* 31: 125–153.

Herd, David, and Anna Pincus, eds. 2016. *Refugee Tales*. Manchester: Comma Press.

Jansen, Yolande. 2015. "Deportability and Racial Europeanization: The Impact of Holocaust Memory and Postcoloniality on the Unfreedom of Movement in and to Europe." In *The Irregularization of Migration in Contemporary Europe: Detention, Deportation, Drowning*, edited by Yolande Jansen et al., 15–30. London: Rowman & Littlefield International.

Jansen, Yolande, Robin Celikates, and Joost de Bloois, eds. 2015. *The Irregularization of Migration in Contemporary Europe: Detention, Deportation, Drowning*. London: Rowman & Littlefield International.

Jeandesboza, Julien, and Polly Pallister-Wilkins. 2016. "Crisis, Routine, Consolidation: The Politics of the Mediterranean Migration Crisis." *Mediterranean Politics* 21 (2): 316–320.

Keen, Suzanne. 2007. *Empathy and the Novel*. New York: Oxford University Press.

Kirby, Emma Jane. 2016. "Compassion Fatigue and the Optician of Lampedusa." *BBC News*, October 7. https://www.bbc.com/news/world-europe-37485824.

———. 2017. *The Optician of Lampedusa: Based on a True Story*. New York: Or Books.

OHCHR (Office of the High Commissioner for Human Rights). 2016. "Protecting the Human Rights of All People in Vulnerable Situations Within Large Movements." June 30. https://www.ohchr.org/Documents/Issues/MHR/MigrantsLargeMovements/StatementGMG.pdf.

Sacco, Joe. 2010. "Joe Sacco: Not in My Country: A Tale of Unwanted Immigrants." *The Guardian*, July 17. https://www.theguardian.com/world/interactive/2010/jul/17/joe-sacco-unwanted-immigrants.

Sanna, Francesca. 2016. *The Journey*. London: Flying Eye Books.

Sayer, Rosemary, ed. 2015. *More to the Story: Conversations with Refugees*. Perth: Margaret River Press.

UNHCR. 2016. "Mediterranean Death Toll Soars, 2016 Is Deadliest Year Yet." October 25. http://www.unhcr.org/afr/news/latest/2016/10/580f3e684/mediterranean-death-toll-soars-2016-deadliest-year.html.

University of Oxford Podcasts. 2014. "Undocumented: The Architecture of Migrant Detention." December 14, 2014. Accessed August 17, 2018. http://podcasts.ox.ac.uk/undocumented-architecture-migrant-detention.

Weizman, Eyal, Paulo Tavares, and Susan Schuppli. 2010. "Forensic Architecture." *Architectural Design* 80 (5): 58–63.

CHAPTER 12

The Gorki Theater's *Exil Ensemble* as State-Sponsored Repudiation of Citizenship

Marike Janzen

In 2016, one year after record-breaking numbers of refugees arrived in Germany, Berlin's state-supported Gorki Theater founded the *Exil Ensemble* (Gorki, "Exil," n.d.).[1] The group comprises seven actors from Syria, Palestine, and Afghanistan who are at the beginning of their careers and forced to live in German exile. The ensemble, which exists as a discrete entity separate from the Gorki's more permanent acting company, offers members the opportunity to pursue their professional training across the time span of two theater seasons. This training includes developing original performances and honing acting practice (Gorki, "Exil," n.d.). In January 2017, the *Exil Ensemble* took a bus tour across Germany in order to gather material for their first production. In collaboration with the Austrian-Israeli playwright Yael Ronen, in-house director at the Gorki, ensemble members developed a play based on their trip titled *Winterreise* (*Winter Journey*). The piece both implicitly and explicitly references canonical German literary works of the nineteenth

M. Janzen (✉)
University of Kansas, Lawrence, KS, USA
e-mail: mjanzen@ku.edu

A. S. Moore and S. Pinto (eds.), *Writing Beyond the State*,
Palgrave Studies in Literature, Culture and Human Rights,
https://doi.org/10.1007/978-3-030-34456-6_12

century—Johann Wolfgang von Goethe's account of his educational journey, or *Bildungsreise*, across Italy, and Franz Schubert's famous 1828 song cycle, titled *Winterreise*—to tell the story of seven actors in German exile on a bus tour across Germany. The Gorki premiered the piece in April 2017. The *Exil Ensemble* brings non-German refugees into cultural institutions (the state-funded theater) and forms (canonical texts of the nineteenth century) that are central to conceptions of German national identity. In doing so, the work simultaneously challenges assumptions that the nation-state is the equivalent of its citizens and highlights the vulnerability, and agency, of its non-citizen subjects.

A critical moment in the play that illustrates how subjects within the nation can simultaneously exist in precarious separation from it comes when the group stops in Dresden. By chance, their visit coincides with weekly Monday demonstrations held in the city by the right-wing organization PEGIDA (*Patriotische Europäer gegen die Islamisierung Europas*, or Patriotic Europeans against the Islamicization of Europe). On the day of the actors' visit, like most Mondays since 2014, PEGIDA members have gathered in Dresden's main square to protest German immigration and border enforcement policies they see as too lax. In this context, the Arabic-speaking actors feel unsafe in public. Instead of seeing the sights, they stay in their hotel and watch the demonstration from their windows. Kenda, from Syria, is frustrated. She wants to go outside and "shout about something [she] really cares about" (Ronen and Exil Ensemble 2017, 31). But just like in Syria, where she was afraid to attend protests for fear of reprisals, she is afraid, in Germany, of the violence that could result from her speaking freely. She does not want to subject herself to attacks by PEGIDA members or arrest by the police providing security. Alone in her hotel room, with no one to hear her, Kenda shouts out what she feels anyway: "No borders, no nations, stop deportations!" (31).

In this scene, German citizens are protected in expressing their Islamophobic opinions. At the same time, Kenda, a non-citizen, is prevented from acting out her right to freedom of expression.[2] Kenda's protest, unheard in the fictive public space of the play, pushes the viewer to consider the extent to which public self-expression requires state citizenship. Or, to put the issue that Kenda's solo demonstration raises another way: can practices of state citizenship silence, and thus dehumanize, the non-citizen? The stakes of this question are amplified in the play, given that its very topic is the place of denizens in a contemporary Germany anxious about determining who can belong in the state in the context of what media and politicians term a *Flüchtlingskrise*, or "refugee crisis."

Kenda's protest demonstrates how conflations of "human" with "state citizen" render certain expressions inaudible, and, as a result, erase central human experiences as defining elements of the category "citizen." The incompatibility between human-ness and state citizenship that Kenda's protest raises, echoes concerns that the political philosopher Hannah Arendt addresses in her reflections on the inhumanity that attends citizenship status. In her 1943 essay "We Refugees," Arendt, a German Jew who fled fascist Germany in 1933 for France and then the US, notes a cruel paradox at work in her fellow refugees' frantic efforts to gain official status in their exile homes. In their struggle, Arendt sees evidence for her argument that at the midpoint of the twentieth century, humans' existence is legitimated and protected through formalized relationship to a state. In such a world, Arendt claims, "human beings as such have ceased to exist" (Arendt 1994, 118). Only those who possess "passports or birth certificates [or even] tax receipts" are granted the distinction of deserving protection, and thus of being human (118).

The conclusion that Arendt draws from this condition is that refugees stop clinging to citizenship—and the belongingness to a community that it confers—as validation of their human-ness. Instead, she calls on them to embrace their status as humans existing outside of a state's purview and consciously reject a normative vision of "human" as "citizen" within which the non-citizen is a "pariah" (119). Arendt's admonition that the refugee be taken seriously, posits the non-citizen as the normative human on which to found social organizations. Though not referencing Arendt directly, *Winterreise* seems to be following the thread of her argument by giving unheard non-citizens like Kenda an actual stage and an audience.

Giorgio Agamben, reflecting on the relevance of "We Refugees" fifty years after its publication, articulates why such calls to disassociate human-ness from connection to "the old trinity of state/ nation/ territory," continue to be so crucial (1995, 117). According to Agamben, as "growing portions of humanity can no longer be represented within [the nation-state]" (117), "the refugee is the sole category in which it is possible today to perceive the forms and limits of a political community to come" (114). As the number of displaced people in the world continues to grow—in 2017 the figure was 68.5 million—states, particularly in the global north, are making it increasingly difficult for non-citizens to exist, let alone participate, within their territory (UNHCR 2018). In the context of this violence, there is an urgent need to reconceptualize the spheres in which humans can find belonging. Kenda's chant, "no borders, no nations, stop deportations," which rejects the state because of the harm it causes, is a demand for such a rethinking. For both Arendt and Agamben—and Kenda—the prospect of organizing a just human community around the concept of state-citizen is not possible.

The Gorki Theater is only one of many German theaters to take up the theme of the refugee. Particularly since the "refugee crisis" took shape in 2015, theaters in the Federal Republic have been key players in the nation's efforts to incorporate and "integrate" large numbers of people who have sought refuge in the country (Wilmer 2018, 201). Yet within the context of the German literary sphere, a space that has traditionally fostered human-ness and citizenship as mutually reinforcing categories, the Gorki Theater's approach to representing refugees on stage bears special attention. Rather than seeking to highlight the refugee's capacity to integrate into the nation, by virtue of her human-ness, *Winterreise* and the institutional form of the *Exil Ensemble* foreground ways of being human that the ordinary categories of state belonging do not contain.[3]

In this paper, I explore how the play *Winterreise*, as well as the Gorki Theater's *Exil Ensemble* that developed and performed the piece, make a move resonant with Agamben, to propose the refugee, and not the citizen, as the building block of a future political community. This occurs at the level of the work's content. The play's protagonists, caught between unsafe homelands and a strange, sometimes unwelcoming, new home, neither yearn for nor move toward incorporation into the state. Belonging, at least for some, derives from their relationship to the theater, not a country. As I demonstrate below, in *Winterreise*, one exiled actor asserts that he considers his home to be any venue for and community of creative performance, rather than a nation or language. This delinking of human from the category "citizen" also occurs at an institutional level. By drawing on state funds to employ a theater ensemble of non-citizens who present material about refugees, the Gorki Theater implicitly calls into question the historical connection between publicly supported cultural institutions and citizen formation in Germany.

In what follows, I examine how *Winterreise* and the Gorki Theater's *Exil Ensemble* work against commonsense connections between humanness and citizenship within Germany. I begin by outlining the relationship of theater to citizenship practices. In particular, I describe how, in Germany, current state-supported literary practice engages the project to train citizens by seeking to interpellate non-citizens as citizens. I then focus on the way that *Winterreise* represents exiles in Germany via genres of German national culture bound up with practices and conceptions of German-ness—the *Bildungsreise* and the *Lied*. In foregrounding the exile in this way, the play maintains a tension between the experience of non-Germans in the country and the role national culture plays in crafting citizens. Finally, I show how the Gorki Theater's *Exil Ensemble* reinforces the play's message at an institutional level in the way it fashions a physical and public space of and in the state for exiled actors to share their voice. In this way, the Gorki Theater asserts the non-citizen as a category with which the state must contend, but not integrate. The Gorki's efforts to assert exile, and being-in-exile, as the normative mode of being human even within the context of national culture and state cultural programs presents a noteworthy rebuke to a state system keeping refugee bodies out of their territories and beyond their sphere of protection.

Theater Interpellating the Citizen

German public support for the arts ranks among the most generous in the world (Canada Council for the Arts 2005), and Germany's 143 publicly funded theaters are beneficiaries of much of this arts funding (Brauneck 2018, 172). The priority Germany places on the theater has to do with its historical significance as a space for training citizens who can exercise critical judgment in the public sphere and become educated in national traditions (Tinius 2013). Since the Enlightenment, literature in German-speaking lands has been valued as a tool that can promote subjects' self-awareness as freethinking individuals, and thus prepare them to participate in rational debate central to a modern state's democratic processes (Habermas 1996). In the nineteenth century, philosophies of education, or *Bildung*, that valorized the autonomous reading citizen aligned with performances of German class and national identity; the educated citizen, or the *Bildungsbürger*, was one who engaged the German literary canon (Boyer 2005, 59). Thus, in Germany, theater serves as a primary site for cultivating a sense of citizenship understood both as a mode of participating in the state's public sphere and as a relationship to a particular cultural and linguistic legacy. Theater interpellates the audience as citizen, and theater subsidies that lower ticket prices facilitate public access to it.

Recent national policy proposals aimed at combating the marginalization of non-citizens in Germany explicitly consider the social role of theater to inform citizenship practices. In 2005, Germany passed comprehensive immigration reform. The "Zuwanderungsgesetz," or "immigration law," which streamlined decades of ad hoc legislation regulations related to residency permits and the mobility of European Union residents, signaled a recognition on the part of the federal government that Germany is a "Zuwanderungsland," or a country made up of immigrants (Auswärtiges Amt, n.d.; Deutsches Historisches Museum, n.d.). Part of the new law's brief required the state to take organized action relating to the so-called "integration" of people with a *Migrationshintergrund*, or "migration background," into the country (Auswärtiges Amt, n.d.). To fulfill this mandate, the German government launched a "Nationaler Integrationsplan," or national integration plan, in 2006 (Sharifi 2017, 373). Its aim is to cultivate stronger ties between immigrants in Germany and their new homeland, for example, by providing "Integrationskurse," or integration courses, that offer instruction in German language and culture, or by teaching German citizens about the cultural backgrounds of their new neighbors (Deutscher Bundestag 2007; "Warum Integration so wichtig ist," n.d.). Theaters, in particular, are seen as especially suited to the project of integration because they can simultaneously serve as venues for orienting non-Germans to German linguistic and national practices, as well as platforms for showcasing non-German cultural traditions that are unfamiliar to a German audience.

Yet the ability of publicly supported German theater to function as a tool of integration has required some advocacy. As scholars of German theater point out, from the middle of the century in the Federal Republic of Germany through German reunification, there were distinct theater scenes for people with a "migration background" and those without one (Sharifi 2018, 329). The former group, often Turks who were in Germany because of its guest worker program with Turkey, developed independent, that is, not state-funded, theater ensembles and projects that took up themes relevant to immigrants (335). These theaters received little publicity or recognition. By contrast, the large majority of theaters, including those receiving state support, were primarily staffed and attended by Germans without a "migration background" (Sharifi 2017, 337). The programming in these institutions hewed more closely to a German national tradition (337). As Azadeh Sharifi explains, it is only within the past decade that theaters in Germany have begun to serve as spaces for both groups (338).

Indeed, the "National Integration Plan" took note that theaters in Germany neither represented nor reached a representative cross section of German society (336). To combat the segregation of Germany's theater scene into discrete spaces, the integration plan proposes that cultural organizations take an active role in fostering integration. State agencies are helping to facilitate this goal. For example, Germany's Ministry for Culture and Media, currently led by Monika Grütters—a member of Angela Merkel's Christian Democratic Union (CDU) party—highlights integration as one of its key priorities. In 2016, the ministry launched what has been termed the "Initiative kulturelle Integration," or "cultural integration initiative" (Initiative kulturelle Integration 2017). This is a project of the *Deutscher Kulturrat*, or German Cultural Council, a federally funded association of cultural associations, to articulate the responsibilities and roles that cultural organizations in the Federal Republic should hold in supporting integration. The initiative grounds the significance of "culture" for integration in terms of its capacity to create social cohesion by transmitting an understanding of the nation's past and present as well as the values held by the community (Initiative kulturelle Integration 2017). Many of the values that the initiative claims that "culture" can, and should, instill, align with Western democratic norms. These include acceptance of Germany's *Grundgesetz*, or Basic Law, and the rights it lays out, as well as a belief in the necessity of freedom of expression and democratic debate that inform the nation's prized "Streitkultur," or "culture of debate" (Initiative kulturelle Integration 2017).

This vision of culture's role in integration informs the kind of funding opportunities the state offers for projects seen to foster reflection on the relationship between "German-ness" and cultural diversity. Such support comes from agencies such as the *Kulturstiftung des Bundes*, or the Federal Cultural Foundation, the country's most highly endowed public foundation. The *Kulturstiftung des Bundes* actively provides monies to multiple theaters across Germany for projects to more fully incorporate voices and perspectives of people with a "migration background" into their ensembles, audiences, and programming. Thus, for example, in addition to funding the Gorki Theater's *Exil Ensemble*, the *Kulturstiftung des Bundes* provides monies to Munich's *Kammerspiele* for the development of its *Open Border Ensemble*, a project to more fully integrate actors with a "migration background" into the theater's troupe (Kulturstiftung des Bundes, n.d.-a, n.d.-b, n.d.-c).

State funds, tied to expectations for shaping a unified conception of German-ness, reinforce the role of theater in Germany as a critical space for crafting the feelings and behaviors seen to attend German citizenship. As Lauren Berlant points out in a different context, practices such as those the German state theater is seen to support, ones that highlight individuals' connection to a geopolitical space and its inhabitants, are key elements in the formation of substantive citizenship (Berlant 2007, 37). In other words, German theater serves as a site that reinforces historical knowledge and behaviors through which members of a community define their belonging to one another and the territory they share. The feeling of substantive citizenship that German theater creates, however, does not equate with formal citizenship, that is, an individual's particular "standing within the law" (37) or status of belonging in a nation. Thus, even though theater in Germany is considered to function as a space that can interpellate the conduct and attitudes of the ideal citizen, it cannot guarantee the rights of those non-citizens performing on stage or attending the theater who, themselves, are participants in citizen-shaping acts and may feel connected to the German theater space. In this way, German state-funded theater sanctions the very kind of behavior that Arendt characterizes as disguising the lie of citizenship: the efforts of exiles to be seen as citizens, even if they don't possess the papers that afford them that identity and the protection of their humanity.

A German Canon and Non-citizens in the *Winterreise*

At first glance, the content of the play *Winterreise* seems to neatly fulfill the mission of culture as a tool of integration and citizenship-development that state organs lay out. In *Winterreise*, exiles—actors with a "migration background" living in Germany—learn about Germany and engage canonical literary forms and texts as they tell about their experiences. These literary models, in turn, are associated with developing individuals' capacities for self-awareness and critical apprehension of their surroundings. In short, the play appears to contain the components that the "Initiative for Cultural Integration" prizes: it teaches about Germany's past and present while cultivating allegiance to the constitutionally described norm of the citizen as an autonomous, freely acting individual.

Rather than producing individuals ready to integrate into the nation, however, *Winterreise* works against the grain of official expectations that knowledge of the nation and experience in the ways it tells stories will lead to feelings of attachment to the nation's values and belonging within the bounds of a geopolitical territory. The play does so by foregrounding exiles' agency and experience as the catalyst for their journey through Germany. The impetus for the bus tour comes from them, and not from citizens without a "migration background." The exiles are not subject to an official "integration" agenda. Further, the self-awareness they achieve as a result of their travel, and communicate to the audience in English and Arabic, not in German, reveals their alienation both from Germany and from the homes they have left; it highlights their status as non-German-speaking exiles. Finally, the "home" to which some describe connection is not a particular nation, but the international space of theater.

The play's form of a bus tour references the German tradition of the *Bildungsreise*, one of whose most famous practitioners was Goethe. In 1816, Goethe published the *Italienische Reise* (*Italian Journey*), a travelogue of his trip across Italy in the 1780s (Goethe 2017). The account is significant for the way Goethe reflects on the way his engagement with classical art shapes his aesthetic. Goethe, in the work, "adopts the stance of the scientist-explorer," who takes in the sights with the aim of "mich an den Gegenständen kennen zu lernen" ("[learning] about myself via the objects") (Baumgartner 2014). This practice of self-formation via engagement with the world that Goethe lays out is not only a practice for artists, but forms the core tenet of German citizen-making project such as the public education model articulated by Wilhelm von Humboldt in the early nineteenth century. For Humboldt, *Bildung*, or education, is not the rote learning of skills, but a process of self-formation that requires both learning from the world and, in turn, shaping it (Humboldt 1904, 326). *Winterreise* plays with citizen forming expectations related to the trope of travel and *Bildung* by presenting non-Germans as eager learners and travelers.

Winterreise emphasizes the exile, not the citizen, as the driving force behind the project of self-formation that travel can provide through a kind of false start. The play's opening scene appears to reinforce the image of the exile as dependent on Germans' help. As *Winterreise* begins, people bundled up in heavy coats and scarves and speaking Arabic slowly gather in the dark. They debate whether they have correctly understood the instructions their German friend Niels sent them about where they should meet. Maryam wonders, "What if we are waiting for him in the wrong place? And he is in the right place waiting for us" (Ronen and

Exil Ensemble 2017, 2), while Karim notes, "Wait, he said in front of the trees, actually we are more to the side of the trees" (3). Though comical, the scene portrays confused, potentially lost, foreigners.

The actors decide, however, that this scene of anxious waiting may be confusing to the audience. Maryam says, "we think we are progressing too fast, stop acting, it's not clear what we're doing here" (4). They decide to back up, to start their account with the time "when we went to [Niels's] house and wanted to talk" (4). The scene changes to Niels's apartment, where the actors enter and confront him about their relationship. In a comic turn of the conventional "relationship talk," in which a partner complains of neglect and asks for more attention, the exiles complain that they are tired of talking about themselves. They want to know more about their German friend and what makes him tick. As Maryam says, "It's always about us … our culture … We are bored with ourselves" (10). The exiles tell Niels: "We want to get to know you, the real you, All of you, not just the Berlin side of you" (12). They pepper their friend with questions: "What's your history?" "What's your background?" "What's your baggage?" "Do you want to take us out?" (12, 14). The exiles are not hapless in Germany, as our first encounter with them might indicate. They are tired of seeing themselves as objects of curiosity, and take the initiative to present themselves as subjects who want to know more about their context.

Niels plans the itinerary of the bus tour, not because he has a specific agenda, but because his exile friends have asked him to do so. Most sites he selects are predictable. He plans visits to cities that played an important role in German literary history. These include Dresden, a center for German Romanticism; Weimar, where Goethe lived and where the Nazis built the concentration camp Buchenwald; and Mannheim, home of the playwright Friedrich Schiller. Niels's rationale for choosing other sites has more to do with his own personal whims. He takes the exiles to Munich's Allianz Arena, home to Germany's most successful soccer team, FC Bayern München, because he appreciates its oval shape: it makes him feel "safe" (36). He decides that the tour should stop in Zurich: a place more "boring" than Germany that will convince his friends that Germany has the potential to be exciting (44). In short, the *Bildungsreise* that Niels organizes for the exiles is a somewhat haphazard one, a tour that draws on schoolbook notions of significant places as well as his idiosyncratic interests. The main impetus of the tour is the exiles' desire to see the country.

While Ronen draws on the *Bildungsreise* as the play's structuring element, the work's content, the exiles' responses to what they see, references another German literary canonical artifact related to the trope of travel as a mode of self-formation. Here, her point of departure is Franz Schubert's 1828 song cycle *Die Winterreise*, the quintessential *Lied*, a central artistic form of nineteenth-century Germany that brought folk traditions to the *Bildungsbürger*. Ronen transforms Schubert's protagonist, a lone and lovelorn man wandering through a desolate winter landscape, into exiles on a bus tour through Germany in wintertime. In her adaptation of the piece, Ronen draws on the trope of travel across bleak spaces as catalyst for self-expression. By applying the prized German practice of introspection through travel that Schubert's *Winterreise* references to a contemporary story of non-Germans' encounter with the country, Ronen underscores the play's larger critique of the idea that citizens necessarily belong to a nation's political—or cultural—forms.

In *Winterreise*, the exiles' encounters with a cold Germany, in terms of weather, unfriendly people, and unpeopled places, spur them to share their own stories: of life in their home countries, their flight to Germany, or their struggles to make sense of German habits. Just as the *Bildungsreise* foregrounds the exiles as agents, the responses to their experiences highlight their self-awareness as exiles. Like Kenda, whose exposure to protests in Dresden leads her to remember protests in Syria, the exiles' site visits spur their reflection on experiences of disruption and loss and their unsettled status in Germany.

Hussein's response to the group's visit to Zurich exemplifies how stops in different places do not merely offer a list of interesting facts to learn about, but instigate the process of reflection and self-examination about the phenomenon of exile. When the bus approaches the border between Germany and Switzerland, Hussein, a Palestinian refugee who had been living in Syria, gets nervous. He fears that he will face trouble because he does not have a passport, just a "traveling document for the Palestinian refugees in Syria" (46). Theoretically, the document allows Palestinians to leave Syria and return to the country, but does not function as a "residency permit." For this reason, holders of such travel documents are ineligible to receive visas to travel to other countries (refworld 2013). Niels asks Hussein what a "travel document" is. Hussein explains it to him, but not without first expressing "how much [he hates] this question" (46). The bus crosses the border without problems, but the tour's Zurich "leg" reinforces to Hussein his status as a double exile: a Palestinian in exile from his exile home in Syria.

Being in Zurich also reminds Hussein of his flight from Syria to Germany; Zurich was his last "station before Germany on [his] never ending journey from Damascus to Lüneburg" (47). Normally, Hussein doesn't like to talk about this experience, but on that day in the hotel where the travelers are resting—close, he thinks, to the place near the train station where he slept during the last time he was there—he wants to tell about his flight. Keeping silent about this memory, he admits, is not justified. That "is how war and injustice continue from generation to another generation" (47). Because he "[hopes] nobody will have to go through what [he] went through in [his] journey" (47), Hussein proceeds to tell his fellow travelers how he fled Syria.

What follows is a story that echoes those of thousands of Syrian refugees, with its references to fake documents, smugglers, dangerous sea-crossings in over-filled boats, and crowded refugee camps.[4] Yet as the only story in the play that describes in detail the route the exiles took from their homes to Germany, it is an important testament to the very experience that turned Hussein into an exile. Furthermore, Hussein's travel tale that lurches from one stroke of luck to the next—a trafficker who can be bribed, a boat that doesn't sink, a fake passport that works—calls into question the very premise of the *Bildungsreise*; travel as a mode of self-betterment for the citizen.

In German canonical genres of travel, the journey that leads to self-examination and self-formation ends in the traveler's return. The returned self, at least in the eighteenth-century model of the *Bildungsreise* if not the nineteenth-century *Lied*, is an improved one, ready to apply lessons learned to her home context. In *Winterreise*, the actors will return to Berlin at the end of their trip. Berlin, however, is not home. Neither does it function as a place in which they will necessarily want to apply their learning. As Mazen declares in the play's closing scene, his home is the theater—not a particular stage, but the theater in general. He remarks: "when I enter a theater anywhere in the world I right away feel home, I feel safe, it feels like its family. I look at my new theater family and I think I can get used to it, they are beautiful" (54).

In *Winterreise*, Ronen inverts the *Bildungsreise* from a story of Germans going out into the world, learning about themselves, and returning home, into a story of exiles traveling through Germany, reflecting on their condition as exiles, and better understanding their "home" as the space of the theater. Through this transformation of the genre, Ronen replaces the German with the exile. As a result, the exile becomes a normative figure, and not an anomaly. At least in terms of its story, *Winterreise* does not interpellate the citizen, but the exile.

The *Exil Ensemble* with and Beyond the State

In a move that parallels the play's realignment of form, the Gorki Theater's *Exil Ensemble* uses national resources to support exiles by hiring them as actors, and giving their voices national and international reach. By prioritizing and amplifying exile subjectivity, the *Exil Ensemble* infrastructure challenges the function of the theater as a space for interpellating citizens, and instead, seeks to interpellate the audience as exiles.

In describing the work that she believes German theater should be doing, the Gorki Theater's director, Shermin Langhoff, critiques perspectives—for example, those reflected in national discourses and policies—that view art as the pathway for migrants and Germans with "migration background" to "integrate" into Germany. In an essay titled "Kultur ist kein Integrationskurs," ("Culture is not an 'Integration Class'") published in one of Germany's major newspapers, the *Süddeutsche Zeitung*, Langhoff argues that culture should not be instrumentalized to serve the project of citizenship training (2016). Such a view, Langhoff claims, not only weakens art's social function as a site of social critique, but connects art to narrow views of German-ness that exclude the cultural and religious practices of people living in the country. According to Langhoff, and other intellectuals like Max Czollek, the fact that recent immigrants and those with a "migration background" inhabit a German space, means that they are necessarily already part of the nation's cultural fabric (2016; Czollek 2018). Instead of serving to integrate Germany's "others" into the nation, art should do the work of a "Desintegrationskurs," or "disintegration class"—Langhoff's play on the term "Integrationskurs" used to describe nationally mandated "integration classes" for migrants—and push for a rethinking of the criteria that count as "German."

The *Exil Ensemble* promotes disintegration by strategically connecting conceptions and embodiments of "exile" to the state stage. One way the theater seeks to accomplish this is by drawing explicit connections between migration and exile with canonical German literary history. From 1933 to 1945, German artists opposed to and endangered by fascism lived in exile across the world. During that time, Zurich's *Schauspielhaus* gave many playwrights and actors in exile, including Bertolt Brecht, a place to perform (Künste im Exil, n.d.). Indeed, in Germany, the term *Exillit-eratur* (exile literature) clearly refers to literature produced by Germans who had escaped National Socialism by leaving the country. In referencing a historical precedent of theater in exile within the Germanophone world, Langhoff simultaneously connects the experience of complicated citizenship status with the history of German letters.

The term "exile" thus marks a connection to and reminder of the significant role that migration and asylum have played in German literary history. At the same time, the word's use to describe a theater ensemble offers a critical intervention in the way that the nomenclature for non-citizens in Germany is currently instrumentalized for political purposes. Writing on the challenges to representing contemporary Germany, Anne Ring Petersen and Moritz Schramm explain that the term "migrant" "no longer [serves as] a purely descriptive term" to characterize a person who moves from "one specific region or country to another" (Petersen and Schramm 2017, 6). Instead, it is combined with other words to both evaluate the degree to which the person deserves to be integrated into the state, and to shore up ethno-nationalist sentiments (Holmes and Castañeda 2016, 16–18). For example, while "political migrants" may be seen as justified in their decision to come to Germany, an "economic migrant" is perceived to be looking for handouts (Petersen and Schramm 2017, 6). Furthermore, the invocation of "migrant" to describe citizens of color in the phrase "people with migration backgrounds," reaffirms notions of the once-migrant as still distinct from the majority.

While "exile" may avoid the valences of "deservingness" that attach to descriptions for migrants, it permits a more accurate characterization of the multiple kinds of legal statuses that migrants can hold. As *Exil Ensemble* member Tahera Hashimi puts it:

> we looked for a terminology, that, on the one hand, holds a historical connection to art for artists who can no longer freely speak and work as they like in their own countries, and for that reason go to another country; and on the other hand, is politically open. Without implying a definition about passports or residency status, because our group represents very diverse [migration] experiences. (Gorki 2017, 20)[5]

"Exile" offers a way to describe an individual's violated relationship to home without invoking state-issued identities.

Beyond creating an institution that inserts, through its name, a consciousness of exile as forming part of Germany's past and present, the *Exil Ensemble* also places exile bodies on the state stage. This strategy of deliberately putting people who exist outside of definitions of "Germanness" in the public space of the theater is one that Langhoff practiced before coming to the Gorki in 2013. From 2008 until 2013, Langhoff was director at Berlin's Ballhaus Naunynstrasse, an independent theater located in the predominantly Turkish neighborhood of Kreuzberg, where she established what she calls "post-migrant" theater (Sharifi 2018, 335). According to Langhoff, post-migrant theater represents on stage "the stories and perspectives of those who themselves have not migrated but who have this migration background as part of their personal knowledge and collective memory" (Sharifi 2017, 327). Significantly, Langhoff asserts the content of post-migrant theater not as marginal to German reality and tradition, but as one of its centrally defining elements.

During her tenure at the Gorki thus far, Langhoff has "transformed the composition of the Gorki Theater ensemble into a post-migrant theater company" by enacting changes such as hiring staff and actors of "migration background" (Wilmer 2018, 195). As a result, the Gorki is no longer a place where only predominantly white, German-speaking actors primarily perform works of the German literary canon, the modus operandi of "the other subsidized theater companies in Germany" (195). Instead, it has become a venue for actors of color to tell their stories in their own languages (Sharifi 2018, 330). The *Exil Ensemble* expands this project by bringing exile voices to the post-migrant theater.

The public funds that serve as the primary source of support for the *Exil Ensemble*, ensure a more robust institutionalization of the exile as part of the German cultural landscape than is possible by independently funded stages, since federal, state, and city arts budgets are less vulnerable to external pressures than those of independent arts organizations (Tinius 2013). The Gorki Theater itself receives money from the city-state of Berlin: it is one of the five theaters that Berlin maintains (Wilmer 2018, 195).[6] Data from 2015 indicates that Berlin's annual spending allotment for its theaters was 107 million Euros—half of its total annual budget for cultural projects. In that year, the Gorki received 10 million Euros (Haydon 2015). Beyond this support for the Gorki, federal, city, as well as private funds support the theater's Exil Ensemble project, launched in 2016. The federal government provides monies from the *Kulturstiftung des Bundes* (Federal Culture Foundation), which itself receives 35 million

Euros annually from the budget of the cultural minister (Kulturstiftung des Bundes, "Die Stiftung stellt sich vor"). The *Lotto Stiftung Berlin* (Berlin Lottery Foundation), also supports the *Exil Ensemble*. This is an entity that annually draws on 20% of money spent on the lottery to fund projects for the public good (Berliner Zeitung 2018). The Mercator foundation offers funds for the *Exil Ensemble* as well. It is a private entity with the stated mission "to prevent dangerous climate change, promote integration, and strengthen arts, education, and to provide fair and equal opportunities so that everyone can participate in today's society" (European Foundation Center, n.d.).

The stability that this funding affords to the *Exil Ensemble* experiment has implications for its potential to effect change in perceptions about the kinds of bodies associated with the state. As Sharifi asserts, "the political conditions of [immigrant] theater makers are crucial and have an impact on their presence in the respective theater scenes. This implies that many immigrant theater makers are excluded from public subsidies due to their residence status" (Sharifi 2017, 322). Although the *Exil Ensemble* actors likely hold different immigration statuses and thus distinct relationships to the German state support system for non-citizens, through their employment at the Gorki they are also employees of the state. This affords a stability both for the actors themselves, who are appointed for two-year terms, as well as for the larger goal to "permanently integrate newly arrived artists into German ensembles" (Kulturstiftung des Bundes; Gorki, "Exil," n.d.).[7] Paradoxically, state support for integration serves the critical project of "disintegration."

Conclusion

Agamben claims that the refugee, and not the citizen, should serve as the foundation of a political community to come. In a way, the Gorki Theater and its *Exil Ensemble* are proposing just such a new kind of community in the space of the theater. It offers both a community of belonging, a theater "home" for the exiled actor Mazen, as well as a space in that community for protected expression, a place where Kenda can shout "No borders! No nations! Stop deportations!"

Even while drawing on the tradition of German theater as a central institution of citizen formation, the *Exil Ensemble* rejects the limitations that definitions of citizen place on bodies. On the one hand, the project calls for a recognition of the exile's human-ness by deploying the theater's social function as a space for hailing citizens, or, to put it another way, community members. On the other hand, the project asserts those bodies that the state seems to want to either integrate into a circumscribed definition of German-ness or expel, as already part of German society.

It will be important to follow what initiatives like those of the *Exil Ensemble* mean for the role of the state and the theater in forming citizens. In the summer of 2018, Munich's city-funded theater, the *Münchner Kammerspiele*, was a key supporter of a large protest against the conservative Christian Socialist Union (CSU) and its anti-immigrant politics (Hutter 2018). In response, CSU politicians called for the theater to recuse itself from the protest: as a publicly-supported institution, it should show political neutrality (Hutter 2018). There was hefty criticism of the CSU's reaction, which was perceived to be a troubling call to limit free speech (Zeit Online 2018). Yet with the increasing popularity of more and more exclusive citizenship criteria, and the possibility that threats like those against the *Münchner Kammerspiele* do not remain empty, it may turn out that projects like the state-sponsored *Exil Ensemble* are more necessary than ever. Indeed, it may be that the German state, with its significant resources and long tradition of shaping citizens, is a required supporter for the rethinking of citizenship and human-ness, not a paradoxical one.

Acknowledgments Research and writing of this essay was supported by funding from the General Research Fund of the University of Kansas.

Notes

1. During 2015, 1.3 million people fleeing war, authoritarian regimes, and the structural violence of so-called failed states "applied for asylum in the 28 member states of the European Union, Norway, and Switzerland" (see "Migrant crisis," BBC News, last modified March 4, 2016, https://www.bbc.com/news/world-europe-34131911). This was the highest number of asylum applications in the region since the break-up of the Soviet Union in 1992 (see "Number of Refugees to Europe Surges," Pew Research Center, last modified August 2, 2016, http://www.pewglobal.org/2016/08/02/number-of-refugees-to-europe-surges-to-record-1-3-million-in-2015/). 40% of this number, 476,659, sought asylum in the Federal Republic of Germany (BBC News 2016).

2. Article 19 of the Universal Declaration of Human Rights states: "Everyone has the right to freedom of opinion and expression; this right includes freedom to hold opinions without interference and to seek, receive and impart information and ideas through any media and regardless of frontiers."
3. I would argue that the widely acclaimed novel by Jenny Erpenbeck, *Gehen, ging, gegangen* (*Go, Went, Gone*) (2015), about a retired professor living in Berlin who befriends and mentors a group of refugee men from Africa aligns with this narrative of humanizing the stranger.
4. With 2000 dollars hidden in his shoes and more money hidden in his bag, Hussein flew to Qamischli, in northern Syria. There, he engaged a smuggler to help him cross the border into Turkey. After hiding in a muddy, mosquito-ridden cornfield for two hours to wait out police patrols, the group he was with made it to the Turkish city of Izmir. There, he paid a smuggler $1000 for a seat on a boat to the Greek island of Samos. The boat ran out of gas, and those onboard paddled with their hands to get to shore. In Samos, Hussein spent ten days in a detention camp for refugees. Since the officials didn't understand his status—he is neither a Palestinian from Palestine nor a Syrian from Syria—they determined that they couldn't deport him to either place, and, instead, sent him to Athens. From Athens, Hussein tried to reach central Europe by land. Both the Macedonian and the Albanian police denied him entrance into their countries. Back in Athens, Hussein tried to secure a fake passport. It took him six different attempts to secure a passport until he was allowed to board a plane to Zurich. From Zurich, he then made his way to Lüneburg.
5. "... wir haben nach einer Terminologie gesucht, die einerseits eine historische Verbindung mit Kunst hat für Künstlerinnen, die in ihrem Land nicht mehr frei sprechen und arbeiten können, wie sie möchten, und deshalb in ein anderes Land gehen, aber andererseits auch politisch offen ist. Ohne eine Definition nach Pässen oder dem Aufenthaltsstatus, weil das sehr divers in unserer Gruppe ist."
6. The other theaters are the Deutsches Theater, the Berliner Ensemble, the Schaubühne, and the Volksbühne.
7. According to the *Kulturstiftung des Bundes*, the "Exil Ensemble" is a space to explore "[wie] neu angekommene Künstler/Innen dauerhaft in die deutschen Ensembles integriert werden [können]."

Works Cited

Agamben, Giorgio. 1995. "We Refugees." *Symposium: A Quarterly Journal in Modern Literatures* 49 (2): 114–119.

Arendt, Hannah. 1994. "We Refugees." In *Altogether Elsewhere: Writers on Exile*, edited by Marc Robinson, 110–119. London: Faber & Faber.

Auswärtiges Amt. n.d. "Zuwanderungsgesetz." Accessed September 16, 2018. https://www.auswaertiges-amt.de/de/einreiseundaufenthalt/zuwanderungsrecht-node.

Baumgartner, Karin. 2014. "Travel, Tourism, and Cultural Identity in Mariana Starke's *Letters from Italy* (1800) and Goethe's *Italienische Reise* (1816–17)." *Publications of the English Goethe Society* 83 (3): 177–195. Taylor & Francis, Online.

BBC News. "Migrant Crisis: Migration to Europe Explained in Seven Charts." Last modified March 4, 2016. https://www.bbc.com/news/world-europe-34131911.

Berlant, Lauren. 2007. "Citizenship." In *Keywords for American Cultural Studies*, edited by Bruce Burgett and Glenn Hendler, 37–42. New York: New York University Press.

Berliner Zeitung. "Lotto-Stiftung: Millionensumme an 22 Berliner Vorhaben." Last modified March 1, 2018. https://www.berliner-zeitung.de/berlin/lotto-stiftung–millionensumme-an-22-berliner-vorhaben-29800146.

Boyer, Dominic. 2005. *Spirit and System: Media, Intellectuals, and the Dialectic in Modern German Culture*. Chicago: University of Chicago Press.

Brauneck, Manfred. 2018. *Die Deutschen und ihr Theater. Kleine Geschichte der 'moralischen Anstalt' – oder: Ist das Theater überfordert?* Bielefeld: transcript Verlag.

Bundesministerium des Innern, für Bau und Heimat. n.d. "Warum Integration so wichtig ist." Accessed September 16, 2018. https://www.bmi.bund.de/DE/themen/heimat-integration/integration/integration-bedeutung/integration-bedeutung-node.html;jsessionid=AC445CB3383A3B23F583E01CAF20242B.1_cid373.

Canada Council for the Arts. 2005. *Comparisons of Arts Funding in Selected Countries: Preliminary Findings*. Ottawa: Canada Council for the Arts.

Czollek, Max. 2018. *Desintegriert Euch!* München: Carl Hanser Verlag.

Deutscher Bundestag. 2007. "Der nationale Integrationsplan: Neue Wege-Neue Chancen." Presse und Informationsamt der Bundesregierung. Berlin.

Deutsches Historisches Museum. n.d. "Zuwanderungsland Deutschland: Migrationen 1500–2005." Accessed September 15, 2018. http://www.dhm.de/archiv/ausstellungen/zuwanderungsland-deutschland/migrationen/.

Erpenbeck, Jenny. 2015. *Gehen, ging, gegangen*. Munich: Albrecht Knaus Verlag.

European Foundation Center. n.d. "Stiftung Mercator GmbH." Accessed September 16, 2018. http://www.efc.be/organisation/stiftung-mercator-gmbh/.

Gorki. 2017. *Materialmappe zum Stück Winterreise*, edited by Mai-An Nguyen. Accessed September 15, 2018. http://gorki.de/de/gorki-x.

———. n.d. "The Exil Ensemble." Accessed September 15, 2018. https://gorki.de/en/exile-ensemble.

Habermas, Jürgen. 1996. *The Structural Transformation of the Public Sphere: An Inquiry into a Category of Bourgeois Society*. Translated by Thomas Burger. Cambridge: The MIT Press.

Haydon, Andrew. 2015. "International: Gorki Theater." *The Stage: Since 1880*. Last modified May 21, 2015. https://www.thestage.co.uk/features/2015/international-gorki-theater/.

Holmes, Seth M., and Heide Castañeda. 2016. "Representing the 'European Refugee Crisis' in Germany and Beyond: Deservingness and Difference, Life and Death." *American Ethnologist* 43 (1): 12–24.

Hutter, Dominik. 2018. "CSU fordert Maulkorb für die Kammerspiele." *Süddeutsche Zeitung*. Last modified July 17, 2018. https://www.sueddeutsche.de/muenchen/ausgehetzt-kundgebung-csu-fordert-maulkorb-fuer-die-kammerspiele-1.4058440.

Initiative kulturelle Integration. "Thesen." Last modified May 16, 2017. https://www.kulturelle-integration.de/thesen/.

Kulturstiftung des Bundes. n.d.-a. "Die Stiftung stellt sich vor." Accessed September 16, 2018. https://www.kulturstiftung-des-bundes.de/de/stiftung.html.

———. n.d.-b. "Exil Ensemble." Accessed September 16, 2018. https://www.kulturstiftung-des-bundes.de/de/projekte/buehne_und_bewegung/detail/exil_ensemble-1.html.

———. n.d.-c. 360°: Fonds für Kulturen der neuen Stadtgesellschaft. Accessed September 16, 2018. https://www.kulturstiftung-des-bundes.de/de/projekte/nachhaltigkeit_und_zukunft/detail/360_fonds_fuer_kulturen_der_neuen_stadtgesellschaft.html.

Künste im Exil. n.d. "Schauspielhaus Zürich." Accessed September 16, 2018. https://kuenste-im-exil.de/KIE/Content/DE/Themen/schauspielhaus-zuerich.html.

Langhoff, Shermin. 2016. "Kultur ist kein Integrationskurs." *Süddeutsche Zeitung*, January 16. https://www.sueddeutsche.de/kultur/serie-was-ist-deutsch-kultur-ist-kein-integrationskurs-1.2814539.

Petersen, Anne Ring, and Moritz Schramm. 2017. "(Post-)Migration in the Age of Globalization: New Challenges to Imagination and Representation." *Journal of Aesthetics and Culture* 9 (2): 1–12.

Pew Research Center. 2016. "Number of Refugees to Europe Surges." Last modified August 2, 2016. http://www.pewglobal.org/2016/08/02/number-of-refugees-to-europe-surges-to-record-1-3-million-in-2015/.

refworld. 2013. "Syria: The legal rights and obligations of a Palestinian who has been issued a Syrian travel document, including whether they must report for military service; whether the rights and obligations apply to Palestinians that have resided outside of the country for the majority of their life and only visited it briefly (2009–November 2013)." Last modified November 22, 2013. http://www.refworld.org/docid/532024234.html.

Ronen, Yael, and Exil Ensemble. 2017. *Winterreise.*

Sharifi, Azadeh. 2017. "Theatre and Migration Documentation: Influences and Perspectives in European Theatre." In *Independent Theatre in Contemporary Europe*, edited by Manfred Brauneck. Bielefeld: transcript Verlag. JSTOR.

———. 2018. "Multilingualism and Postmigrant Theatre in Germany." *Modern Drama* 61 (3): 328–351. Project MUSE.

Tinius, Jonas L. 2013. "Patronage and Crisis: German Theatre and Cultural Politics." Last modified February 13, 2013. http://kingsreview.co.uk/articles/patronage-and-crisis-german-theatre-and-cultural-politics/.

UNHCR, The UN Refugee Agency. 2018. "Forced Displacement Above 68 m in 2017, New Global Deal on Refugees Critical." Last modified June 19, 2018. http://www.unhcr.org/en-us/news/press/2018/6/5b27c2434/forced-displacement-above-68m-2017-new-global-deal-refugees-critical.html.

United Nations. n.d. "Universal Declaration of Human Rights." Accessed September 15, 2018. http://www.un.org/en/universal-declaration-human-rights/.

von Goethe, Johann Wolfgang. 2017. *Italienische Reise.* Berlin: Fischer Verlag.

von Humboldt, Wilhelm. 1904. *Wilhelm von Humboldts Werke, zweiter Band 1796–1799*, edited by Albert Letzmann. Berlin: B. Behr's Verlag.

Wilmer, S. E. 2018. *Performing Statelessness in Europe.* Basingstoke: Palgrave Macmillan.

Zeit Online. "Der CSU-Protest gegen den Protest." Last modified July 22, 2018. https://www.zeit.de/gesellschaft/zeitgeschehen/2018-07/muenchen-ausgehetzt-csu-theater-demonstration-rechtsruck.

CHAPTER 13

Toxicity, Speculation, and Rights: Political Imagination in Mixmedia, Literary, and Cinematic Futurescapes

Hanna Musiol

We Fuel the Future.
—GE Oil and Gas (General Electric 2018)

Science fiction is metaphor…. The future, in fiction, is a metaphor.
—Ursula Le Guin (2018, 46)

Neoliberalism signifies the movement of governmental rationality from a logic of anticipation and prevention to one of speculative preemption: it goes beyond a generic concern with the future and is oriented to the pragmatic uses of instability, uncertainty, and crisis …
—Martijn Konings (2018, 110–111)

H. Musiol (✉)
Norwegian University of Science and Technology, Trondheim, Norway
e-mail: hanna.musiol@ntnu.no

A. S. Moore and S. Pinto (eds.), *Writing Beyond the State*,
Palgrave Studies in Literature, Culture and Human Rights,
https://doi.org/10.1007/978-3-030-34456-6_13

Toxic Imagination

"The present," writes José Esteban Muñoz (2009), "is not enough" (27). He calls it "insolvent" (30), "impoverished[,] and toxic for queers and other people, who do not feel the privilege of majoritarian belonging, normative tastes, and rational expectations" (27). In 2020 his observation is as prescient as ever and, of course, extends, quite literally, to most of nonhuman life, too. The rapid disappearance of species makes our time, an era of normalization of gross human rights violations, also the era of the "sixth extinction" (Kolbert 2014), of "biological annihilation" (Haraway 2015; Ceballos et al. 2017), in which biological, sociopolitical, and cultural forms of devastation coincide (Grear and Gearty 2014; Klein 2014). In the realm of rights discourse, however, the heteronormative sociocultural and economic violence that Muñoz writes about and biological extinction often occupy disparate terrains. And yet, cultural, economic, and environmental injustice are not only interconnected but co-constitutive (Alaimo 2016; Armiero 2018; Armiero and de Angelis 2017; Grear and Gearty 2014; Whyte 2016; Tsing et al. 2017; Santos 2015). Muñoz, like others, does not trivialize the importance of targeted, immediate legal work to expand access to rights, but he warns against reducing justice to existing and "pragmatic [legal] strategies"[1] that cannot imagine the world beyond what is currently possible via litigation. He rallies, then, against legal instrumentalism, which produces selective victories while still sustaining "toxic" habits of thought and "insolvent" modes of social existence.[2] Such an understanding of poisonous practices of thought and aesthetic and political imagination that often precede and enable biosocial harm[3] informs the discussion of speculative works, across media, that follows (Alaimo 2010, 2016; Armiero and de Angelis 2017; Armiero 2018; Muñoz 2009; Solnit 2014).

Political Work of Speculation and the Space-Time of Rights

Most rights-expansion imaginings share a utopianist, future-facing orientation. Post–World War II international human rights are perhaps the most iconic examples of "writings beyond the state" that imagine in 1948 in a very utopian fashion that "[a]ll human beings are born free and equal in dignity and rights" in a transnational *somewhere* (United Nations 1948).[4] Promoted as "universal" and trans-, if not yet post-, state, such imagined rights were underwritten by capitalist, anthropocentric, and heteronormative ethoi and heavily dependent on states for ratification, implementation, and survival.[5] Nonetheless, exercising legal rights at existing juridical levels is as important as imagining political ecologies of rights beyond what is legal or possible in the present (*Donna Haraway* 2017; Muñoz 2009; Tsing et al. 2017; Whyte 2016). In that sense, rights are also a matter of cultural imagination and aspiration, and, thus, depend on the future,[6] which is continuously in the making, continuously being reimagined, but also "preempted," capitalized on, and foreclosed in the present (Konings 2018, 111). Thus, while rights and futuristic speculation are inseparable, speculation is not solely the vehicle for aspirational emancipatory politics. Toxic, gendered, corporate, econolegal, transnational, and nationalist futurescaping and future-dreaming are, in fact, far more pervasive, politically influential, and terraforming than international human rights "lawscapes" (Philippopoulos-Mihalopoulos 2014). Speculation in "strategic" business or military "innovation," as Stefano Harney and Fred Moten show us (2013, 88–89) in the interlinked transnational finance, energy culture, or politics, is not only pervasive, alluring, and rights-shaping "beyond the state" but, often, literally, a mode, a genre of politics (Jameson 2005). Fredric Jameson (2005, xi) references, for instance, Boris Groys's (1992) classic work about the deployment of utopian thinking in totalitarian politics of the past, while Martijn Konings (2018) sees speculation as a central tool of present-day neoliberal transnational governance (110–111). Acknowledged or not, in other words, speculation motors finance and business, and national and international politics. Thus, when General Electric Oil and Gas (GE Oil and Gas) defines their business practice as "imagination at work" that "fuel[s] the future," its speculative work becomes a form of governmentality that reshapes the future *and* the extractive present (General Electric 2018). Using speculation "pragmatically," (Konings 2018, 111), GE "greens" current-day industrial practices that hasten climate-change-induced devastation and "biological annihilation" (Ceballos et al. 2017), making a certain kind of corporate present and future possible,[7] but also enabling an end for other forms and arrangements of social and biological life.

Of course, many realms of cultural, economic, and political activity have their speculative expressions and modes of world-building, which transform what rights are and where they can be exercised, but their sociopolitical "impact factor" is not equal. Moreover, not all transmodal speculations across politics and human–nonhuman divides offer radical ways of recognizing the present or envision the consequences of their imaginings (Nixon 2011; Lepore 2017, n.p.; Jameson 2005; Jensen et al. 2018, n.p.). Thus, when scholars, artists, and activists alike, turn their attention to the understated but potent political work of nonhegemonic "critical dystopias" (Jameson 2005, xi–xii, 198–199), they look for how "critical fantasies" (Butler 2004, 29)—literary, visual, sonic, philosophical, and multimodal—refract and critique the present and imagine other worlds and times of intersectional justice, transspecies allegiances, or decolonized human rights.[8] For Muñoz (2009), the "queer utopia" of "anticipatory illuminations of the not-yet-conscious … [and] of art" (3, 28, 87) are precisely the tools of liberation that can help us "reclaim imagination" (Jensen et al. 2018, n.p.), and free us "from … the stultifying hold of the present" (Muñoz 2009, 179). Similarly, if one agrees with Konings's (2018) diagnosis that capital, and not, say, Ursula Le Guin, dominates or "owns" political speculation now with disastrous planetary-scale effects, nurturing the "polemical," dialogical character of critical speculation and its capacity to emphasize the "consequences" of political acts is of vital cultural and sociopolitical importance (Stengers in Jensen et al. 2018, n.p.; Dunne and Raby 2013).

This chapter turns to such critical, polemical, speculative, and multimodal imaginings and futurescapes—Johannes Heldén and Håkan Jonson's *Encyclopedia* (2017),[9] Jennifer Egan's "Black Box" (2012), and Boots Riley's *Sorry to Bother You* (2018)—as they invoke and revoke toxic institutional, trans- and national(ist) rights scripts, expand the limits of their respective genres and media, and explore the critical affordances of speculation. All three projects engage critically with the contested aspects of rights discourse, its anthropocentric exceptionalism, its erasure of cultural, racial, and gender difference, its co-optation in militaristic expansion, and its failure to address systemic economic exploitation and legacies of colonialism in the Global North. "Toxicity, speculation, rights" attends specifically to the socioenvironmental imaginaries that Heldén and Jonson (2017), Egan (2012), and Riley (2018)[10] construct, with a particular focus on the spatiotemporal location of their imagined ecologies. It examines how they engage with the tensions between anthropocentric, often raced, heteronormative, and gendered limits of Western human rights and other kinds of transnational rights scripts, and environmental, transspecies, noncapitalist justice concepts, which emerge from queer, feminist, and decolonial thought and civic activism (Whyte 2017; Gómez-Barris 2017; Tsing et al. 2017). The chapter also reflects on the diverse analytical affordances of speculative work. Muñoz (2009) argues, for instance, like Ursula Le Guin before (2018, 46), that the present can become legible through an investigation of "our perceptions" of futurity (Muñoz 2009, 27),[11] and this chapter explores this refractive, investigative, diagnostic, and para-documentary capacity of speculative fiction, which often operates as a "realism of the 21st century" (Lea 2015, n.p.; Le Guin 2018, 46; Nixon 2011). It then turns to exploring how these works reimagine "the critical promise of fantasy" by staging embodied scenarios or acts of anticipation, which demand active participation of their audiences (Butler 2004, 29). Ultimately, while these futuristic speculations are read critically against progressivist, neoliberal, and often colonial notions of "justice time," this chapter searches for emancipatory gestures and alternatives, where it finds them, within the otherwise catastrophic, dystopian worlds.

Speculating Extinction as "Biocultural Fact"

One of the main challenges of human rights discourse is its focus on preserving the physical integrity of humans disentangled from the environmental context and political practices, which would actually make such preservation possible (Grear 2017[12]; Musiol 2015, 2016; Whyte 2016). Speculative fiction in literature and visual arts often traces the effects of environmental injustice on nonhumans and humans alike, and it does not derive from the central tenets of human rights architecture, the sanctity of the "possessive" human individual in relation to property.[13] Instead, it challenges storytellers to push "storytelling beyond the [human] individual" in an expressly transnational, transdisciplinary fashion, and across the scientific and creative genres and media of "storytelling and observation" (Tsing et al. 2017, M3). As such, speculative fiction often exposes the major shortcomings of human-rights-law-based concepts of justice, and is, therefore, lauded in environmental humanities for its capacity to narrate complex and stretched-over-time ecological destruction that is hard to observe and comprehend, let alone care about (Nixon 2011; Stengers in Jensen et al. 2018). It is, then, recognized equally for its communicative, generative, *and* affective power, as it fosters the ability of communities of readers and spectators to understand, imagine, but also *sense* ecological change. Finally, it is invaluable in investigating the *anticipated* effects of current technopolitical processes and testing out econopolitical scenarios

(Nixon 2011; Alaimo 2010; *Donna Haraway* 2017). Isabelle Stengers calls it, rightly, "an art of consequences" (in Jensen et al. 2018, n.p.).

Encyclopedia, a collaborative science fiction work by Johannes Heldén and Håkan Jonson (2017), is precisely that (Fig. 13.1). This taxonomic, archival, and speculative project indexes, documents the anticipated consequences for, ***and*** imagines the futures of, the nonhuman world. It is composed of unique encyclopedia entries, printed on separate index cards. Each entry, written by its human authors, Heldén and Jonson, and a nonhuman automated text generator, describes one unique creature. The *Encyclopedia*, however, is not a book or a compendium in a traditional sense but a multidimensional, performative textual-digital imaginarium, composed of an infinite collection of index cards arranged and displayed symmetrically on a large wall (Fig. 13.1). The rigid spatial arrangement and taxonomic impulse that shapes the text on each index card is disrupted by the species introduced to readers through each entry. All of its

Fig. 13.1 The *Encyclopedia* installation (Photo by Aage A. Mikalsen, Kunsthall Trondheim, 2017)

documented creatures are unique and fictive, and reading their descriptions, it is hardly possible to resist a sense of magic, discovery, and wonder at the multiplicity of different animals, their features, habitats, and habits. For instance, the *Encyclopedia* introduces us to unknown, mysterious beings, such as *Peremeles Buffo*, a creature with "long and sharp incisors" who lived across "boreal forests, high plateaus, and the deserts" and whose "skin was … used to make rugs" (Heldén and Jonson 2017); or to the five-meter-long herbivorous *Ardeide obscurus,* that "formed herds of mixed sexes of up to 70 members" and could aggressively defend its territory (against human encroachment). Like all other organisms in *Encyclopedia*, they were "made extinct by humans": *Peremeles Buffo* disappears in 2308 AD, and *Ardeidae obscurus* in 2079 AD (Heldén and Jonson 2017).

Encyclopedia is a work of science *and* fiction, a play on the supposedly closed science genre and the open one of speculative fiction. In its cataloging effort and scientific scrutiny, Heldén and Jonson's work is reminiscent of the big data *Catalogue of Life* (Roskov et al. 2018), a collaborative global scientific compendium that provides a comprehensive nomenclature, taxonomy, and classification of all species, and that boasts of "tracking 95% of species known to science," a most comprehensive undertaking to document and preserve the biodiversity of the world. Yet, Heldén and Jonson's *Encyclopedia* is both more and less finite in that each entry is unique and nonreplicable, and, thus, each iteration of *Encyclopedia* contains a different combination of human- and machine-generated entries, describing a collection of new organisms never imagined or documented before. In that sense, it celebrates the infinity of biodiversity imagination. At the same time, their work is also firmly a catalog of death, a record of imaginary species' extinctions, as each animal's *bildung*—short, reductive, and written to emphasize the organism's utility to humans, but sometimes allowing for a less instrumentalist description, too—ends with a set annihilation date at the bottom of the index card. The use of the phrase "made extinct" in caps, and in a decisive passive form,[14] adds a sense of finality to the predicted human-induced devastation and annihilation of all the creatures that the project documents.

Thus, the ecological *Encyclopedia* straddles the line between documentation and ephemerality in its compendium of organisms not only fantastic but also always vanishing.[15] This distressing human-imagined and machine-generated catalog of extinction cannot imagine beyond the "end of future" for all its nonhuman organisms, because it cannot imagine a different kind of human-nonhuman relation. Land and water creatures in *Encyclopedia*, all precious to humans because of their meat, skins, bones, habitats, fur, and so on, are however not the only protagonists. Each index card concludes with a record of *human* activity—plunder, killings, extraction of any animal-derived resource, destruction of species' habitats—which seems habitual, systemic, extractive, relentless, and unstoppable.[16] Animal names and habits change but the human practices do not. Heldén and Jonson's work does not flirt with the possibility of animal resurrection, the kind, for example, that the Che Guevara–inspired cows led to slaughter partake in Dana Lyons's classic 1996 "Cows with Guns."[17] Nor do they differentiate between the humans who inflict devastation and those who suffer from it, a major limitation, critics of the Anthropocene's historical nuance- and politics-erasing narrative would say, that must be accounted for to address impending extinction (Armiero and de Angelis 2017; Haraway 2015; Tsing et al. 2017; Whyte 2016, 2017). Still, their cataloging of the creation and destruction of biodiversity, the collapsing of the fictive and the scientific, is a literal *exercise* in futurescaping,[18] and it draws attention to the invariably human subjectivity or "voice" that encyclopedias privilege, and to the extinction genre, in art and politics, in which that narrative voice tells the same story of relations that always ends with the nonhuman disappearance. The nonhuman animal, unlike the nonhuman machine, has no narrative agency in this genre. Much of sci-fi responds to the failure of the state or transnational systems to contain violence or forestall extinction. Here no alternative regulatory social, state- or supranational, or extraterrestrial system exists. This is the future as well as the present for those left out from *human* rights.

Feminist Survival and Human Rights Interventions

If *Encyclopedia* cannot imagine a regulatory rights framework and traps audiences in a mock, nostalgic choreography of spectatorship, the hyperstate and international rights regime is the landscape of Jennifer Egan's future. It literally scripts the life of the female protagonist of "Black Box," a satirical sci-fi spy Twitter story, but the audience is imagined as a key and active actor, too. At the center of the story is a predicament well diagnosed by Rebeca Solnit (2014), who notes that "[e]very woman who appears wrestles with the forces that would have her disappear[,] tell her story for her, or write her out of the story, the genealogy, the rights of man, the rule of law" (71), and, thus also, out of the future.[19] *Buffo Peremeles* is often, in other words, not the only threatened animal.[20] Jennifer Egan takes on this kind of erasure and disappearance in "Black Box," composed as a list of Twitter-post-length "dispatches" (Egan in Treisman 2012, n.p.) and survival instructions recorded by a nameless female cyborg-spy on a mission in the near-future South of France. Yet, she documents practices which ensure that "women do not register in [the] field of [political] vision" (sec. 23), while *also* examining the brutal entanglements of Western feminism and human rights military interventionism. As such, she narrates the complicity of women in perpetuating political violence, in ways reminiscent of Coco Fusco's visceral *Field Guide for Female Interrogators*, and addresses their struggle against political victimization (Fusco 2008).[21] "Black Box" is, in a sense, also a post-catastrophic archive of that brutal entanglement.

The female citizen-agent of the future, we learn in the story, is instructed to assume the role of a "Beauty" on her mission to infiltrate and collect evidence from a "violent and ruthless ... Designated Mate" (Egan 2012, sec. 7, 2). To succeed, she must perform her gender in a familiar fashion: she must "be both irresistible and invisible" (sec. 1), "simpleminded" (sec. 18), and "forgotten[,] yet still present" (sec. 23). Her body, with its performative, biological, and technologically enhanced capacities—"giggles; bare legs; shyness" (sec. 1), a "microphone ... implanted just beyond the first turn of [her] right ear canal" (sec. 13), a "Subcutaneous Pulse System ... embedded behind the inside ligament of ... right knee" (sec. 15), "the camera implanted in [her] left eye ... operated by pressing ... left tear duct" (sec. 25), or a "Universal [Data] Port" between her "right fourth and pinky toes" (sec. 35)—is weaponized and incorporated as an intelligence-gathering apparatus. Her "physical person," in other words, is a shell, a medium, [the government's] "Black Box," that she is to deliver to authorities (sec. 38).

"Black Box," built on nationalist, militarist, heterosexist jargon, extracts unending female heroism, uncompensated labor, nationalist affect, sex, and submission. Often in contradictory ways. The spy must make use of her body surfaces—seductive and young-looking— and transcend, disassociate herself from her body, and literally blend into the environment. Early instructions, for instance, command future female spies to "Mirror Designated Mate's attitudes, interests, desires, and tastes" to "become *part of his atmosphere*" (sec. 9, emphasis mine). Designated Mate is her "context"; she, his atmosphere (sec. 21). As a successful agent, she must possess other action-film-star's skills, operating a motorboat, handling advanced technology and firearms, not to forget using her "martial-arts experience," which may help her "occlude the windpipe" of the Designated Mate (sec. 35) at a strategic moment. Most crucially, however, her intelligence-gathering relies on strategic heterosexual sex work,[22] described as an unpaid act of patriotic "sacrifice" (sec. 32) for her country, the US.[23] The spy is also expected to suffer beatings, bouts of short-term memory loss, unconsciousness (sec. 35), "crushing onslaught of pain" (sec. 42), and, ultimately, death. She is, also, expected and trained to inflict violence on others, much like the female victimizers in Abu Ghraib or Guantánamo (Fusco 2008), but her victims might be also include civilian women and children (Egan 2012, sec. 37). Her survival, in other words, coincides with and depends on her strategic role in nationalist, militarist interventions. The mechanized voice of the narrator (at times, indistinguishable from the protagonist of the text), subjective and "very conventionally feminine and very human" (Precup 2015, 181), anticipates also the ubiquitous appropriation of female voices of Siri, Alexa, or Google Assistant, to soften and feminize corporate interventions.[24]

In "Black Box," the protagonist absorbs, quotes, and reproduces the ideological script that disappears her and other women in exchange for the promise of national inclusion and glory. "Some of you will not survive, but those who do will be heroes [who will] change the course of history," reads her military primer in contradiction of its own instructions suggesting that the violent anti-feminist future will replicate (sec. 5). In fact, in the more troubling section 21, quotation marks around instructions disappear, and this absence may mark the moment when the spy internalizes such toxic instructions she had been given and takes them as her own voice:

> In the new heroism, the goal is to merge with something larger than yourself. (sec. 23) … In the new heroism, the goal is to renounce the American fixation with being seen and recognized … (sec. 21)

And yet, Egan then blends these institutional indoctrinations with the spy's seemingly more personal observations. Filled with commands for what a woman of the future "must" or "should" do, "Black Box" is also subverted by random musings, and often poignant coping advice. For instance, after the spy is warned that "knowing your latitude and longitude is not the same as knowing where you are" (sec. 22), the language softens and drifts into a more personal realm. If it "calms you to imagine your husband tracking your dot of light [on a screen], then imagine it" (sec. 22); it can be "oddly reassuring" (sec. 22). The blurring of past and anticipated missions mirrors the shift from dry, official instructions to more personal, intimate, meditative speculations. At times, it becomes impossible to distinguish between the *she* who tells and the *she* who is being told, as Egan reimagines the encounter with instructions as an interaction between women sharing survival strategies.

The female spy can and should be read as a tainted figure, a white Western feminist assassin on a covert and violent transnational human rights mission (and the story references the documented use of human rights discourse and violence in such international operations[25]). Yet, the story's dispatches from the future narrate it, if not in the wake of a catastrophe—although the symbolism of the black box surely legitimizes such a reading—then from the precipice of a disaster, continuously alluded to, averted, approximated, mourned, and averted again. The narrator's weaving of subjective observations into the least malleable techno-militarist discourse, her direct address to other women who are to be employed on similarly violent sacrificial missions, unfixes the text's ideological viewpoint. After all, "Black Box" is a survival and training manual instructing future female agents to identify and manipulate nationalism and misogyny in potentially insurgent ways. The spy must respond to the militaristic and nationalist rhetoric, whose reach always extends beyond the state, and the reductive formalities of the genre, and is initially complicit in the violent and extractive political and cultural economy she inhabits. Thus, her revolt is neither obvious nor anticipated. However, while the story beams with what Egan calls, sarcastically, "a rich, deep crawl space of possibilities" (sec. 21), it also suggests ways to resist their toxic imaginings, a way out of the nationalist "crawl space." If Egan's speculative work offers a way to resist toxic nationalism, it is through her transformative work on the reader inside and outside of her text. In Egan's world, barring prosthetic technological enhancements, the gravitas of futurity is placed, in other words, on the reader, clearly the only figure of the future, who can rewrite it. The initial release of "Black Box" as a series of tweets (before being published as complete story), and the experimental nature of this story's format and its dissemination context, is important here.

Egan admitted to wanting to explore the potential of Twitter as "a delivery system for fiction" (qtd. in Treisman 2012, n.p.), as a public but also, paradoxically, an intimate transmission medium, delivering her text directly and immediately to readers. In Egan's hands, however, the truncated story delivered over 10 days in individual tweets—one a minute for an hour per day—not only slowed down the process of reading but also transformed *how* her text is read: not as prose, in paragraph-long chunks, but more deliberately, closely, and slowly, as poetry, word by word and line by line. Futuristic technological propaganda of efficiency and pompous patriotic newspeak begin to sound amusing and to crumble under such scrutiny. While the tenor of the satirical "Black Box" is dystopian—even more dystopian now than when originally published—it offers an escape route through these aesthetic experiments. Forcing reflective pauses between her Twitter lines, creating the new space for, and a mode of, reading and following instructions, Egan points out the reader's capacity to interrupt, rewrite, the script. The story ends with what appears to be a rescue mission, and yet, the narrator-protagonist warns that the rescue will be particularly "painful," "menacing," "jarring," so much so that some "citizen spies" choose not to be "saved" (sec. 44). Yet, what opens the final section of the story is the crucial "*if you wish* to return to your body [author's emphasis]," a white, female, heterosexual, militarized body, questioning the necessity of the spy to participate in the rescue mission to return to national and domestic bliss. Despite the nine steps that follow the initial *if you wish*, the spy, and the reader of the story, forced-persuaded to see "hope" in the faces of her rescuers, is given a chance to escape reproducing the future, to opt out of the nationalist script and to choose a different one. So is her reader, reimagined as a subject with interpretative and political power.

Labor Organizing, Racial Justice, and "Human Rights Cities"

Literary and cinematic speculative fiction markets may be not as segregated as when Samuel Delaney and Octavia Butler were breaking into the sci-fi fold,[26] but despite the commerical success of *Black Panther* (2018) or Nnedi Okorafor's fiction (2007), intersectional justice scripts are yet to become a mainstream sci-fi film genre in the Global North. Boots Riley's sci-fi film *Sorry to Bother You* (2018), lauded for its innovative, "ultraprogressive, radical storytelling" (Yoshida 2018, n.p.) and called "one of the year's sharpest pieces of political art" in 2018 (Parham 2018, n.p.), addresses this gap and clearly writes racial and social justice into Riley's futurescapes. Many reviewers recognize that the writer-director-songwriter Boots Riley's science fiction satire "punk film" (Yoshida 2018, n.p.) unapologetically constructs a world that reclaims political imagination from popular genres of extractive and racialized neoliberal speculation. A.O. Scott literally describes it as "a raft," and not simply "another postmodern playhouse out of borrowings and allusions" (2018, n.p.). If it is a raft, it is not built on techno-fetishistic or nationalist dreams, interplanetary colonization, or utopian urban development. Instead, it turns to the intra-national histories of local, cities-level economic social justice activism, to the arts, and to music. In that, it challenges the progressive and future-centric orientation of rights discourse—emancipation as only a future possibility—not simply by returning to the past, but by reclaiming its site-specific and transmodal archive of radical politics. It returns rights futures to forgotten practices of political, artistic, and civic engagement.

Sorry to Bother You (2018), set in the near-future Bay Area of California, introduces us to Cassius "Cash" Green (Lakeith Stanfield), "a black telemarketer with self-esteem issues and existential angst" (Boots Riley, quoted in "Interview" 2018), who desperately needs a job. When Cash secures a position at the San Francisco–based RegalView telemarketing company, he is instructed to adopt a "white voice" to perform a particular racial and class identity (*Sorry to Bother You* 2018, 00:13.05 min). Like the female spy in "Black Box," he is asked to "stick to the script"—an actual workplace motto displayed in his RegalView office—to do his job. In his co-worker's words, this means not simply sounding white, "proper" and "nasal," but sounding "like you don't have to care ... [, like] you have your bills paid [and] never been fired, just laid off ..." (*Sorry to Bother You* 2018). Like Egan's spy, Cash must make the atmosphere pleasant, nonthreatening; he is told to sound "breezy" and unburdened (*Sorry to Bother You* 2018) as a "Power Caller" at RegalView's parent company, WorryFree. WorryFree peddles an undeniably attractive vision of the future: it promises employees lifelong employment, shelter, food, and economic safety—a utopian promise in the US and globally. But its big corporate clients are actually drawn to a different promise and praxis: WorryFree achieves its efficient methods of labor extraction and cost reduction by contracting its work to desparate, unpaid, indentured slave laborers, who trade their work, time, and bodies to the company. WorryFree also takes its economic "innovation" further and mutates its employees into "equisapiens," monstrously strong horse-man workers. Equisapiens, reasons WorryFree CEO Steve Lift (Armie Hammer), "a Silicon Valley libertarian tech-bro visionary dirtbag" (Scott 2018, n.p.), will reduce labor costs and eliminate the danger of workers' protests. In exchange for the job promotion, Cash sells out his co-workers, who wants to unionize,[27] but snorts the animalizing serum (which he mistakes for a line of coke at a company party) and pays the price for his disloyalty in flesh. Yet, over the course of the film, he also undergoes a political awakening. He exposes WorryFree's business practices on live TV and rejoins the protesters in the streets with the equisapiens he frees from WorryFree. Ultimately, the protesters escape the violence of the police, win more rights at RegalView, and Cash and his friends restore their bonds.

Sorry to Bother You addresses the widespread and rapid erosion of human, civil, and environmental rights; the plight of racially and economically segregated cities; and the near-total occupation of the discourse of futurity by toxic neoliberal dreams with speculative audacity *and* documentary-like precision. As Jason Parham (2018) notes, its "racial horror" and its world "arise from the best kind of fiction, one inspired from the fury and turbulence of real life" (n.p.). Thus, following on Harney and Moten's (2015) and Muñoz's (2009) observations, it is pertinent to search for our sociopolitical present in Riley's work. Riley's near-future world is shaped by familiar national and international processes: a merciless assault on labor rights, the racialization of poverty, the integration of unethical corporate economic practices—sweatshops, deregulation, environmental destruction—into the very fabric of social life and governance[28]—and the retreat from environmental and social justice and human rights as policy considerations and ambitions.[29] Yet, the film is equally attentive to the site-specific social, human, cultural, and environmental justice strategies of resistance: unionization, socially engaged guerilla art, and the rich archives of city-based activism.

The location of the story in Oakland, a still poor if gentrifying, iconic black city and the birthplace of the Black Panthers movement, whose political agenda depended on racial and socioeconomic justice, is of central significance to this story. Riley did not turn Oakland into a background set that actors pass through. In the words of Omari Hardwick, he "figured out the Bay in its full capacity" and "saturated" the characters and the world of film with Oakland's character and legacy.[30] Invoking the city's radical African American social history, as well as the current strategies that rights advocates employ to address the state- and international-level retreat from human and civil rights law, points in the film to the recognition of cities-based rights advocacy and governmentality.[31] Moreover, California has been the setting for intersectional, multiethnic labor activism, and the film's futurism both invokes this history and imagines a social alliance of labor and racial justice advocacy, which are often seen as incompatible. Cash, a black man who initially has no political inclinations and is motivated by economic need; his political activist- and artist-girlfriend, Detroit (Tessa Thompson),[32] a secret member of the radical Left Eye, a Black Lives Matter–like social justice collective; and their friend, Squeeze (Steven Yeun), an Asian American union organizer, point to the possible future of such intersectional rights, without United Nations (UN) forces or white saviors present. Not less important is the sonic soundscape—Riley's own soundtrack is audible to lead characters as another "voice" that accompanies and may propel them into activism (Howard 2018). Importantly, although the film concludes with Cash mutating into an equisapien, this ending does not foreclose the possibility of radical politics. In the final scenes, equisapiens and humans (Cash included)—originally pitted against each other—unite and join the struggle for economic and political rights together, in recognition of their shared position in the systemic exploitation that targets humans—especially humans of color, women, and the poor—as resources. As such, the film imagines local, intersectional, radical, and transspecies political allegiances in the future. Riley's futurism, in other words, excavates and celebrates important environmental and civil rights work, recovering the past, often local, more intersectional, or anti-capitalist archives of labor, gender, and rights activism, recovering and reimagining justice as a communitarian and archival project.[33]

That union organizing and intersectional social justice work must be imagined as science fiction and as an unrealizable utopia in 2018 and that, at the same time, the audacious violence and exploitation that *Sorry to Bother You* portrays are vividly believable (Parham 2018, n.p.) are some of the greatest ironies of our time. So is imagining female survival as possible only if conditioned by nationalism and humanitarian militarism; so is cataloging the extinction of everything nonhuman, of everything imagined as the only genre of transspecies storytelling.

Time of Survival and Emancipation

Jill Lepore (2017) may be correct to bemoan the seductions of catastrophic, dystopian imagination and to urge more utopian works as a way out of sociocultural paralysis. However, the catastrophic multimodal futurescapes that Egan, Heldén and Jonson, and Riley construct are not failures of "civic imagination" (Nussbaum 1997, 85). To the contrary, they seem to imply that emancipatory imaginings must still begin with a denaturalization of dominant, corporate, nationalist, and transnational forms of speculation, as the only possible genres of political being. Hegemonic speculation, Egan, Heldén and Jonson, and Riley show, is toxic, "preemptive" and world forming (Konings 2018, 110). It does not expand a horizon of possibility; it forecloses it. As such, the pressing concern of radical speculation may still now well rest not just on constructing utopian alternatives but, first, on making legible the dominant modes of futurescaping (Le Guin 2018); and fostering critical, old and new, habits of interpretation and transmodal imagining, are key to this enterprise. Moreover, Riley's, Egan's, and Heldén and Jonson's projects challenge the temporal dimensions of rights discourse, the simultaneous separation of sociocultural and environmental "justice times," and the location of justice thinking in some nondescript, elusive future (Whyte 2017; Nixon 2011).[34] The utopian future can, and often does, function as a pernicious reproductive metaphor for progress and innovation, they warn, and the temporal dislocation in all three projects shows that most of their characters—the nonhuman animals, women, people of color, the poor, egalitarian communities—do not fit on the developmentalist grid of rights "progress." They all are shadow characters, without a present and without a future. In his seminal "Our Ancestors' Dystopia Now" (2017), Kyle Powys Whyte urges us to rethink precisely this relationship between colonial imagination, the capitalist understanding of time, the political dimensions of dystopia, and our very concepts of rights and of environmental justice, especially for those who have "travel[ed] through the membrane of death" (Harjo 2001, 20; Rifkin 2017) and must survive in a (post)dystopian future of someone else's making. All three projects recognize that time is valued and counted differently for different biosocial actors, and, thus, their futures signify in complex ways. The futuristic setting or orientation may work as a magnifying mirror metaphor for the present; as a site of a scientifically predicted and politically approved disappearance and devastation; as a time from which we must retreat; as a fiction of inevitable future, which, paradoxically, forces characters to bank and lose their present on (Konings 2018); as a "biocultural fact" woven of sacrificial bodies, stories, grounds, and imaginings of our time (Appadurai 2013); and as a site of perpetual yet unacknowledged, colonial replication. All three works invest, therefore, in narrating the consequences resulting from conflicting understandings of time—apolitical, nationalistic, straight, corporate, extractive, racialized—and from the self-destructive allegiances to aspirational futures that some characters (Egan's spy, or Cash) must make in exchange for a promise of survival. If anything, Egan's futuristic female human rights mercenary (2012), Heldén and Jonson's (2017) predatory humans ever-replicating the transational script of ecological death, and Riley's neo-slave corporate world of WorryFree (2018) warn us of the ease with which corporate, extractive, gendered, raced, and militaristic toxic scripts and futures reproduce, of the lethal force of "preemptive" hegemonic speculation, and trust in some abstract "justice time" in some right-ahead somewhere (Konings 2018, 110–111). To escape such periled futures, they recontextualize and re-politicize time, human and nonhuman flesh, and expose if not always reconstitute their relations. Their emancipatory speculation emerges from archives of resistance and civic imagination they salvage (*Sorry to Bother You* 2018), from encouraging an aesthetico-political transmodal literacy and fostering an active and critical engagement with aesthetics as a form as cultural and political activism (Egan 2012; Heldén and Jonson 2017; *Sorry to Bother You* 2018).

Acknowledgments I thank Lucia Brooks, Rebecca Tiger, Kari Kraus, and other rights advocates, for their work that reimagines rights futures; the participants of 2016 Futurescapes, for inspiration and conversations that continue; Kunsthall Trondheim, for mind- and space-expanding collaborations; Alexandra Schultheis Moore and Samantha Pinto, for their thoughtful comments on an earlier version of this chapter; and Kristen Ebert-Wagner, for editorial help.

Notes

1. He is particularly critical of the use of the heterosexist econopolitical model of marriage as a template for gay rights and liberation movement leading to the 2015 US Supreme Court decision in *Obergefell v. Hodges* (Obergefell v. Hodges 135 S. Ct. 2584).
2. Some legal practitioners disagree with this argument and point to the incremental nature of legal and political change. The national director

of the American Civil Liberties Union (ACLU), David Cole, argues, for instance, that one must "learn to absorb defeats and recognize that change comes incrementally, that the dam only ever breaks after constant, sustained [legal] pressure" (quoted in Lovell 2018, n.p.). On the other hand, other accomplished civil and human rights legal practitioners, such as *The New Jim Crow*'s author, Michelle Alexander, recognize that using the oppressive legal system—the racialized legal system in the US context of her work—to gain justice has well-defined limits, and that justice work must involve a radical reimagining of existing legal frameworks.

3. For a discussion of the imaginative and physical toxicity of the big data industry, see Cieplowski (2015).
4. Note that while my chapter highlights the presence of speculative imagination *across* disciplines and media, it does not aim to erase the obvious impact differences between the necessarily normative function of law and the less normative, perhaps unfortunately, force of critical speculative arts.
5. Rights are, after all, most effective when they can be exercised in the broadest and most localist jurisdictions (Santos 1987). International rights frameworks are a jurisdictional supplement to the law of state, and their procedures are activated only *after* the affordances of state legal apparati are exhausted (Santos 1987). Paradoxically, then, the state still plays a crucial role in regulating the de facto access to rights, and contemporary human rights activists fight to return *the here* to the human rights elsewhere or nowhere, to focus on "intra-national" human rights (Musiol 2016; Santos 1987).
6. For a critique of such "reproductive futurism" and queerness, see Edelman (2004, 2–4).
7. On the co-constitutive relation between extraction and art, see Barrett and Worden (2014).
8. See Stengers in Jensen et al. (2018, n.p.); *Donna Haraway* (2017).
9. While there are earlier versions of *Encyclopedia*, this chapter focuses explicitly on the 2017 site-specific installation to acknowledge the uniqueness and the performative character of each *edition* of *Encyclopedia*.
10. The complex reception these speculative fictions have generated deserves more space than this chapter allows.
11. Konings argues that the present is *made* by such future imaginings (2018).
12. Grear (2017) notes the limitations of human rights but also points to the possibilities of expanding the very category of human at the center of it.
13. In fact, it challenges the privileged position of the human, especially the one residing in the Global North, which it recognizes as one of the agents of devastating ecological *and* human rights crises.
14. The use of a more tentative conditional grammatical structure could offer some hope.

15. Their science fiction narrates deathly, impending temporalities at a time when the 2018 *Catalogue of Life*, incomplete and not predictive, still features 61,361 extinct species to 1,753,852 living ones (the ratio is swiftly changing, of course).
16. In the end, readers can collect a unique index card to preserve and treasure, although it is only a description of vanishing species (and a complicated gesture in the history of specimen collections).
17. A short version of the film is included in *Donna Haraway* (2017).
18. Note the embodied, performative, even theatrical, character of the installation. To access some of the entries displayed in the highest rows of *Encyclopedia*, one must climb a ladder, much like scientists and library users had to climb ladders to reach information before it became more horizontally, fingertips-level available via the internet.
19. While Haraway admits that feminist science fiction influenced her theory work (*Donna Haraway* 2017), mainstream future-oriented ontologies perpetuate a toxic social imagination, despite the near ubiquitous praise that speculative work receives in one of the key frontiers of critical rights work—climate-change advocacy and environmental justice. In other words, science fiction (and various genres of action and adventure), useful in addressing environmental concerns, can simultaneously revive heterosexist fantasies of gender norms and roles. Still, feminism and queer theory are some of the most significant paradigm shifters in environmental humanities work. See Alaimo (2010); *Donna Haraway* (2017); Haraway (2015); Tsing et al. (2017).
20. Lee Edelman (2004) would view escaping the heteronormative "reproductive futurism" (3) as redeeming. Egan might agree.
21. Fusco's multimodal project addressed the active participation of women in new and official rituals of torture during the War in Terror.
22. Her husband's job as a national security expert demands no such sacrifices, and, one presumes, it is paid.
23. "Black Box" offers advice on how to bear the discomfort of sexual acts using a "Dissociation Technique" while also warning that dissociating from her body might become permanent, which would jeopardize both the mission and her life. She is told that she "will sometimes be expected to change hands," yet is also comforted that her "job is identical regardless of whose hands [she is] in" (sec. 30).
24. The story also anticipates the adoption of social media and Twitter, in particular, for ideological mass indoctrination in the era of the Twitter US presidency.
25. The procedural instructions are vague and flexible when it comes to inflicting harm on "others." It is okay to kill a civilian mother and hurt her child, even though the spy is reminded to "hew to our principles" (sec. 37). Yet, instructions are "no more than guidelines," especially "[w]hen

self-preservation requires that you harm the innocent." "As Americans" the primer reads, "we value human rights above all else and cannot sanction their violation" and "a wider leeway becomes necessary ... [w]hen someone threatens *our* human rights ..." (sec. 37).

26. Infamously, bookstores would not stock Delaney's speculative work featuring androgynous, polyamorous, and racially and sexually ambiguous characters (Delaney 1998; Ghansah 2011).
27. They make very modest demands that the company provides living wages and humane working conditions.
28. In the US, Department of Justice [DOJ] resistance to the racial-profiling guidelines established in the aftermath of Michael Brown's death and the ensuing Ferguson, Missouri, riots to curtail police brutality (Musiol 2016) endanger the so-called consent decrees, DOJ's agreements with police departments to stem our racial-profiling practices.
29. The US withdrawal from the 2015 Paris Agreement on Climate-Change Mitigation on June 1, 2017, and from the United Nations Human Rights Council in 2018 (Tyler and Rachko 2018) is a culmination of this trend. As a hegemon with global influence, the US influences human rights and the environment globally, and not simply nationally.
30. The director and actors discuss the importance of shooting the film in Oakland, and not LA (Coley 2018; "Interview" 2018).
31. Barbara Oomen et al. (2016) call this trend the "rise of human rights cities," a strategy of turning urban sites into human and environmental rights sanctuaries, using urban legal, cultural, and political resources to resist the violent targeting of vulnerable populations, including migrants, people of color, the LGBTQ+ community, women, and the poor. This strategy has evolved in response to the ineffectiveness of state and international rights regimes, and it is a key tactic ensuring the preservation and expansion of rights within fractured national and international legal rights ecosystems. While it has a long history, the strategy has intensified in the aftermath of the 2016 US election, the 2017 Muslim travel ban, the removal of environmental protections and defunding of climate-change mitigation, and the war on (im)migrants in the US—led by Immigration and Customs Enforcement (ICE).
32. Her complexly symbolic name invokes another important American city decimated economically by the corporate logic of outsourcing, as well as black resistance and a site that embodies the violent history of white and black working-class conflict.
33. Macarena Gómez-Barris (2017) emphasizes the need for a "'decolonial queer femme' method" to "valorize[] nonnormative embodied femininity as sources of knowing and perceiving" (9).

34. The interconnected pushes to decolonize, queer, make intersectional international human rights and environmental theoretical frameworks and practices are important directions of critical legal studies / human and environmental rights work (Grear 2017; Gómez-Barris 2017; Musiol 2015, 2016; Tsing et al. 2017; Santos 2015; Whyte 2017).

Works Cited

Alaimo, Stacy. 2010. *Bodily Natures: Science, Environment, and the Material Self.* Bloomington: Indiana University Press.

Alaimo, Stacy. 2016. *Exposed: Environmental Politics and Pleasures in Posthuman Times.* University of Minnesota Press.

Appadurai, Arjun. 2013. *The Future as Cultural Fact: Essays on the Global Condition.* London: Verso.

Armiero, Marco. 2018. "An Environmental Historian Among the Activists: The Political, the Personal, and a Project of Guerilla Narrative." In *Italy and the Environmental Humanities: Landscapes, Natures, Ecologies*, edited by Serenella Iovino, Enrico Cesaretti, and Elena Past, 163–172. Charlottesville: University of Virginia Press.

Armiero, Marco, and Massimo de Angelis. 2017. "Anthropocene: Victims, Narrators, and Revolutionaries." *South Atlantic Quarterly* 116 (2): 345–362.

Barrett, Ross, and Daniel Worden, eds. 2014. *Oil Culture.* Minneapolis: University of Minnesota Press.

Black Panther. 2018. Dir. Ryan Coogler. Marvel Studios, Walt Disney Pictures.

Butler, Judith. 2004. *Undoing Gender.* New York and London: Routledge.

Ceballos, Gerardo, Paul R. Ehrlich, and Rodolfo Dirzo. 2017. "Biological Annihilation via the Ongoing Sixth Mass Extinction Signaled by Vertebrate Population Losses and Declines." *Proceedings of the National Academy of Sciences* 114 (30): E6089–6096.

Cieplowski, Maciej. 2015. "Haunted by Data." *O'Reilly*, October 4. Accessed August 30, 2017. https://www.youtube.com/watch?v=GAXLHM-1Psk.

Coley, Jacqueline. 2018. "UNCUT 'Sorry to Bother You' Director and Cast Interview." *Rotten Tomatoes*, August 10. https://www.youtube.com/watch?v=buXtTTeI2H0.

Delaney, Samuel. 1998. "Racism and Science Fiction." *New York Review of Science Fiction* 120, August 1998. Accessed November 4, 2014. http://www.nyrsf.com/racism-and-science-fiction-.html.

Donna Haraway: Storytelling for Earthly Survival. 2017. Dir. Fabrizio Terranova. New York: ICARUS films.

Dunne, Anthony, and Fiona Raby. 2013. *Speculative Everything: Design, Fiction, and Social Dreaming.* Cambridge, MA: MIT Press.

Edelman, Lee. 2004. *No Future: Queer Theory and the Death Drive*. Durham, NC: Duke University Press.

Egan, Jennifer. 2012. "Black Box." *The New Yorker*, June 4. Accessed July 12, 2015. https://www.newyorker.com/magazine/2012/06/04/black-box-2.

Fusco, Coco. 2008. *A Field Guide for Female Interrogators*. New York: Seven Stories Press.

General Electric. 2018. "GE Digital." Accessed August 1, 2018. https://www.ge.com/digital/.

Ghansah, Rachel Kaadzi. 2011. "Samuel R. Delany, the Art of Fiction" [Interview]. *The Paris Review* 197 (Summer). Accessed November 1, 2013. https://www.theparisreview.org/interviews/6088/samuel-r-delany-the-art-of-fiction-no-210-samuel-r-delany.

Gómez-Barris, Macarena. 2017. *The Extractive Zone: Social Ecologies and Decolonial Perspectives*. Durham, NC and London: Duke University Press.

Grear, Anna. 2017. "Human Rights and New Horizons? Thoughts Toward a New Juridical Ontology." *Science, Technology & Human Values* 43 (1): 129–145.

Grear, Anna, and Conor Gearty, eds. 2014. *Choosing a Future: The Social and Legal Aspects of Climate Change*. Cheltenham, UK: Edward Elgar.

Groys, Boris. 1992. *The Total Art of Stalinism: Avant-garde, Aesthetic Dictatorship and Beyond*. Princeton, NJ: Princeton University.

Haraway, Donna. 2015. "Anthropocene, Capitalocene, Plantationocene, Chthulucene: Making Kin." *Environmental Humanities* 6: 159–165.

Harjo, Joy. 2001. "A Map to the Next World." In *A Map to the Next World: Poems and Tales*, edited by Joy Harjo, 19–21. New York: Norton.

Harney, Stefano, and Fred Moten. 2013. *The Undercommons: Fugitive Planning and Black Study*. Wivenhoe and New York: Minor Compositions.

———. 2015. "Michael Brown." *boundary 2* 42 (4): 81–87.

Heldén, Johannes, and Håkan Jonson. 2017. *Encyclopedia*. Exhibited at Kunsthall Trondheim.

Howard, Annie. 2018. "Boots Riley on Creating Music to Appeal to 'Sorry to Bother You' Audience: 'We Don't Sell Platinum Records.'" *Hollywood Reporter*, November 15. Accessed February 3, 2019. https://www.hollywoodreporter.com/news/boots-riley-creating-music-sorry-bother-you-audience-1163387.

"Interview with 'Sorry to Bother You' Director Boots Riley and Star Lakeith Stanfield." 2018. *IMDB*, July 5. Accessed June 30, 2018. https://www.youtube.com/watch?v=o6ZJI34TdD8.

Jameson, Fredric. 2005. *Archaeologies of the Future: The Desire Called Utopia and Other Science Fiction*. London: Verso.

Jensen, Casper Bruun, Line Marie Thorsen, and Isabelle Stengers. 2018. "Reclaiming Imagination: Speculative SF as an Art of Consequences (an Interview with Isabelle Stengers)." *Nature Culture*. Accessed January 21, 2019. https://www.natcult.net/interviews/reclaiming-imagination-speculative-sf-as-an-art-of-consequences/.

Klein, Naomi. 2014. *This Changes Everything: Capitalism vs. the Climate*. New York: Simon & Schuster.

Kolbert, Elizabeth. 2014. *The Sixth Extinction: An Unnatural History*. New York: Henry Holt.

Konings, Martijn. 2018. *Capital and Time: For a New Critique of Neoliberal Reason*. Currencies: New Thinking for Financial Times. Stanford: Stanford University Press.

Le Guin, Ursula. 2018. "Introduction to *The Left Hand of Darkness,* 1976." In *Dreams Must Explain Themselves: The Selected Non-fiction of Ursula K. Le Guin*, 46–49. London: Gollancz.

Lea, Richard. 2015. "Science Fiction: The Realism of the 21st Century." *Guardian*, August 7. Accessed August 13, 2018. https://www.theguardian.com/books/2015/aug/07/science-fiction-realism-kim-stanley-robinson-alistair-reynolds-ann-leckie-interview.

Lepore, Jill. 2017. "A Golden Age for Dystopian Fiction." *New Yorker*, June 5 and 12. Accessed August 1, 2018. https://www.newyorker.com/magazine/2017/06/05/a-golden-age-for-dystopian-fiction.

Lovell, Joel. 2018. "Can the A.C.L.U. Become the N.R.A. for the Left?" *New York Times*, July 2. Accessed July 7, 2018. https://www.nytimes.com/2018/07/02/magazine/inside-the-aclus-war-on-trump.html.

Muñoz, José Esteban. 2009. *Cruising Utopia: The Then and There of Queer Futurity*. New York: NYU Press.

Musiol, Hanna. 2015. "Sites of Human Rights Theory." In *Routledge Companion to Human Rights and Literature*, edited by Sophia McClennen and Alexandra Schultheis Moore, 389–397. London: Routledge.

———. 2016. "Willful Targets of Rights." In *Discursive Framing of Human Rights: Negotiating Agency and Victimhood*, edited by Jonas Ross Kjærgård and Karen-Margrethe Simonsen, 148–166. London: Routledge.

Nixon, Rob. 2011. *Slow Violence and the Environmentalism of the Poor*. Cambridge, MA: Harvard University Press.

Nussbaum, Martha. 1997. *Cultivating Humanity*. Cambridge, MA: Harvard University Press.

Okorafor, Nnedi. 2007. *The Shadow Speaker*. New York: Jump at the Sun/Hyperion Books.

Oomen, Barbara, Martha F. Davis, and Michele Grigolo, eds. 2016. *Global Urban Justice: The Rise of Human Rights Cities*. Cambridge: Cambridge University Press.

Parham, Jason. 2018. "*Sorry to Bother You*: A Dizzying Satire That Hungers for Truth." *WIRED*, July 7. Accessed July 31, 2018. https://www.wired.com/story/sorry-to-bother-you-review/.

Philippopoulos-Mihalopoulos, Andreas. 2014. *Spatial Justice: Body, Lawscape, Atmosphere*. London: Routledge.

Precup, Amelia. 2015. "The Posthuman Body in Jennifer Egan's 'Black Box.'" *American, British, and Canadian Studies* 25: 171–186.

Rifkin, Mark. 2017. *Beyond Settler Time: Temporal Sovereignty and Indigenous Self-Determination*. Durham, NC: Duke University Press.

Roskov, Y., L. Abucay, T. Orrell, D. Nicolson, N. Bailly, P. M. Kirk, T. Bourgoin, R. E. DeWalt, W. Decock, A. De Wever, E. van Nieukerken, J. Zarucchi, and L. Penev, eds. 2018. *Species 2000 & ITIS Catalogue of Life, 2018 Annual Checklist*. Accessed August 8, 2018. Digital resource at www.catalogueoflife.org/annual-checklist/2018. Species 2000: Naturalis, Leiden, the Netherlands.

Santos, Boaventura de Sousa. 1987. "Law: A Map of Misreading. Toward a Postmodern Conception of Law." *Journal of Law and Society* 14 (3): 279–302.

———. 2015. *Epistemologies of the South: Justice Against Epistemicide*. Abingdon: Routledge.

Scott, A. O. 2018. "Review: 'Sorry to Bother You,' But Can I Interest You in a Wild Dystopian Satire?" *New York Times*, July 2. Accessed July 31, 2018. https://www.nytimes.com/2018/07/02/movies/sorry-to-bother-you-review-lakeith-stanfield.htm.

Solnit, Rebecca. 2014. *Men Explain Things to Me*. Chicago: Haymarket Books.

Sorry to Bother You. 2018. Dir. Boots Riley. Cinereach; Forest Whitaker's Significant Productions; MACRO; MNM Creative; The Space Program.

Treisman, Deborah. 2012. "This Week in Fiction: Jennifer Egan." *The New Yorker*, May 25. Accessed September 3, 2018. https://www.newyorker.com/books/page-turner/this-week-in-fiction-jennifer-egan.

Tsing, Anna, Heather Anne Swanson, Elaine Gan, and Nils Bubandt, eds. 2017. *Arts of Living on a Damaged Planet: Ghost and Monsters of the Anthropocene*. Minneapolis: University of Minnesota Press.

Tyler, Jasmin, and Thomas J. Rachko, Jr. 2018. "US Turning Its Back on Human Rights: Withdrawal from UN Body Mirrors Abuses at Home." *Human Rights Watch*, June 29. Accessed July 29, 2018. https://www.hrw.org/news/2018/06/29/us-turning-its-back-human-rights.

United Nations. 1948. *The Universal Declaration of Human Rights*. Accessed January 23, 2019. http://www.un.org/en/documents/udhr/resources.shtml.

Whyte, Kyle Powys. 2016. "Our Ancestors' Dystopia Now: Indigenous Conservation and the Anthropocene." In *The Routledge Companion to the Environmental Humanities*, edited by Ursula K. Heise, Jon Christensen, and Michelle Niemann, 206–215. New York: Routledge.

Yoshida, Emily. 2018. "The Raucous *Sorry to Bother You* Is the Punk Film 2018 Deserves." *Vulture*, July 5. Accessed July 29, 2018. http://www.vulture.com/2018/07/review-sorry-to-bother-you-is-the-punk-film-2018-deserves.html.

Whyte, Kyle Powys. 2017. "Indigenous Climate Change Studies: Indigenizing Futures, Decolonizing the Anthropocene." *English Language Notes* 55 (1–2): 153–162.

Epilogue

Alexandra S. Moore and Samantha Pinto

Like Theo Marboah's image that we write about at the start of this volume, so much of what lies within the pages of *Writing Beyond the State* sees form and structure as sites of critique, but also of imaginatively unmaking the political imaginary beyond the boundaries of sovereignty. In the pages above, this collection focuses on the crumbling and indeed often fictional and mythic structures of the sovereign nation, including secured borders, citizenship, and laws; the material structures of ships and of detention centers, to name but a few sites of securitization; and the literary and cultural forms of art that challenge sovereignty as both a material reality that does violence to human subjects and their environments, and as a goal of human rights moving forward. The artistic forms and the criticism appended to them in these essays challenge the limits of human rights representation and affect, moving them away from repair through national law and international aid and sympathy. Instead, much of the cultural production discussed herein presents not utopic, but complicated layered experiences within the complex institutions of human rights. These works assume not a static negotiation with a sovereign state as the ultimate human rights framework, but instead a series of moving, flexible, networked, and changeable relations—some predicated on violence, and other on the possibilities beyond it.

A. S. Moore and S. Pinto (eds.), *Writing Beyond the State*, Palgrave Studies in Literature, Culture and Human Rights,
https://doi.org/10.1007/978-3-030-34456-6

This sense of rights as systems of relational movement is embodied in the cover image, from Jason deCaires Taylor's 2018 "The Sculpture Coralarium" in the Maldives an artwork that existed (before its forcible removal by the government for being "anti-Islamic" in its depiction of human figures) in the realm of the "tidal," its structure of "high-grade marine stainless steel and pH-neutral cement [that] ... reference coral patterns while also being engineered to allow currents and marine life to pass through it" (Haridy 2018). The installation stood as a dynamic artwork both as it aimed to take on the long-term change that marine living brings to its surfaces and also in the daily flux of the tides that would render its form alternately exposed and submerged.[1] Like the Marboah diptych, "The Sculpture Coralarium" stages the creative possibilities of the syncretic time of contemporary art and literature in the post-sovereign moment with its ability to signal material structures of power while making visible the overlapping presence of different historical and even geologic moments. At the same time, it marks the vulnerability of both persons and structures as subjects of and subject to rights, as well as of and to interpretative protocols. Perhaps no large-scale installation artwork embodies the present interpretive difficulties of audience, form, and affiliation in human rights studies than deCaires Taylor's 2017 Museo Atlántico (also discussed by Terri Tomsky in Chapter 11 of this volume). As a series of sculptures situated underwater, Museo Atlántico offers us a new and largely inaccessible gallery space, one managed by the cost and bureaucracy of divers and guides to visit "in person." And yet, by expressly creating environmentally aware art to "revitalize" devastated areas that rely on wealthy tourism, deCaires Taylor also refuses to deny the capitalist systems that grid our porous natural world as well as forge globalization that challenges the nation state as the foremost organizing structure and site of reform for human rights. Museo Atlántico could be read as creating and sustaining more marine life, calling attention to climate change through its surface area of what deCaires Taylor calls his "artificial reefs" (2018) of underwater sculpture. But its sculptural attentions yoke the history and present of human interaction with—and traffick on—the sea.

Through deCaires Taylor's photographs of his own underwater installation—billed as a museum of the Atlantic, connoting both high art and history—those not privy to the guided diving tours of the coast Lanzarote, one of the Canary Islands, can gain sight of that which lies beneath the surface of the water. In one section of the installation, entitled "Crossing the Rubicon," a group of human figures walks toward a wall of sorts, but one with an open door, a portal into undefined underwater space. In another section, a group of refugees sits on a raft. Yet another sculpture is a wreath of wasted bodies, nearly skeletal, that evokes the middle passage. All of these figures and structures sit under the sea, hosting sea life, acting as homes for other organisms that will invariably transform them. The sculpture here has no enduring, permanent surface—the installation marks a history and a present that will both last and, in its presence under the water, be inexorably changed by time, and by its conditions.

As the figures in "Crossing the Rubicon" move toward but never reach the stone gates knotted with iron-like tree limbs under the African Atlantic, both the structure of the "border" and the representation of subjects stand resolutely un-sovereign; they are inhabited by oceanic species that invade their interiors and coat their exteriors, making different that which still stands, as well as those poised to journey to or through those structures, those violences, and those histories. The reference to the Rubicon—a river in Italy made famous by Caesar's military campaign that led to civil war and the consolidation of his power, thought to be the contemporary river with the same name flowing from the Adriatic Sea—positions refugee crossings within a particularly long durée of power struggles over sovereignty, marked through a series of transgressions and migrations, rather than coherence or belonging.

That history of violent sovereignty and the transgressions and migrations it spawns also find expression in deCaires Taylor's "Raft of the Lampadusa" with its formal invocation of Theodore Gericáult's 1819 painting, "The Raft of Medusa." The events they chronicle invoke a racialized history and legacy of European imperial ambition along the coasts of Africa: Gericáult imaginatively depicts the few survivors of an 1816 French navy vessel, shipwrecked on a colonizing venture to Senegal; and deCaires Taylor addresses the 2013 loss of an estimated 366 African migrants and asylum seekers when their raft sank near the island of Lampedusa on the journey across the Mediterranean from Libya (also discussed by Naimou in Chapter 10). Whereas Gericáult's painting displays the intense emotion and tumultuous, dangerous sea and sky typical of Romanticism, deCaires Taylor's reimagining of the tableau sits quietly—its figures in the stillness of contemplation or death—on the floor of the sea. These affective differences turn viewers' attention away from the formal equivalencies of the doomed life raft and toward their different historical and material contexts, a turn amplified by the choice deCaires Taylor makes to alter the temporality of the moment. In Gericáult's painting, the composition gains its balance and dynamism from strong diagonals created, on the left, by the top of the sail, outstretched arms, and, on the right, by the edge of the raft and reaching bodies, all of which lead to the offset focal point of a young man, perched high above the horizon, waving a red flag in a failed attempt to attract the attention of a receding rescue boat—a Romantic sublime of hope and despair. Significantly, deCaires Taylor avoids representation of a potentially analogous moment, when the captain of the Mediterranean raft doused a blanket with gasoline and lit it to attract the attention of the Italian coast guard or fishing boats. In doing so, *The Guardian* reports, “the fire burnt his hand, making him drop the blanket. Petrol had spilled on the deck and instantly ignited. Flames shot into the air” (Nelson 2014). The resulting panic capsized the raft, trapping underwater those below deck and plunging those above board, most of whom could not swim, into the sea. Thus, deCaires Taylor’s sculpture, anchored to the seafloor, imagines an impossible time of life in, after, and through death where the intense affect and humanitarian pseudo-identification of the painting have no place.

The haunting underwater photographs of deCaires Taylor’s work portray both horrors (in his death-like figuration of human forms) and wonders (sculpture teeming with non-human life), eschewing the affect of sentimental realism—of “feeling” like “them” in the ways that so many of the essays herein critique as a mode of human rights engagement. Museo Atlántico cannot and does not try to escape its museum-ness—its touristic draw, its historical narration through objects, and its own place in art history—but it does insist that both object and structure—subject and institution—are transformed by the environment and by (human) acts in slow time. DeCaires Taylor’s work draws attention to the devastation rendered in “slow violence,” as Rob Nixon (2011) terms environmental devastation, but also the possibilities of building and creating alternate forms of relationality that will take root in the post-sovereign future even as they offer a critique of sovereignty in the present moment. Museo Atlántico then undermines the idea of museum as archive and canon, offering instead a shifting cartography of not just how to represent human rights and their loss, but the need to represent human rights imaginaries beyond a singular, sovereign event or act of repair. In our reading, the work does not just to broaden the archive or the canon, but helps to imagine alternative vocabularies and structures of human rights’ representational systems.

This work of imagining otherwise, exemplified in deCaires Taylor’s project and addressed in the essays herein, disrupts the normativity of human rights as exclusively a matter of positive law or imperial ambition. Thus, in many ways, the approaches to reading and representing human rights in this volume partake in the longer tradition of poststructuralist analysis by foregrounding the discursive and representational forms of rights in historical, political, and social context. Although poststructuralism has been critiqued for failing to attend to the material realities of the knowledges, texts, and subjects whose meanings are linked to institutional positionality and discursive play/production, the authors in this volume consistently work against this ostensible divide between discursive and material worlds to show the impact of egregious violations of human rights on forms, lives, and bodies. These readings open up space for what Jacques Rancière, over the past two decades, has described as the political staging of dissensus, of the disruption of normativity, staging which does not depend on a sovereign subject: "There is no man of the Rights of Man, but there is no need for such a man. The strength of those rights lies in the back-and-forth movement between the first inscription of the right and the dissensual stage on which it is put to the test" (Rancière 2004, 305). For many of the authors in this volume, dissensus is also understood as crucial to a more explicitly decolonizing approach to human rights. This volume takes dissensus and decolonizing approaches as starting points from which to consider alternative imaginaries of freedom, emancipation, and flourishing.

Note

1. For more on the intersection of eco-criticism and postcolonial literature and theory, see Caribbean Poet Kamau Braithwaite's generative methodology of global history that he terms "tidalectics" (1999, 34), which was translated into an interpretative tool by postcolonial scholar Elizabeth DeLoughrey (2007, 2).

Works Cited

Brathwaite, Kamau. 1999. *ConVERSations with Nathaniel Mackey*. New York: We Press.

DeLoughrey, Elizabeth. 2007. *Routes and Roots: Navigating Caribbean and Pacific Island Literatures*. Honolulu: University of Hawaii Press.

Haridy, Rich. 2018. "The Sculpture Coralarium: The World's First Semi-Submerged Tidal Art Gallery." *New Atlas*, July 19. https://newatlas.com/sculpture-coralarium-jason-taylor-maldives-underwater-gallery/55542/.

Nelson, Zed. 2014. "Lampadusa Boat Tragedy: A Survivor's Story." *The Guardian* (UK), March 22. https://www.theguardian.com/world/2014/mar/22/lampedusa-boat-tragedy-migrants-africa.

Nixon, Rob. 2011. *Slow Violence and the Environmentalism of the Poor*. Boston: Harvard University Press.

Rancière, Jacques. 2004. "Who Is the Subject of the Rights of Man?" *The South Atlantic Quarterly* 103, no. 2: 297–310.

Taylor, deCaires. 2017. Selected works. Museo Atlántico. Lanzarote, Canary Islands.

———. 2018. "Artificial Reefs." https://www.underwatersculpture.com/environment/artificial-reefs/.

Index

A. S. Moore and S. Pinto (eds.), *Writing Beyond the State*, Palgrave Studies in Literature, Culture and Human Rights, https://doi.org/10.1007/978-3-030-34456-6

The manufacturer's authorised representative in the EU is Springer Nature Customer Service Centre GmbH, Europaplatz 3, 69115 Heidelberg, Germany. If you have any concerns regarding our products, please contact ProductSafety@springernature.com

Printed and bound by CPI Group (UK) Ltd, Croydon, CR0 4YY

30/09/2026

02225644-0009